Studies in Liturgical Musicology
Edited by Dr. Robin A. Leaver

1. Frans Brouwer and Robin A. Leaver (eds.). *Ars et Musica in Liturgia: Essays Presented to Casper Honders on His Seventieth Birthday.* 1994.

2. Steven Plank. *"The Way to Heavens Doore": An Introduction to Liturgical Process and Musical Style.* 1994.

3. Thomas Allen Seel. *A Theology of Music for Worship Derived from the Book of Revelation.* 1995.

4. David W. Music. *Hymnology: A Collection of Source Readings.* 1996.

Hymnology
A Collection of Source Readings

by
David W. Music

Studies in Liturgical Musicology, No. 4

The Scarecrow Press, Inc.
Lanham, Md., and London

SCARECROW PRESS, INC.

Published in the United States of America
by Scarecrow Press, Inc.
4720 Boston Way
Lanham, Maryland 20706

4 Pleydell Gardens, Folkestone
Kent CT20 2DN, England

Copyright © 1996 by David W. Music

British Cataloguing-in-Publication Information Available

Library of Congress Cataloging-in-Publication Data

Music, David W., 1949-
Hymnology : a collection of source readings / by David W. Music
p. cm. — (Studies in liturgical musicology ; no. 4)
1. Church music. 2. Hymns—History and criticism. I. Title.
II. Series.
ML3000.M87 1996 781.71—dc20 96-1827 CIP

ISBN 0–8108–3148–1 (cloth : alk. paper)

Contents

Editor's Foreword

MANY hymns possess a timeless quality, an existential reality for the worshiper who sings them. But these hymns were created within specific time frames. They were therefore culturally, theologically, and liturgically shaped by the environment within which they were written. Thus the orthodox hymnody of Ambrose contradicted the heterodox hymnody of Arius and his followers. The sequences of Notker and others were created out of pragmatic musical concerns in the ninth century. The development and success of metrical psalmody owed much to Calvinist theology and worship practice in the sixteenth and succeeding centuries. The hymns of the generation of Charles Wesley and John Newton were a direct outgrowth of the evangelical revival of the eighteenth century.

Although hymns frequently enshrine deeply personal concerns, they have repeatedly been the subject of public and corporate scrutiny in councils and committees of the churches, such as the Council of Laodicea in the fourth century, the Westminster Assembly in the seventeenth century, and the theological faculty of Wittenberg University in the eighteenth century.

Those who wrote hymns were frequently promoting agendas other than the obvious one of providing new religious songs for individual and corporate worship. Thus the compilers of the Bay Psalm Book were more concerned with pedagogy than with poetry, their aim being to provide accurate verse, faithful to the original inspired Hebrew of the Psalms. On the other hand, Isaac Watts, while accepting the Calvinist principle of metrical psalmody, exploded the genre by refusing to be limited to the subject matter of the Hebrew Psalms and therefore incorporated a New Testament understanding of grace and salvation into his psalm versions.

Hymns are encountered, learned, and sung as individual compositions, yet, during the modern period, they were not circulated as broadsides, single-sheet copies, but as singular items in anthologies of such texts, that is, in hymnals. Prefaces to these hymnals help us to understand the immediate context within which the hymns were introduced and/or promoted, the liturgical purposes they were designated to fulfil, and the motives behind the publication of each distinctive collection. John Wesley's *Collection of Hymns for the Use of the People Called Methodists* (1780) focused on personal spirituality, especially conversion and assurance from an Arminian theological standpoint, whereas John Newton's *Olney Hymns* (1779) promoted a distinctive Calvinist theological stance. In the following century Thomas Helmore and John Mason Neale were concerned with a more Catholic spirituality in their *Hymnal Noted* (1852-1854), a direct product of the Tractarian Movement. *The English Hymnal* (1906), a self-consciously Anglo-Catholic anthology, was different again. It was, among other things, a manifesto for good music, which, according to the music editor, Ralph Vaughan Williams, is a moral issue.

Discussions of these matters can, of course, be found in numerous studies of the development of hymnody, but documentary sources, which present the issues within the then contemporary thought-forms and presuppositions, have been inaccessible in a single source until the publication of this volume. For example, the two prefaces of Isaac Watts, vitally important for an understanding of his aims and objectives, as well as the direction of subsequent English hymnody, have hitherto been unavailable together for comparison and study. David W. Music has therefore compiled a most useful anthology of basic documentary source material relating to the historical development of hymnody. It will greatly assist the student of hymnology and significantly inform anyone with an interest in hymns.

Robin A. Leaver, Series Editor
Westminster Choir College of Rider University
and Drew University

Acknowledgments

APPRECIATION is expressed to the copyright owners listed below for allowing the use of copyrighted material in this book.

The Liturgical Press for permission to quote from Robert F. Hayburn, *Papal Legislation on Sacred Music: 95 A.D. to 1977 A.D.*

Dr. Dianne M. McMullen for permission to quote from her doctoral dissertation, "The *Geistreiches Gesangbuch* of Johann Anastasius Freylinghausen."

Farrar, Straus & Giroux, Inc., for permission to quote from *The Diary of Samuel Sewall 1674-1729*, edited by M. Halsey Thomas.

International Commission on English in the Liturgy for permission to quote excerpts from the English translation of *Documents on the Liturgy, 1963-1979: Conciliar, Papal, and Curial Texts* © 1982, International Commission on English in the Liturgy, Inc. All rights reserved.

Oxford University Press for permission to quote extracts from Ralph Vaughan Williams's preface to the *English Hymnal*.

Epworth Press for permission to quote from *The Letters of the Rev. John Wesley, A.M.*, ed. by John Telford.

Franciscan Press for permission to quote from *St. Francis of Assisi: Writings and Early Biographies. English Omnibus of the Sources for the Life of St. Francis*, ed. by Marion A. Habig.

Catholic University of America Press for permission to quote from Simon P. Wood's translation of Clement of Alexandria, *Christ the Educator*, and from Agnes Clare Way's translation of Saint Basil, *Letters*.

Paulist Press for permission to quote from *Egeria: Diary of a Pilgrimage*, translated by George E. Gingras © 1970, Paulist Press; and from *Palladius: The Lausiac History*, translated by Robert T. Meyer © 1965. Used by permission of Paulist Press.

University of California Press for permission to quote from Richard Crocker, *The Early Medieval Sequence*. Copyright © 1977 The Regents of the University of California.

Introduction

THIS book represents an attempt to help modern students, leaders, and singers of hymns view the history of congregational song through the perspective of its original writers, leaders, singers, and commentators. As the title suggests, it is a collection of source documents from various periods of church history. The writings have been selected to illustrate certain aspects of the philosophy and/or practice of hymnody in these eras.

Such an approach is certainly not new in the study of church history, music history, or, indeed, church music history. Henry Bettenson's *Documents of the Christian Church* (London: Oxford University Press, 1943), Oliver Strunk's *Source Readings in Music History* (New York: W. W. Norton & Company, 1950), Piero Weiss and Richard Taruskin's *Music in the Western World: A History in Documents* (New York: Schirmer Books, 1984), and Elwyn A. Wienandt's *Opinions on Church Music* (Waco: Markham Press Fund of Baylor University Press, 1974) are but a few of the excellent works of this kind.

However, these and similar volumes deal only peripherally with documents relating to hymnody. In contrast, the scope of the present book is confined essentially to congregational song.

Many of the readings presented here have been available in various modern sources for some time. It is hoped that their being brought together within a single volume will be a considerable convenience for the reader. Other documents have not been readily accessible in the past, and their inclusion in this book will hopefully bring fresh insights to the subject.

The arrangement of the book is essentially chronological, but within a topical framework. Beginning with early church song, the volume proceeds through the various branches of the Reformation, English hymnody, American hymnody, and Vatican Council II. Each section except the last one is broken down into smaller units, which likewise take a chronological/topical approach. This arrangement is similar to that of currently available histories of hymnody and should enhance the book's usefulness as a supplement to such materials. At the same time, it will allow the hymnological specialist or general reader to concentrate on the topics or time periods that are of the most personal interest.

It might be argued that some of the readings in this volume, particularly in Part I, relate more directly to solo or choral song than to the large-group involvement usually implied by the term "congregational." Such criticisms are entirely justified. The reasons these items have been included are threefold: (1) They demonstrate the continuity of Christian song from the early church to the twentieth century, (2) the forms under consideration are the closest thing to true congregational song that has come down to us from that era, and (3) examples of the materials referred to have been subsequently adapted for use as congregational hymns.

Obviously, such a collection as the present one must be selective in nature. Many other interesting documents could have been included, but the consequent increase in the size and scope of the book would have been counterproductive. Some important types of hymnody are not covered at all or are barely touched upon, while others are represented by numerous and/or lengthy examples. In some cases, no significant documents dealing with a particular type of hymnody appear to be available. On the other hand, no apology is made for including large amounts of material by Martin Luther, Isaac Watts, John Wesley, and other central figures in the history of Christian hymnody.

It will be noted that compared with the other eras represented in the book, very few writings from recent times have been included, and that only one of these dates from after the first decade of the twentieth century. This has been done deliberately. While there have been many interesting developments in hymnody during the twentieth century, we are perhaps as yet too close to the events to tell which of them will prove to be of lasting significance and which will turn out to be mere blips on a local scene. Much that has happened in twentieth-century hymnody has been a rediscovery or revitalization of earlier forms covered elsewhere in the book. And, while the twentieth century has seen a tremendous increase in the amount of writing about hymnody, there are few works that have had the profound impact of the preface to the *English Hymnal* or the Constitution on the Sacred Liturgy of Vatican Council II.

Whenever possible, the compiler has included complete documents or major sections of documents in order to provide context and continuity. This is particularly true in the case of such landmark writings as the prefaces to Watts's *Hymns and Spiritual Songs* and *Psalms of David Imitated in the Language of the New Testament.* For some writings, however, it has seemed expedient to provide a judicious selection in order to avoid unnecessary repetition or extraneous or inconsequential material. When less than a complete document or section is presented, the bibliographic citation begins with the word "from." Otherwise, it may be assumed that the entire document or section listed in the source note has been reproduced. Omissions within the text of a partial document are indicated by ellipses.

For many of the readings, recourse has been had to original printings or facsimile copies of the documents. However, no attempt has been made to be pedantic in this area, and liberal use has been made of scholarly editions and modern reprints. Thus, some of the readings will include archaic spellings and grammatical constructions, while others from the same era will be couched in modern terms. When a modern edition has been used, that fact is noted in the bibliographic citation; where no such note appears it may be assumed that an original document or facsimile was employed.

It has been the goal of the compiler to let the writings essentially speak for themselves. Thus, the sources from which the writings are taken have been reproduced as faithfully as possible, including misspellings, poor grammatical constructions, factual errors, etc. In a few instances, such as the preface to Coverdale's *Goostly Psalmes and Spirituall Songes*, certain archaic abbreviations have been fleshed out without comment. An occasional correction or addition to the text of a document is given in brackets where the meaning of the original would be unclear if left uncorrected. The numbering of the psalms follows that of the sources themselves; in documents using the Latin Vulgate system, the number of the psalm in Protestant bibles is given in brackets following the original reference. When a scholarly edition or modern reprint of a document has been used, all parenthetical comments and footnotes by later editors or translators have been omitted.

Several writings that were originally in languages other than English have been translated, apparently for the first time. In some cases, non-English works that have been previously available in translation appear in new renderings. The work of other translators is acknowledged in the source notes; where no reference is given to a translator, the rendering may be assumed to be the work of the compiler.

While the temptation to include explanatory footnotes has been strong, the resulting clutter would have disturbed the continuity and readability of the text and resulted in confusion with notes found in the documents themselves. Thus, the only footnotes contained here are those of the original writers. In some instances, these have been renumbered for the present edition. At times, the footnotes were originally not footnotes at all, but notes in the margins. These have been numbered and their approximate position in relation to the text indicated.

As a replacement for editorial footnotes, the compiler has opted to preface each selection or group of selections with an introduction. This attempts to set the context for the writing, often including information on the biography of the author, the historical background to the selection, the importance of the writing, and a brief summary of its important points. Where several writings of a single author appear in succession, they are introduced as a group. The goal of these introductions is to provide only basic information necessary to àn understanding of the passage at hand. For further information, the reader should consult the works listed in the bibliography at the end of the book. This is particularly true for biographical details on Luther, Calvin, Watts, Wesley, and other significant figures, which can be found readily elsewhere.

It remains my pleasant task to acknowledge the assistance of a number of people who generously provided materials or advice for this work. I am grateful to S. Sue Johnson of Riverside, California, and Paul R. Powell of Princeton, New Jersey, for making available to me copies of the first edition prefaces to Watts's *Psalms of David Imitated* and *Hymns and Spiritual Songs*, respectively. The staffs of the Roberts and Bowld Libraries at Southwestern Baptist Theological Seminary also rendered much support in tracking down hard to find sources.

Thanks are due to Alan Buescher of Fort Worth, Texas, for his assistance with the Hebrew fragments found in the book and to my colleague Dr. William Colson of the Southwestern Seminary faculty for help in the translation of the Bucer extract.

Two other colleagues, Dr. William J. Reynolds and Dr. J. Stanley Moore, read early drafts of the book and made many valuable suggestions, as did Dr. Robin A. Leaver, the editor of the volume. Sandra J. Perrodin did yeoman service in typing the entire manuscript.

The assistance of these people has improved the book immeasurably, but it should be noted that the responsibility for any errors found herein is mine alone.

Finally, I would like to acknowledge the patience and understanding of my wife, Doris, and my children, John, Caroline, and Colleen, who not only endured neglect while the book was in progress but had to listen to me talk about it as well. *Misericordias Domini in aeternum cantabo* (Ps. 89:1).

Abbreviations

CCSL   *Corpus Christianorum. Series Latina.* 176 vols. Turnholt: Brepols Editores Pontificii, 1954-1965.

WA   *D. Martin Luthers Werke.* 64 vols. Weimar: Hermann Böhlau, 1883-1990. [*Weimar Ausgabe*]

WA Br   *D. Martin Luthers Werke. Briefwechsel.* 18 vols. Weimar: Hermann Böhlau, 1930-1985. [*Weimar Ausgabe, Briefwechsel*]

NPNF   Philip Schaff and Henry Wace, eds., *A Select Library of Nicene and Post-Nicene Fathers of the Christian Church.* 2nd series. 14 vols. New York: The Christian Literature Company/Charles Scribner's Sons, 1890-1900.

PL   J.-P. Migne, ed. *Patrologiae Cursus Completus . . . Series Latina.* 221 vols. Garnier Fratres, 1878-1890.

WJW   The Works of John Wesley. 14 vols. London: Wesleyan Conference Office, 1872.

Part I

The Early Church and the Middle Ages

1
Psalm and Hymn Singing Practices in Early Christianity

Pliny the Younger (c. A.D. 62-c. 113)

PLINY the Younger (Caius Plinius Caecilius Secundus), Roman statesman and literary figure, wrote ten books of letters that provide much information on Roman law, life, and customs of the first and second centuries. The tenth book, written while he was serving as governor of the Roman province of Bithynia (111-c. 113), contains his official correspondence with the Emperor Trajan on various administrative matters.

The following letter from the tenth book includes one of the earliest post-New Testament references to Christian singing and serves as an important link in tracing Christian song between the close of the first century and the writings of the later church fathers. The phrase here given as "to utter in turn songs to Christ as to a god" (*carmenque Christo quasi deo dicere secum invicem*) is often taken to refer to antiphonal singing, though other meanings are also possible.

1   Letters, Book 10, No. 96. *Source: C. Plini Caecili Secundi Epistularum Libri Novem Epistularum ad Traianum Liber Panegyricus.* Revised by Mauritius Schuster (Leipzig: B. G. Teubneri, 1933), pp. 363-365.

C. Pliny to the Emperor Trajan

It is my practice, sir, to refer all doubtful matters to you. For who is better able to guide my uncertainty or inform my ignorance?

I have never been present at a trial of Christians. Thus, I do not know how and to what extent they are usually punished or interrogated. I am not at all sure to what extent I should distinguish between ages, weak and strong, to pardon those who repent, or whether merely bearing the name Christian or only the crimes associated with it is a punishable offense.

Meanwhile, I have used the following method in dealing with those who are charged with being Christians. I ask them if they are Christians. Those who confess it I ask the question again and a third time, threatening the death penalty. The ones who persist are ordered away for execution. For there can be no doubt that, whatever the nature of their profession, stubbornness and obstinate inflexibility ought to be punished. Others displaying similar folly, who are Roman citizens, are set apart for sending on to Rome.

Soon the mere investigation, as usually happens, led to spreading accusations, with more examples being brought to light. An accusatory pamphlet appeared—without a signature—which contains many names. I considered for release those who denied that they are or have been Christians and followed me in a prayer to the gods and your image (which for this purpose I had ordered to be carried in), who made supplication with wine and incense, and finally cursed Christ—which, I am told, no one who is a true Christian can possibly be made to do.

Others named by the informant admitted they were Christians and then denied it; they had been indeed, but had ceased, some more than three years ago, some even longer, and a few as many as twenty years ago. These also all venerated your image and those of the gods and cursed Christ.

But they assured me that the sum of their fault or error was that they usually met before light on an appointed day to utter in turn songs to Christ as to a god, afterward taking an oath—not for the purpose of wickedness, but in fact to abstain from theft, banditry, committing adultery, lying, and witholding a deposit when it is claimed. At the conclusion of this time they separated, reassembling to take food of an ordinary and innocent kind; but they had ceased this after my edict, issued according to your order banning secret societies.

Believing it all the more necessary to get at the truth, I interrogated two maidservants, whom they call deaconnesses, through torture. I discovered nothing else from this but perverse and immoderate superstition.

Therefore, I broke off the investigation to ask your advice. The matter certainly seemed to me to be worthy of this consultation, especially in view of the numbers endangered by it. Very many of all ages, all classes, and both sexes have been accused and put in peril. The contagion is found not only in the cities, for the superstition has spread even to the villages and countryside; but it seems possible to stop and redirect it. Certainly, the temples, which had been almost desolate, now begin to be crowded, and the sacred festivals, which were neglected for a long time, have been resumed; sacrificial animals, which hitherto seldom had a buyer, are available everywhere. From this it can easily be surmised that many people might be reformed if given an opportunity to repent.

Clement of Alexandria (c. 150-c. 215)

Clement of Alexandria (Titus Flavius Clemens) was born in Athens, the son of pagan parents. After his conversion to Christianity he moved to Alexandria, Egypt, where he achieved renown as a teacher and scholar. He has been described as a "Christian Gnostic" because of his belief that, though salvation comes by faith, the addition of "knowledge" to that faith results in increased good to the believer. Clement's treatise, *Paedagogus* (The Instructor), is concluded by a Greek poem, which, in Henry M. Dexter's translation, "Shepherd of tender [or 'eager'] youth," is still found in modern English-language hymnals. Earlier in the book, Clement contrasts the drunken orgies of the heathen with the chasteness of Christian celebrations. In so doing, he calls his readers to purity, restraint, and nobility in their singing, leaving "overcolorful melodies" to "shameless [literally, 'colorless'] carousals."

2   From *Paedagogus*, Book 2, Chapter 4. *Source*: Translated by Simon P. Wood in Clement of Alexandria, *Christ the Educator*. Vol. 23 of *The Fathers of the Church* (New York: Fathers of the Church, Inc., 1954), pp. 129-130, 132-133.

In the feasts of reason that we have, let the wild celebrations of the holiday season have no part, or the senseless night-long parties that delight in wine-drinking. The wild celebration ends up as a drunken stupor, with everyone freely confiding the troubles of his love affairs. But love affairs and drunkenness are both contrary to reason, and therefore do not belong to our sort of celebrations. And as for all-night drinking parties, they go hand-in-hand with the holiday celebration and, in their wine-drinking, promote drunkenness and promiscuity. They are brazen celebrations that work deeds of shame. The exciting rhythm of flutes and harps, choruses and dances, Egyptian castanets and other entertainments get out of control and become indecent and burlesque, especially when they are re-enforced by cymbals and drums and accompanied by the noise of all these instruments of deception. It seems to me that a banquet easily turns into a mere exhibition of drunkenness. The Apostle warned: "Laying aside the works of darkness, put on the armor of light. Let us walk becomingly as in the day, not occupying ourselves in revelry and drunkenness, not in debauchery and wantonness."

. . .

But make sure that the sociability arising from our drinking is twofold, in keeping with the direction of the Law. For, if "Thou shalt love the Lord thy God," and after that, "thy neighbor," then intimacy with God must come first, and be expressed in thanksgiving and chanting of psalms. Only then are we free to show sociability toward our neighbor in a respectful comradeship. "Let the word of the Lord dwell in you abundantly," the Apostle says. But this Word adapts Himself and adjusts Himself to the occasion, person, and place; in our present discussion, He is the congenial companion of our drinking. The Apostle adds further: "In all wisdom teach and admonish one another by psalms, hymns and spiritual songs, singing in your hearts to God by His grace. Whatever you do in word or in work, do all in the name of the Lord Jesus, giving thanks to God His Father." This Eucharistic feast of ours is completely innocent, even if we desire to sing at it, or to chant psalms to the lyre or lute. Imitate the holy Hebrew king in his thanksgiving to God: "Rejoice in the Lord, O ye just; praise becometh the upright," as the inspired psalm says: "Give praise to the Lord on the harp, sing to Him with the lyre"—an instrument with ten strings—"Sing to Him a new canticle." There can be little doubt that the lyre with its ten strings is a figure of Jesus the Word, for that is the significance of the number ten.

It is fitting to bless the Maker of all things before we partake of food; so, too, at a feast, when we enjoy His created gifts, it is only right that we sing psalms to Him. In fact, a psalm sung in unison is a blessing, and it is an act of self-restraint. The Apostle calls the psalm "a spiritual song." Again, it is a holy duty to give thanks to

God for the favors and the love we have received from Him, before we fall asleep. "Give praise to Him with canticles of your lips," Scripture says, "because at His command, every favor is shown, and there is no diminishing of His salvation." Even among the ancient Greeks, there was a song called the skolion which they used to sing after the manner of the Hebrew psalm at drinking parties and over their after-dinner cups. All sang together with one voice, and sometimes they passed these toasts of song along in turn; those more musical than the rest sang to the accompaniment of the lyre.

Yet, let no passionate love songs be permitted there; let our songs be hymns to God. "Let them praise His name in choir," we read, "let them sing to Him with the drum and the harp." And the Holy Spirit explains what this choir is which sings: "Let His praise be in the church of the saints: let them be joyful to their king." And He adds: "For the Lord is well-pleased with His people." We may indeed retain harmonies, but not so those tearful songs which are too florid in the overdelicate modulation of the voice they require. These last must be proscribed and repudiated by those who would retain virility of mind, for their sentimentality and ribaldry degenerate the soul. There is nothing in common between restrained, chaste tunes and the licentiousness of intemperance. Therefore, overcolorful melodies are to be left to shameless carousals, and to the honeyed and garish music of the courtesan.

Tertullian (c. 160-c. 240)

Quintus Septimus Florens Tertullian was born and spent his entire life in Carthage, North Africa, the son of a Roman government official. Converted to Christianity about 195, he became a vigorous defender of the faith against all opponents, and is generally acknowledged to have been one of the most important early Latin Christian apologists. Disaffected with what he considered to be the laxity of the church hierarchy, he later joined the Montanists, a rigorously ascetic and millenarian sect that claimed to receive new revelations from God through trances and visions. His particular brand of Montanism ultimately led to the establishment of a new group, the Tertullianists.

Both of the writings extracted below date from Tertullian's orthodox period. In the treatise *Ad Uxorem* (To His Wife), he describes the equality of Christian marriage partners; one sign of this equality is the mutual singing of "psalms and hymns." In the *Apology*, the author defends believers against charges of lewdness, political subversiveness, extravagance, and excessive drinking by describing the Christian *agape*: "Our meal can be understood by its very name, for it is called by the Greek word for 'love.'" One proof of Christian sobriety at these meals was the ability to sing biblical psalms and canticles or newly composed songs.

3   From *Ad Uxorem*, Book 2, Chapter 8. *Source*: *CCSL*, I, pp. 393-394.

Where there is one flesh, there is one spirit: they pray together, have the same desires, mutually perform fasts, each teaches the other, each encourages the other, each sustains the other. Side by side they are together in God's church, together at God's banquet, together in difficulty, in persecution, in weariness. Neither keeps a secret from the other, neither shuns the other, neither is harsh to the other. They freely visit the sick and support the needy. They give alms without fear, sacrifice without care, daily industry without hindrance; they have no hidden signs, no insincere greetings, no withholding of blessings. Psalms and hymns sound between the two, and they challenge each other to see which one will better sing to the Lord. Christ sees and hears such with joy. He sends his peace to them. Where the two are, there he is also: where he is, there is no evil.

4   From *The Apology*, Chapter 39. *Source*: *CCSL*, I, pp. 152-153.

None take their places at the table without first tasting prayer. They eat what they need to satisfy their hunger; they drink as much as is fit for the modest. Thus they have enough, for they remember that they will worship God during the night; they talk knowing that God hears them. After handwashing and lamplighting, each is given an opportunity to stand in the middle and sing to God from the divine scriptures or from his own invention: this proves the limits of his drinking. The meal closes as it began, with prayer. From there they disperse, not as bands of evildoers, nor as groups of rioters, nor as beginners of licentiousness, but as those who give attention to modesty and purity, as if they had been to a school of discipline instead of dining at a banquet.

Ambrose of Milan (c. 340-397)
Ambrose of Milan served as the Roman governor of the city. His administrative abilities were so widely recognized that in 374 he was made Bishop of Milan, though at the time he was still a catechumen. Ambrose was quickly baptized and turned his attention to administering the church's affairs.

One of Ambrose's greatest challenges came in 386, when he and his people withstood attempts by the empress dowager Justina to impose Arianism on the city. The bishop and his people took up quarters in the basilica, surrounded by Justina's soldiers. The faithful occupied themselves in their confinement with the "reciting" of psalms. That the psalms were sung and not merely spoken is evident from the fuller description of the same event given by Augustine (see below).

5   From Letter No. 20. *Source*: *PL*, XVI, p. 1001.

The whole of that day was spent in our sorrow; the royal hangings were cut by boys in their play. I was not able to return home because of the soldiers who surrounded the basilica, keeping it under guard. We recited psalms with the faithful in the smaller basilica of the church.

Augustine of Hippo (354-430)
Augustine was the son of a pagan father and a Christian mother. While attending school in Carthage, he became a member of the Manicheans, a pseudo-Christian gnostic sect, and subsequently immersed himself in Greek philosophy. In 384, Augustine became professor of rhetoric in Milan, where he came under the twin influences of Neoplatonic philosophy and the preaching of Ambrose; these led to a dramatic conversion experience in 386. Ordained a priest in 391, he became Bishop of Hippo in 396, a post he held until his death. A prolific author, Augustine is best known today as the author of the *Confessions* and *De Civitate Dei* (The City of God).

The oft-quoted passage from the *Confessions* found below gives a somewhat fuller account of the event referred to in the previous selection. At the end of chapter 6, Augustine described the death of his son, Adeodatus, and the comfort he received from the singing of the "hymns and canticles" of the church. In the subsequent chapter, Ambrose is credited with establishing "the singing of hymns and psalms in the manner of the eastern parts." The implications of this are unclear. The traditional view is that Ambrose introduced the custom of antiphonal singing as practiced in the eastern churches, though other interpretations are also possible. At any rate, Augustine's colorful description serves as an eloquent testimony to the importance placed on singing by two of the greatest figures of fourth-century Christianity.

Following the passage from the *Confessions* is an extract from one of Augustine's letters, which contrasts the plain singing of orthodox Christians with the orgiastic performances of the Donatists, a schismatic sect centered mainly in North Africa. He also notes a great variety of usage of singing among the churches and points out that some of the North African churches had unduly neglected it.

6   From *Confessions*, Book 9, Chapters 6 and 7. *Source*:
       CCSL, XXVII, pp. 141-142.

How many tears I shed at the pleasant sound of hymns and canticles sung by the impassioned voices of your church! Their voices poured into my ears and dissolved truth in my heart, and a feeling of devotion welled up from it; my tears flowed, and I was happy with them.

Not long before, the church at Milan had begun to practice this method of comfort and encouragement through the joyful singing of the brethren with voices and hearts. It was about a year, or not much longer, since Justina, the mother of the boy emperor Valentinian, having been led into heresy by the Arians, persecuted your servant Ambrose. Faithfully standing guard in the church, the people were ready to die with their bishop, your servant. On that occasion, my mother, your maidservant, became a leader in the concerns and vigils, living on prayer. We were still cold, without the warmth of your spirit, yet were astonished at the disturbances and confusion in the city. At that time, the singing of hymns and psalms in the manner of the eastern parts was established to keep the people from wasting away through the weariness of sorrow. Since then, this has been imitated by many and is common among nearly all your flocks throughout the world.

7   From Letter No. 55, Chapter 18. _Source_: _PL_, vol. 33,
        pp. 220-221.

I am amazed at your request for me to write to you about practices which vary from place to place, when it is not necessary for me to do this, and there is a single helpful rule to keep in mind, that when they are not contrary to faith nor to good morals, but help exhort us to a better life, that wherever we see them or know of their existence, we do not criticize them, but praise and imitate them, unless this will be a hindrance to those whose faith is weak. But even on that account, if there is greater hope of gain than fear of loss, they should be performed without question, especially when they can be strongly defended from the scriptures; as, for instance, the singing of hymns and psalms, for which the examples and precepts of not only the Lord himself but also the apostles are recorded. Of this method, which is so useful for moving the soul to devotion and igniting divine love in the emotions, there are different customs, and a good many members of the African church are sluggish about it. Thus, the Donatists find fault with us, because we soberly psalm the divine songs of the prophets, while they intoxicate themselves by singing psalms composed by human cleverness, which inflame them like the stirring sounds of war trumpets. But when the faithful congregate in the church, is not any time appropriate for holy singing, except when there is reading, or discussion, or praying aloud by the presiding priest, or common prayer announced by the deacon's voice?

Basil (c. 330-379)
      Basil "the Great" was elected bishop of Caesarea and archbishop of Cappadocia in 370 and was a staunch defender of orthodox Christianity against Arian tendencies in the East. He leaned toward asceticism and was influential in the development of eastern monasticism. In his letter "To the Clergy of Neocaesarea," Basil defended himself and his

people against several charges, including their procedure of
singing the psalms. The letter not only describes the manner
in which the psalms were performed, but points out that the
practices of Basil's followers were common throughout the
eastern church.

8   From Letter 207, "To the Clergy of Neocaesarea."
       Source: Translated by Agnes Clare Way in Saint
       Basil, *Letters*. Vol. 28 of *The Fathers of the Church*
       (New York: Fathers of the Church, Inc., 1955), vol.
       2, pp. 82, 83-84.

Now, if they are asked the reason for this unheralded and truceless
war, they mention psalms and a manner of chanting which differs
from the practice prevailing among you, and similar things, of which
they ought to feel ashamed. Moreover, a charge is brought against
us that we maintain men of ascetic life who have renounced the
world and all worldly cares, which the Lord compares to thorns,
since they do not permit the word to come to fruition. . . .
However, I wish you to know that we profess to have orders of men
and women whose conduct of life is heavenly, who have crucified
the flesh with its passions and desires, who are not solicitous about
food and clothing, but, being free from distractions and constantly
waiting on the Lord, continue in their prayers night and day. Their
mouths do not speak idly of the works of men, but they chant
hymns to our God continuously, working with their hands in order
that they may be able to share with those who are in need.
    As to the charge regarding psalmody, by which especially our
slanderers terrify the more simple, I have this to say, that the
customs now prevalent are in accord and harmony with those of all
the churches of God. Among us the people come early after
nightfall to the house of prayer, and in labor and affliction and
continual tears confess to God. Finally, rising up from their
prayers, they begin the chanting of psalms. And now, divided into
two parts, they chant antiphonally, becoming master of the text of
the Scriptural passages, and at the same time directing their
attention and recollectedness of their hearts. Then, again, leaving
it to one to intone the melody, the rest chant in response; thus,
having spent the night in a variety of psalmody and intervening
prayers, when day at length begins to dawn, all in common as with

one voice and one heart, offer up the psalm of confession to the Lord, each one making His own the words of repentance. If, then, you shun us on this account, you will shun the Egyptians, and also those of both Libyas, the Thebans, Palestinians, Arabians, Phoenicians, Syrians, and those dwelling beside the Euphrates—in one word, all those among whom night watches and prayers and psalmody in common have been held in esteem.

Egeria (4th-5th centuries)

Egeria was a Christian woman who made a three-year pilgrimage to the Holy Land and recorded her impressions in an *itinerarium*, or travel diary. Very little is known about the author, including her birth and death dates and place of residence, though there is some evidence that she might have been from Spain; even the form of her name is not wholly certain. Her diary probably dates from the first half of the fifth century.

Despite the uncertainties surrounding Egeria and her diary, this writing is a significant source of information on liturgy and music in the Christian churches of fifth-century Jerusalem and the surrounding area. Chapter 24 of the diary describes the observance of the daily offices at the Basilica of the Holy Sepulchre in Jerusalem. These were centered primarily in the Anastasis, a church built over the grotto that was the reputed site of Christ's burial. The services were apparently performed primarily by those in religious orders, but several passages also suggest the use of congregational singing by others attending the services.

9   *Itinerarium*, Chapter 24. *Source:* Translated by George E. Gingras in *Egeria: Diary of a Pilgrimage*. No. 38 of *Ancient Christian Writers* (New York: Newman Press, 1970), pp. 89-93.

Knowing how pleased Your Charity would be to learn what is the ritual observed day by day in the holy places, I considered it my duty to make known to you the details. Each day before cockcrow, all the doors of the Anastasis are opened; and all the monks and virgins come down—the *monazontes* and the *parthene* as they are called here—and not only they, but laymen as well, men and women who wish to rise very early. From this hour until dawn, hymns are sung, and responses are made to the Psalms, and likewise to the antiphons; and after each hymn a prayer is said. Priests in groups of two or three, and a like number of deacons, take turns on successive days in coming at the same time as the monks, and after each hymn or antiphon they recite prayers. At the time when it begins to grow light, they start singing the morning hymns. Then you see the bishop come in with his clergy. He immediately goes into the grotto, and from within the railings he recites first a prayer for all the people; then he himself mentions the names of those whom he wishes to commemorate, and he blesses the catechumens. Then, after he has said a prayer and blessed the faithful, the bishop comes out from the grotto sanctuary, whereupon all present come forth to kiss his hand, and he blesses each of them in turn as he goes out. And so the dismissal is given, and by now it is daylight.

Once again at the sixth hour, everyone returns a second time to the Anastasis, where Psalms and antiphons are sung while the bishop is being summoned. When he comes in, he does not sit down but, as before, goes immediately within the railings inside the Anastasis, that is to say, within the grotto where he had been in the early morning. As happened earlier, he first says a prayer and then blesses the faithful. And as he leaves the grotto sanctuary, everyone comes forth once again to kiss his hand. The same thing takes place at the ninth hour as at the sixth hour.

At the tenth hour, which is here called *licinicon*, or, as we say, vespers, a great multitude assemble at the Anastasis. All the torches and candles are lighted, and this makes a tremendous light. The light, however, is not brought in from outside, but is taken from inside the grotto, that is, from within the railings where night and day a lamp always burns. Vesper Psalms and antiphons as well are sung for some time, and then the bishop is called. When he comes in, he sits down, and the priests as well sit in their places. Hymns and antiphons are sung; and, when they have been completed according to the custom, the bishop rises and stands in front of the railings, that is, in front of the grotto, while one of the deacons makes a commemoration of each individual as is the custom. Every time the deacon mentions the name of someone, the many children standing about answer: *Kyrie eleison*, or as we say: "Lord, have mercy," and their voices are legion. As soon as the deacon has finished what he has to say, the bishop first says a prayer, and he prays for everyone; and then everyone prays together, both the faithful and the catechumens. Next the deacon cries out that each catechumen, wherever he is standing, must bow his head, whereupon the bishop, who is standing, pronounces the blessing over the catechumens. A prayer is said and the deacon raises his voice anew to admonish each of the faithful present to bow his head; then the bishop blesses the faithful and the dismissal is given at the Anastasis; and everyone comes forth in turn to kiss the bishop's hand.

After this, singing hymns, they lead the bishop from the Anastasis to the Cross, and all the people go along also. When they have arrived there, first of all he says a prayer and blesses the catechumens; then he says a second prayer and blesses the faithful. Afterwards, both the bishop and the whole multitude go immediately behind the Cross, where everything just done before the Cross is done anew. Just as everyone at the Anastasis and before the Cross came forward to kiss the bishop's hand, so they do likewise behind the Cross. Numerous large glass lamps hang everywhere and there are many candelabra, not only in front of the Anastasis, but also before the Cross and even behind the Cross. This is the ritual that takes place daily on the six weekdays at the Anastasis and the Cross.

On the seventh day, however, that is, on Sunday, before the cockcrow, a whole multitude, whatever number can be accommodated in this place and as many as at Easter, gather outside the forecourt adjoining the Anastasis, where for this reason there are lamps hanging. Fearing that they will not arrive in time for cockcrow, the people come beforehand and sit there, singing hymns and antiphons and reciting prayers after each hymn and antiphon. Because of the multitude which assembles, there are always priests and deacons ready to hold the vigil, for, by custom, the holy places are not opened before cockcrow.

As soon as the first cock has crowed, the bishop immediately comes down to the church and goes into the grotto at the Anastasis. All the doors are then opened, and the multitude goes into the Anastasis, where countless lights are already glowing. And as soon as the people have entered, one of the priests sings a Psalm and they all make the response; afterwards, a prayer is said. Next one of the deacons sings a Psalm, and again a prayer is said, whereupon a third Psalm is sung by one of the minor ministers, followed by a third prayer and a commemoration of all. When the three Psalms and prayers have been said, then the censers are brought into the grotto of the Anastasis, with the result that the whole basilica of the Anastasis is filled with odors of incense. Then the bishop stands within the railings, takes up the Gospel, and goes toward the door; there the bishop himself reads the Resurrection of the Lord. As soon as the reading of it has begun, so much moaning and groaning is heard, and there is so much weeping among all the people, that the hardest of men would be moved to tears because the Lord has endured so much on our behalf.

Once the Gospel has been read, the bishop goes out, and singing hymns they lead him to the Cross, and with him go the people. There another Psalm is sung and a prayer said. Then he blesses the faithful, and the dismissal is given. As the bishop leaves, all come forth to kiss his hand. The bishop then withdraws to his house, and from that time on all the monks return to the Anastasis to sing Psalms and antiphons until dawn, and to recite a prayer after each Psalm or antiphon. Each day priests and deacons take turns in holding the vigil at the Anastasis with the people. Among the laity there are men and women who wish to remain there until dawn, while others, not wishing to do so, return to their homes to sleep and to rest.

Palladius (368-431)

Palladius, a native of Galatia, was a desert ascetic who was made bishop of Bithynia by John Chrysostom. Imprisoned twice during political upheavals in the eastern empire, Palladius was banished to Egypt for a time. After his release, he was appointed bishop of Aspona in Galatia. During his last years, he busied himself writing biographies of early monastics. In the *Lausiac History*, he relates the story of the ascetic Adolius—who is unknown except for this reference—and his use of psalmody.

10   *Historia Lausiaca*, Chapter 43. *Source*: Translated by Robert T. Meyer in *Palladius: The Lausiac History*. No. 34 of *Ancient Christian Writers* (Westminster, Maryland: The Newman Press, 1965), pp. 119-120.

1. I also knew Adolius at Jerusalem. He was a Tarsian by birth

who had come to Jerusalem by an altogether different way, not at all by the way we traveled, but cut out for himself a strange way of life. For his ascetic practice was beyond man to such a degree that the very demons trembled at his strictness of life and no one dared to rival him. Because of his excessive self-control and all-night vigils he was actually suspected of being a monster.

2. For in Lent he would eat only every five days, although at other times he ate every other day. But the big thing he did was this: From the time of evening until the brotherhood gathered again in its house of prayer, he would stand on the Mount of Olives, on the Hill of Ascension, the place where Jesus was taken up. There he would stand, singing psalms and praying, and even if it snowed or rained, or there was a frost, he would remain there unshaken.

3. After he had completed his usual time he would knock at the cells of all with the clapper he used in waking them. He would bring them together in houses for prayer and at each oratory join them in singing one or two psalms antiphonally. After he had prayed with them he would go off to his cell before it was day. As a matter of fact the brethren often undressed him, wrung out his clothes as though they were just from the laundry, and put others on him. So then he would rest until the hour of psalmody, and he would keep busy until evening. This, then, was the virtue of Adolius the Tarsian who attained perfection in Jerusalem and there went to sleep.

Council of Laodicea (c. 343-381)

The precise date of the Council of Laodicea is not known, but it was probably held sometime between 343 and 381. Concern over heretical tendencies in hymnody led to the strictures of Canons XV and LIX on the personnel and materials to be used in the church's song. Laodicea was a local, not an ecumenical, council; thus, the prohibitions stated here did not apply to the church as a whole, though they were perhaps representative of a widespread distrust of hymnody at the time. Canon XVII was evidently intended to prevent monotony in the singing of psalms.

11   From Canons of the Council of Laodicea. *Source*: Translated by Henry R. Percival in *NPNF*, 2nd series, vol. 14, pp. 132, 133, 158.

Canon XV

No others shall sing in the Church, save only the canonical singers, who go up into the ambo and sing from a book.

Canon XVII

The Psalms are not to be joined together in the congregations, but a lesson shall intervene after every psalm.

Canon LIX

No psalms composed by private individuals nor any uncanonical books may be read in the church, but only the Canonical Books of the Old and New Testaments.

2
Early Definitions of "Hymn"

Augustine of Hippo

THE most often quoted definition of the word "hymn" is that found in Augustine's commentary on Psalm 72 [73]. In the version of the psalms used by Augustine, the last verse of Psalm 71 [72] formed part of the title of the succeeding psalm. While Augustine was defining the word "hymn," it must be remembered that he was referring to a category of psalms.

12   From *Ennarationes in psalmos*, Psalm 72 [73]. *Source*: *CCSL*, vol. 39, p. 986.

This psalm has an inscription, that is, a title: *The hymns of David, the son of Jesse, have failed. A Psalm of Asaph himself.* The name of David is written in the titles of many psalms, but nowhere is "the son of Jesse" added except in this one alone. Which, we believe, was not done in vain nor uselessly; for God gives us a sign everywhere, and calls us to understand it through the godly study of love. What is: *The hymns of David, the son of Jesse have failed*? Hymns are praises of God with singing: hymns are songs containing the praise of God. If there is praise, but not of God, it is not a hymn; if there is praise, and praise of God, but no singing, it is not a hymn. Therefore, if it is a hymn, it will properly have these three things: not only praise, but of God, and singing. What, therefore, is: *The hymns have failed*? The praises sung to God have failed. He seems to speak of something that is painful and, so to speak, sorrowful. The one who sings praise not only praises, but also praises cheerfully; the one who sings praise not only sings, but also loves the one of whom he sings. In praise one's confession is announced, in singing is the affection of one loving.

Cassiodorus (c. 485-c. 580)

Flavius Magnus Aurelius Cassiodorus Senator spent the earlier part of his life in public service and his later years in the service of the church. Among the works written during the latter period was his *Expositio psalmorum*, a commentary on the 150 psalms of the Old Testament. His discussion of the third verse of Psalm 39 [40] observes that hymns consist of "praise composed in poetic form." However, like Augustine's definition quoted above, it should be noted that Cassiodorus is discussing the word in the context of the psalms.

13   *Expositio psalmorum*, Psalm 39 [40], verse 3. *Source*: *CCSL*, vol. 97, pp. 363-364.

And he put a new song in my mouth, a hymn to our God; many shall see and fear and hope in the Lord. The preceding part of the psalm relates that God brought humanity, plunged in the mire of the world, to firm ground, namely the Christian religion. Which this verse now makes clear by saying: *And he put a new song in my mouth*, that is the most holy proclamation of the New Testament. But *new* is well said, for no previous age had seen the incarnate Lord with bodily eyes. Certainly, nothing is new for God, since he foresaw the makeup of the universe before he established the world. Now *hymn* is from the Greek language, and means praise composed in poetic form. And because there were hymns which the Gentiles shouted to idols, it adds *to our God*; thus, we can clearly observe the kind of hymn that is meant. *Many shall see and fear*. This speaks of the miracles effected during the time of the holy incarnation. For example, when the Jews saw such miracles they feared, and when Christ the Lord preached the crowds of people believed. But they *hoped in the Lord* when they became Christians, for they were converted after their fear of the miracles and demonstrated that they had steadfast hope in the Lord.

Isidore of Seville (c. 560-636)

Isidore of Seville, the leading Spanish churchman of his day, became bishop of Seville in 600. His writings exerted a profound influence on the theologians of his own and subsequent generations. Many of Isidore's works were encyclopedic in nature, including his *De ecclesiasticis officiis* (The Church Offices), which described the liturgy and various ranks of clergy and laity in the church. Among the terms discussed by Isidore were "choirs," "canticles," "psalms," "hymns," "antiphons," and "responses." The fluidity of definitions at this early period is evident from the opening paragraph of the following extract, which, purporting to discuss "hymns," gives examples of what are usually called psalms or canticles. In the second and third paragraphs, however, the author takes note of the productions of post-biblical authors, finally concluding, like Augustine, that hymns may be generically defined as "songs . . . in praise of God."

14   *De ecclesiasticis officiis*, Book 1, Chapter 6. *Source*: *CCSL*, vol. 113, p. 7.

On Hymns

Clearly, David the prophet was the first to write and sing hymns, followed by the other prophets. Later, when the three children were put into the furnace, they called upon all creation to sing hymns to the creator of all. Furthermore, in the singing of hymns and psalms, not only the prophets, but also the Lord himself and the apostles give examples and precepts of this useful manner of stirring a spirit of devotion and inflaming divinely-approved affection.

However, divine hymns have also been composed through human ingenuity. Hilary, bishop of Gaul, a native of Poitiers, distinguished for his eloquence, first blossomed forth in the poetry of hymns. After whom, bishop Ambrose, a man of great glory in Christ and a renowned teacher in the church, collected many of these sorts of songs; and thereafter the hymns which first began to resound in the church in Milan during his time were called "Ambrosian" after his name; this festive devotion has subsequently been observed in all the western churches.

However, any songs which are uttered in praise of God are called hymns.

3
Hymns and Heresy

Ephraim Syrus (c. 306-c. 373)

EPHRAIM Syrus was born at Nisibis in Syria. A staunch defender of orthodox positions on the deity of Christ, he attended the Council of Nicaea. In 363 he moved near Edessa, where he established a theological school. Ephraim was the first significant orthodox hymn writer of Syria and organized choirs of women to sing his hymns. These activities led to his being nicknamed the "Harp of the Spirit."

One of Ephraim's chief opponents in doctrinal controversy was the Syrian Bardasanes. Bardasanes was a hymn writer, and it was apparently in reaction to both the doctrines and popularity of Bardasanes' hymns that Ephraim himself begin to engage in this activity. In the following extract from one of Ephraim's metrical sermons, he points out that Bardasanes sought to imitate David, even to the extent of composing his own rival psalter. Ephraim also frets about the possible effect of Bardasanes' hymns on "the simple."

15   From Homily No. 53, *Against Heretics. Source: Sancti Ephraem Syri, Hymni et Sermones,* ed. and trans. into Latin by Thomas Josephus Lamy (Mechliniae: H. Dessain, 1886), vol. 2, p. 66.

He made hymns naturally,
To that end he adapted measures,
And composed songs,
And introduced meters,
And in weighty proportions separated verses.
Thus, he passed on to the simple poison tempered with sweetness.
The sick do not naturally choose healthy food.

He aimed to follow David,
That he might adorn himself with his beauty
And be commended for his imitations.
This man also composed one hundred and fifty songs.

Sozomen (c. 375-c. 447)

Sozomen was a third-generation Christian. Born at Bethelia,
near Gaza, in Palestine, he subsequently practiced law in
Constantinople. Sozomen wrote two books of church history,
the first (now lost) covering the period from the ascension of
Christ to A.D. 324, and the second (left incomplete) dealing
with the years 324 to 440. Sozomen's second history is
generally thought to have been based at least partly on the
similar work by Socrates (see below), whom he undoubtedly
knew (both practiced law in Constantinople at the same
time), though he sometimes corrected and amplified his
contemporary's work. In the first extract from Sozomen's
book, it is Harmonius, the son of Bardasanes, not Bardasanes
himself, who is "credited" with having first written heretical
hymns in the Syriac language. The passage also describes
how Ephraim fought these heretical hymns by composing his
own, using the meters of Harmonius so they could be sung
to the same tunes. The second selection indicates some of
the difficulties involved in later periods when adherents of
different doctrinal positions tried to sing together.

16   From *Ecclesiastical History*, Book 3, Chapter 16.
         Source: Translated by Edward Walford in Sozomen,
         The Ecclesiastical History (London: Henry G. Bohn,
         1855), p. 135.

I am not ignorant that there were some very learned men who
flourished in Osroene, as, for instance, Bardasanes, who originated
a heresy designated by his name, and Harmonius his son. It is
related that this latter was deeply versed in Grecian erudition, and
was the first to compose verses in his vernacular language; those
verses he delivered to the choirs, and even now the Syrians
frequently sing, not the precise verses written by Harmonius, but
others of the same metre. For as Harmonius was not altogether
free from the errors of his father, and entertained various opinions

concerning the soul, the generation and destruction of the body, and the doctrine of transmigration, which are taught by the Greek philosophers, he introduced some of these sentiments in the lyrical songs which he composed. When Ephraim perceived that the Syrians were charmed with the elegant diction and melodious versification of Harmonius, he became apprehensive, lest they should imbibe the same opinions; and therefore, although he was ignorant of Grecian learning, he applied himself to the study of the metres of Harmonius, and composed similar poems in accordance with the doctrines of the church, and sacred hymns in praise of holy men. From that period the Syrians sang the odes of Ephraim, according to the method indicated by Harmonius. The execution of this work is alone sufficient to attest the natural endowments of Ephraim.

17   From *Ecclesiastical History*, Book 3, Chapter 20.
          Source: Ibid., pp. 142-143.

Besides, the heterodox perceived that, although the government of the churches was in their hands, all the clergy and people did not conform to their doctrines. When they sang hymns to God they were, according to custom, divided into choirs; and, at the end of the hymns, each one declared what were his own peculiar sentiments. Some offered praise to "the Father *and* the Son," regarding them as co-equal in glory; others glorified "the Father *by* the Son," to denote that they considered the Son to be inferior to the Father. Leontius, the bishop of the opposite faction, who then presided over the church of Antioch, did not dare to prohibit the singing of hymns to God which were in accordance with the Nicene doctrines, for he feared to excite an insurrection of the people. It is related, however, that he once raised his hand to his head, the hairs of which were quite white, and said, "When this snow is dissolved, there will be plenty of mud." By this he intended to signify that, after his death, the different modes of singing hymns would give rise to great seditions, and that his successors would not show the same consideration to the people which he had manifested.

Ambrose of Milan
    In one of his sermons, Ambrose observes that his hymns

have been criticized by the Arians for "deceiving the people."
Ambrose considers this a compliment and acknowledges that
hymns are a powerful weapon in fighting heresy.

18   From *Sermo contra Auxentius*. *Source*: *PL*, vol. 16,
            pp. 1017-1018.

[They say that] the poetry of my hymns has led the people into
deception. I certainly do not deny it. This is an important formula
and there is none more powerful. What indeed is more powerful
than the confession of the Trinity, which the people repeat many
times each day? All strive to be faithful in acknowledging the
Father, Son, and Holy Spirit in verse. This has made them all
teachers, who are scarcely capable of being followers.

Socrates (c. 380-450)
    Socrates, not to be confused with the famous Greek
    philosopher, was born at Constantinople and spent most of
    his life there practicing law. He undertook to write a
    continuation of the well-known church history by Eusebius of
    Caesarea (c. 260-339), which had left off at the year 325.
    The following passage from Socrates' history describes how
    the "Homoousians"—those who held the orthodox view that
    the Father and Son were of the same essence or
    substance—under the leadership of John Chrysostom (c. 347-
    407) opposed the singing processions of the Arians by
    organizing singing processions of their own—sometimes with
    disastrous results. These events occurred sometime between
    398 and 403, while John was bishop of Constantinople. An
    important feature of the description is Socrates' quotation of
    part of an Arian hymn. This is one of the few extant
    examples of Arian hymnody, most of which has been lost due
    to suppression and centuries of neglect. Socrates concludes
    the passage by ascribing the "invention" of antiphonal singing
    in the eastern church to Ignatius of Antioch (d. c. 110).

19   *Ecclesiastical History*, Book 6, Chapter 8. *Source*:
           Translated by A. C. Zenos in *NPNF*, 2nd series, vol.
           2, p. 144.

The Arians, as we have said, held their meetings without the city. As often therefore as the festal days occurred—I mean Saturday and Lord's day—in each week, on which assemblies are usually held in the churches, they congregated within the city gates about the public squares, and sang responsive verses adapted to the Arian heresy. This they did during the greater part of the night: and again in the morning, chanting the same songs which they called responsive, they paraded through the midst of the city, and so passed out of the gates to go to their places of assembly. But since they did not desist from making use of insulting expressions in relation to the Homoousians, often singing such words as these: "Where are they that say three things are but one power?"—John fearing lest any of the more simple should be drawn away from the church by such kind of hymns, opposed to them some of his own people, that they also employing themselves in chanting nocturnal hymns, might obscure the effort of the Arians, and confirm his own party in the profession of their faith. John's design indeed seemed to be good, but it issued in tumult and dangers. For as the Homoousians performed their nocturnal hymns with greater display,—for there were invented by John silver crosses for them on which lighted wax-tapers were carried, provided at the expense of the empress Eudoxia,—the Arians who were very numerous, and fired with envy, resolved to revenge themselves by a desperate and riotous attack upon their rivals. For from the remembrance of their own recent domination, they were full of confidence in their ability to overcome, and of contempt for their adversaries. Without delay therefore, on one of these nights, they engaged in a conflict; and Briso, one of the eunuchs of the empress, who was at that time leading the chanters of these hymns, was wounded by a stone in the forehead, and also some of the people on both sides were killed. Whereupon the emperor being angered, forbade the Arians to chant their hymns any more in public. Such were the events of this occasion.

We must now however make some allusion to the origin of this custom in the church of responsive singing. Ignatius third bishop of Antioch in Syria from the apostle Peter, who also had held intercourse with the apostles themselves, saw a vision of angels hymning in alternate chants the Holy Trinity. Accordingly he introduced the mode of singing he had observed in the vision into the Antiochian church; whence it was transmitted by tradition to all the other churches. Such is the account [we have received] in relation to these responsive hymns.

4

Medieval Religious Song

Notker Balbulus (c. 840-912)

NOTKER Balbulus ("Notker the Stammerer") was a monk
at the Benedictine monastery of St. Gall in Switzerland. His
Liber hymnorum (Book of Hymns) was the earliest significant
collection of sequences, a form of Latin religious song that
became very popular in the late Middle Ages. (All but four
sequences were eventually banned by the Council of Trent in
the sixteenth century; a fifth was approved for use in the
eighteenth century.) The preface to Notker's book describes
how the sequence first came to his attention and details his
own early efforts to write in the form. The account suggests
a Frankish origin for the sequence, and implies that it was
originally intended to serve a mnemonic function by adding
words to melismata in "alleluia" melodies.

20   Preface to *Liber hymnorum*. *Source*: Translated by
Richard L. Crocker in *The Early Medieval Sequence*
(Berkeley: University of California Press, 1977), pp.
1-2.

To Liutward, who for his great sanctity has been raised in honor to
be a high priest, a most worthy successor to that incomparable man,
Eusebius, Bishop of Vercelli; abbot of the monastery of the most
holy Columbanus, and defender of the cell of his disciple, the most
gentle Gallus; and also the arch-chaplain of the most glorious
emperor Charles, from Notker, the least of the monks of St. Gall.

When I was still young, and very long melodies—repeatedly
entrusted to memory—escaped from my poor little head, I began to
reason with myself how I could bind them fast.

In the meantime it happened that a certain priest from Junieges
(recently laid waste by the Normans) came to us, bringing with him

his antiphonary, in which some verses had been set to sequences; but they were in a very corrupt state. Upon closer inspection I was as bitterly disappointed in them as I had been delighted at first glance.

Nevertheless, in imitation of them I began to write *Laudes Deo concinat orbis universus, Qui gratis est redemptus*, and further on *Coluber adae deceptor*. When I took these lines to my teacher Iso, he, commending my industry while taking pity on my lack of experience, praised what was pleasing, and what was not he set about to improve, saying, "The individual motions of the melody should receive separate syllables." Hearing that, I immediately corrected those which fell under *ia*; those under *le* or *lu*, however, I left as too difficult; but later, with practice, I managed it easily—for example in "Dominus in Sina" and "Mater." Instructed in this manner, I soon composed my second piece, *Psallat ecclesia mater illibata*.

When I showed these little verses to my teacher Marcellus, he, filled with joy, had them copied as a group on a roll; and he gave out different pieces to different boys to be sung. And when he told me that I should collect them in a book and offer them as a gift to some eminent person, I shrank back in shame, thinking I would never be able to do that.

Recently, however, I was asked by my brother Othar to write something in your praise, and I considered myself—with good reason—unequal to the task; but finally I worked up my courage (still with great pain and difficulty) that I might presume to dedicate this worthless little book to your highness. If I were to learn that anything in it had pleased you—as good as you are—to the extent that you might be of assistance to my brother with our Lord the Emperor, I would hasten to send you the metrical life of St. Gall which I am working hard to complete (although I had already promised it to my brother Salomon) for you to examine, to keep, and to comment upon.

Francis of Assisi (c. 1182-1226)

Francis of Assisi is undoubtedly the most beloved religious figure of the late Middle Ages. His gentle nature, extraordinary love of and respect for all creation, and simple, self-denying lifestyle have become legendary. Vowing a life of poverty, he gave away nearly all his possessions and gathered about him a group of followers who devoted themselves to the same ascetic principles. In the 1220s, the pope officially recognized this group as a religious order, which subsequently became known as the Franciscans. Francis is known to hymnology primarily through the ascription to him of an Italian poem, the "Canticle of the Sun." In English-speaking churches, this is usually sung in William H. Draper's paraphrase, "All creatures of our God and King."

The following reports of Francis's activities are taken from two near-contemporary accounts of his life. Thomas of Celano (c. 1200–c. 1255), a member of the Franciscan order during its founder's lifetime, wrote two biographies of Francis. _The Second Life_, completed by 1247, includes a chapter describing Francis's singing of hymns in the vernacular, in this case French. The _Legend of Perugia_ is found in an early fourteenth-century manuscript from Perugia, Italy. The section of the manuscript that contains the present extract is thought to contain recollections by one of Francis's closest associates, Brother Leo (d. 1271). This passage describes the origin of the "Canticle of the Sun" and Francis's appointment of some of his followers to be "jongleurs of God." Medieval jongleurs were itinerant professional entertainers, whose repertoire typically consisted of secular music. Francis's jongleurs may have sung _laudi spirituali_ ("spiritual praises"), a type of nonliturgical vernacular devotional song that was closely connected with the Franciscans during the thirteenth century.

Both of these excerpts show that vernacular hymnody, while not forming part of the official services of the medieval church, could and did flourish in the popular devotions of the people.

21   Thomas of Celano, _The Second Life of St. Francis_, Book 2, Chapter 90. _Source_: Translated by Placid Hermann in Marion A. Habig, ed., _St. Francis of Assisi: Writings and Early Biographies. English Omnibus of the Sources for the Life of St. Francis_ (Chicago: Franciscan Herald Press, 1973), p. 467.

Sometimes Francis would act in the following way. When the sweetest melody of spirit would bubble up in him, he would give exterior expression to it in French, and the breath of the divine whisper which his ear perceived in secret would burst forth in French in a song of joy. At times, as we saw with our own eyes, he would pick up a stick from the ground and putting it over his left arm, would draw across it, as across a violin, a little bow bent by means of a string; and going through the motions of playing, he would sing in French about his Lord. This whole ecstasy of joy would often end in tears and his song of gladness would be dissolved in compassion for the passion of Christ. Then this saint would bring forth continual sighs, and amid deep groanings, he would be raised up to heaven, forgetful of the lower things he held in his hand.

22   From *The Legend of Perugia*. *Source*: Translated by
           Paul Oligny in ibid., pp. 1020-1022.

The Canticle of the Sun

During his stay in this friary, for fifty days and more, blessed Francis could not bear the light of the sun during the day or the light of the fire at night. He constantly remained in darkness inside the house in his cell. His eyes caused him so much pain that he could neither lie down nor sleep, so to speak, which was very bad for his eyes and for his health. A few times he was on the point of resting and sleeping, but in the house and in the cell made of mats, that had been made ready for him, there were so many mice running around here and there, around him and even on him, that they prevented him from taking a rest; they even hindered him greatly in his prayer. They annoyed him not only at night but also during the day. When he ate, they climbed up on the table, so much so that he and his companions were of the opinion that it was a diabolical intervention, which it was.

     One night, as he was thinking of all the tribulations he was enduring, he felt sorry for himself and said interiorly: "Lord, help me in my infirmities so that I may have the strength to bear them patiently!" And suddenly he heard a voice in spirit: "Tell me, Brother: if, in compensation for your sufferings and tribulations you were given an immense and precious treasure: the whole mass of the earth changed into pure gold, pebbles into precious stones, and the water of the rivers into perfume, would you not regard the pebbles and the waters as nothing compared to such a treasure? Would you not rejoice?" Blessed Francis answered: "Lord, it would be a very great, very precious, and inestimable treasure beyond all that one can love and desire!" "Well, Brother," the voice said, "be glad and joyful in the midst of your infirmities and tribulations: as of now, live in peace as if you were already sharing my kingdom."

The next morning on rising, he said to his companions: "If the emperor gave a kingdom to one of his servants, how joyful the servant would be! But if he gave him the whole empire, would he not rejoice all the more? I should, therefore, be full of joy in my infirmities and tribulations, seek my consolation in the Lord, and give thanks to God the Father, to his only Son our Lord Jesus Christ, and to the Holy Spirit. In fact, God has given me such a grace and blessing that he has condescended in his mercy to assure me, his poor and unworthy servant, still living on this earth, that I would share his kingdom. Therefore, for his glory, for my consolation, and the edification of my neighbor, I wish to compose a new "Praises of the Lord," for his creatures. These creatures minister to our needs every day; without them we could not live; and through them the human race greatly offends the Creator. Every day we fail to appreciate so great a blessing by not praising as we should the Creator and dispenser of all these gifts." He sat down, concentrated a minute, then cried out: "Most high, all-powerful, and good Lord. . ." And he composed a melody to these words which he taught his companions.

His heart was then full of so much sweetness and consolation that he wanted Brother Pacificus, who in the world had been the king of poets and the most courtly master of song, to go through the world with a few pious and spiritual friars to preach and sing the praises of God. The best preacher would first deliver the sermon; then all would sing the "Praises of the Lord," as true jongleurs of God. At the end of the song, the preacher would say to the people: "We are the jongleurs of God, and the only reward we want is to see you lead a truly penitent life." Then he added: "Who are, indeed, God's servants if not jongleurs who strive to move men's hearts in order to lead them to the joys of the spirit?" When he spoke in this way of "the servants of God," he especially had in mind the Friars Minor who had been given to the world to save it.

He called these "Praises of the Lord," which opened with the words: "Most high, all-powerful, and good Lord," the "Canticle of the Sun." The sun was the most beautiful of all the creatures, the one which, better than all the others, could be compared to God. He said: "At sunrise, every man ought to praise God for having created this heavenly body which gives light to our eyes during the day; at evening, when night falls, every man ought to praise God for that other creature, our brother fire, which enables our eyes to see clearly in the darkness. We are all like blind people, and it is through these two creatures that God gives us light. Therefore, for these two creatures and for the others that serve us each day, we ought to praise their glorious Creator in a very special way." He himself did so with all his heart, whether sick or well, and he gladly invited the others to sing the glory of the Lord. When he was laid low by sickness, he often intoned this canticle and had his companions take it up; in that way he forgot the intensity of his sufferings and pains by considering the glory of the Lord. He did this until the day of his death.

Part II

The Reformation

5

The Lutheran Chorale

Martin Luther (1483-1546)

THE beginning of the Reformation is generally dated from
October 31, 1517, when Martin Luther, an Augustinian monk
and university professor, nailed his ninety-five theses to the
door of the cathedral church in Wittenberg, Germany.
Through his study of the New Testament, Luther had
become convinced of the doctrine of justification by faith.
His attempt to reform the church's teaching and practice was
rejected by the ecclesiastical hierarchy, and Luther and his
followers were forced to separate themselves from it. The
movement begun by Luther quickly swept over Germany and
led to the formation of the German Evangelical ("Lutheran")
Church, as well as various north European national churches
that adhered to the reformer's views.

One of Luther's desires was to reemphasize congregational singing in the church. His activities in this regard
are reflected in the readings given below. Luther's *Formula
Missae et Communionis* (Form of the Mass and Communion),
a Latin version of the Mass that expunged elements of
Catholic practice that he found objectionable, made a place
in the liturgy for vernacular congregational singing. His
letter to Georg Spalatin shows him inviting others to write
hymns for use in the new church, while his preface to Johann
Walther's *Gesangbüchlein* (Little Songbook) reveals his
concern that young people have worthwhile spiritual songs to
sing. Luther's "New Preface" to Rauscher's *Geistliche lieder
auffs new gebessert* (Spiritual Songs Improved) expresses his
displeasure at those who have altered his hymns without
consent, using a coarse German proverb to compare the
alterations to "mouse dung in the pepper."

23   From *Formula Missae et Communionis* (1523). *Source*:
           WA, vol. 12, p. 218.

Also, I wish we had more songs in the vernacular for the people to
sing during mass, either immediately after the gradual or the
Sanctus and Agnus Dei. For who doubts that once the voices of all
the people did this, which now only the choir sings or responds to
the blessings of the bishop? In fact, the bishops may arrange these
songs thus, either after the Latin songs, or alternately in Latin on
one day and sung in the vernacular on another, until the whole
mass is brought out in the vernacular. But poets are missing among
us, or are not yet known, who can produce devout and spiritual
songs (as Paul calls them),[1] which are worthy of frequent use in
God's church. Meanwhile, one may acceptably sing "Gott sey
gelobet und gebenedeyet, der uns selber hatt gespeyset," etc. after
communion. Omit that despicable part, "Und das heylige
sacramente, an userm letzten ende, aus des geweyeten priesters
hende," which was added by some worshiper of S. Barbara, who
having thought little of the sacraments during his whole life, hoped
that at death this good work would give him life without walking in
faith. For both the meter and musical style prove it to be
superfluous. Besides this, "Nu bitten wyr den heyligen geyst" may
be effective. Also, "Eyn kindelin so lobelich." For not many are
found which partake of a serious spirit. I say this in case any of our
German poets are afraid to create devotional poems for us.

24   Letter to Georg Spalatin (late 1523). *Source*: *WA Br*,
           vol. 3, p. 220.

Grace and peace. It is our intention, following the example of the
prophets and ancient church fathers, to write vernacular psalms for
the masses, that is, spiritual songs, that the word of God may
continue among the people even in song. Therefore, we look
everywhere for poets. Since you are certainly gifted with both
fluency and elegance in the German language, and have refined it
through much use, I beg you to work with us in this cause, and try
to transform any of the psalms into songs, just as you have in my

---

[1]Col. 3, 16.

present example. However, I would prefer that you omit new words and those used at court, in order to appeal to the masses of plain people, yet at the same time using words that are choice and proper to be sung, having a clear meaning and related as closely as possible to the psalm. Accordingly, exercise your freedom, keeping the meaning, abandoning exact wording, arranging your translation by using other words. I do not have as much ability to do this as I wish. Therefore, I shall find out if perhaps you are a Heman or Asaph or Jeduthun. I will also ask Johanne Doltzicko—who is himself fluent and elegant—the same thing, if the two of you have the time for it, which I suspect is not true just now. But you have my seven penitential psalms and commentaries, from which the sense of the psalm can be obtained, or if it pleases you, you may be assigned the first of these psalms, "Lord, not in wrath," or the seventh, "Lord, hear my prayer." I assign the second psalm, "Blessed are they whose" to Jo. Doltzicko, since I have versified "Out of the depths," and "Have mercy on me" has already been accounted for. Or if these are too difficult, then take these two: "I will bless the Lord at all times" and "Rejoice, you righteous, in the Lord," that is, [Psalms] 33 and 32. Or Psalm 103: "Bless the Lord, my soul." Anyway, reply so we can know what to expect from you. Goodbye in the Lord.

25   Preface to Johann Walther, *Gesangbüchlein* (1524).
Source: *WA*, vol. 35, pp. 474-475.

That it is good and acceptable to God to sing spiritual songs, I believe, is obvious to Christians, since everyone has not only the example of the prophets and kings of the Old Testament (who praised God with singing and playing, with poems and stringed instruments), but also the common use of psalmody in early Christianity. Indeed, St. Paul appointed it in 1 Cor. 14 and admonished the Colossians to sing spiritual songs and psalms from their hearts to the Lord. By these means, God's word and Christian doctrine may be instilled and practiced on a regular basis.

For this reason I also, together with some others, in order to make a good beginning and encourage others who can do it better, have brought together some spiritual songs, so that the holy gospel, which by God's grace is again opened, may be carried on and made to increase, that we ourselves might also be able to boast, as Moses did in his song, Ex. 15, that Christ is our praise and song, and that we ought to know nothing to sing or say but what Paul says, 1 Cor. 2, that Jesus Christ is our Savior.

And, moreover, they have been arranged into four voices, for no other reason than that I fervently wish that young people, who should and must be trained in music and the other fine arts, had something to make them abandon love tunes and carnal songs and in their place learn something wholesome, and thus fill the good with pleasure, as is best for the young. Furthermore, I am not of the opinion that all the arts should be beaten down and fade away because of the gospel, as some of the superspiritual suggest, but I would gladly see all the arts, particularly music, in the service of him who has given and created them. I ask, therefore, that every pious Christian would let himself be pleased with this, and where God has granted more or the same, to help further. Unfortunately, it is otherwise in the world, which is lax and forgetful about attracting and teaching the poor youth, which should be one of our primary aims. God give us his grace. Amen.

26   "A New Preface," in Andreas Rauscher, *Geistliche lieder auffs new gebessert* (1531). *Source*: *WA*, vol. 35, pp. 475-476.

Now some have proven their abilities and increased the number of songs so that they have left me behind and become my masters. But others have done little good in this cause. And since I see that no end is in sight to everyone following their own indiscriminate opinion, moreover, that the first of our songs also become more corrupted with every printing, I am afraid it will be the same with this little book as it has been with all good books: it will be overwhelmed and devastated by the clumsiness of emptyheads, the good will be lost from it and only the useless retained, as we see in St. Luke, chapter one, that at the beginning everyone wanted to write a gospel, until the true gospel was nearly lost under so many gospels. The same has happened also to Sts. Jerome and Augustine, and to many other books. In sum, there will be mouse dung in the pepper.

Now since we want very much to prevent this, I have again looked over this little book and printed our songs in order together with the authors' names, which I previously avoided as willful boasting, but now must do out of necessity, so that strange, unfit songs may not be sold under our names; after that are given those which we esteem the best and most useful written by others. I ask and admonish all who have the pure word of love to no longer improve or add to our little book without our knowledge. But if one would improve it without our knowledge, let the people know that it is not our Wittenberg publication. To be sure, anyone can put together his own little book of songs and leave ours alone, as we ask, demand, and herewith certify to be our desire. For, indeed, we want our money to retain its worth, not disallowing anyone to make a better one for himself, to the sole praise of God's name and not our own.

Frid. Nausea Blancicampianus (16th century)

In reaction to the schism caused by the Reformation, Pope Paul III (1468-1549) called for a general council to attempt to heal the division, reform the church, and set up defenses against the Turks. The Council of Trent was convened in 1545 and met periodically until 1563. By this time, of course, the Protestant Reformation was irreversible, but the Council of Trent did succeed in clarifying the Roman Catholic position on many issues and reforming some of the abuses of which Luther and others had complained. Indeed, the council may be said to have set the basic direction of Roman Catholicism for the next 400 years.

Discussions of music in the church played a relatively minor part at the council, and its decisions on this subject were couched in general terms. However, two years before the convening of the council, Frid. Nausea Blancicampianus, the bishop of Vienne, France, sent a letter to Pope Paul III suggesting topics that should be discussed at the meeting. One section of Blancicampianus's letter, reproduced below, refers to the German songs that were so effective in inculcating Lutheran doctrine, noting that these would have to be done away with before reunion could be achieved. The bishop's remarks are interesting as giving the perspective of a contemporary Roman Catholic on the hymns of Luther and his followers.

27   From letter to Pope Paul III (1543). *Source*:
        Translated by Robert F. Hayburn in *Papal Legislation
        on Sacred Music: 95 A.D. to 1977 A.D.* (Collegeville,
        MN: The Liturgical Press, 1979), p. 26.

I say in addition that it will not be very easy for them (namely the
Protestants) to agree with us, because it will be necessary after
peace is established to do away with those German songs, which
they use very much in many of their churches. Not a few of these
are hymns which go contrary to the authority of the Supreme
Pontiffs, the Mass, the good works, and the established customs of
religious people on the one hand and praise their new rites and
dogmas on the other. Who can say how many persons have easily
been drawn away already from the true religion by these same
chants, to which they have already become accustomed for twenty
years or more? But if the use of songs of this type must remain
publicly in the churches, joined with a certain envy and levity, it will
not be possible for long to have unity, since many of the words of
the same songs are plainly contrary to the Catholic songs.

Johann Anastasius Freylinghausen (1670-1739)

During the late seventeenth and early eighteenth centuries,
Lutheranism in Germany was rent into two opposing factions:
1) Orthodoxy, which centered on intellectual adherence to
correct doctrine as expressed in the creeds and confessions
of the church and the writings of trustworthy theologians, and
2) Pietism, which emphasized a personal experience of
religion and holy living. Johann Anastasius Freylinghausen,
a Pietist minister and teacher, spent his career in Halle,
where he served as an assistant and successor to August
Hermann Francke, one of the chief figures in early German
Pietism. Freylinghausen's most important contribution to the
Pietist cause was undoubtedly his two hymnals, *Geistreiches
Gesangbuch* (1704) and *Neues Geistreiches Gesangbuch*
(1714). The popularity of the first collection is evident from
the fact that it went through nineteen editions during the
eighteenth century.

In the following extracts from the preface to the fourth
edition of *Geistreiches Gesangbuch*, Freylinghausen points out
that the book contains both old and new songs, and identifies

the subject headings under which the hymns are arranged. These subject headings demonstrate typical Pietist emphases on personal religion and mystical union with Christ, the bridegroom.

28   From Preface to *Geistreiches Gesangbuch*, 4th ed. (Halle: Wäysenhause, 1708).

> Glory and worship, thanks and praise
> be to our God and to the Lamb!
> Dear Reader!

The holy scripture of the Old and New Testaments, church history, and experience itself well attests that it has always been a mark of singular grace that God has visited his people—which he still promises for the future—when and where psalms and hymns of praise and spiritual loving songs have flowed from the mouth of spiritual children and infants.

. . .

Just as every previously quoted example demonstrates the truth of the earlier propositions, confirmation of them can be further increased by the experience of our times, in which the good hand of our God has led us to serve. In the past several years he has let the preaching of atonement and the gospels resound with new strength, particularly in our Germany, and has sealed the same with no little fruit (which not to recognize or wish to recognize is a sign of an extremely dangerous blindness). He has also placed a new song in the heart and mouth of many of his children with which to praise him and elevate both the present and still future grace; this is evident from the new songbooks of the day, such as those from Urfurt, Halle, Darmstadt, and Berlin, which have been used here as well as other places with good profit and edification.

. . .

And for the same purpose the present new songbook of all saints, chosen and beloved of God, will appear in the fourth printing in the good hope that such will be attained through the grace of the Lord, and that my arrangement and compilation of the songs contained in it will be a practical little service to those who are pleasing in Christ Jesus.

For the edification of the eager reader or singer it is necessary to inform him of a few things about the content, arrangement, and other matters. The content of this songbook is evident from the title page: both old and new songs are found in it, and some measure of the intended subjects is indicated. For in the Revelation of John, chapter 14, the great host is presented and exhibited in both the old and new, namely, playing and singing the Song of Moses and the Lamb, besides which the holy scripture old and new (Matt. 13:52) combines the current and ancient fruit of Solomon's vineyard (Song of Solomon 7:13). The gratitude due to God requires that we both hold to the counsel of the old and yet not disdain the new, since both are his gift and present. Furthermore, it cannot be denied that one may find a noticeable difference between old songs as well as new ones, some of which are spiritual and powerful, and thus accommodated to edification and the awakening of Christian devotion. This has been obvious to the one who with due deliberation has collected and compiled the songs, who has consequently included not only new songs, but a sufficient number of both old and new in this convenient and ordered songbook, which presents and communicates herein the desired core of old and new songs. It is not at all denied that one can find many old and new songs besides those contained in this songbook, indeed, substantial ones, which is not said to the prejudice or disadvantage of this book. But someone who says that because of that this is not a complete songbook has to consider that because of the great quantity of old and new songs, as also that several authors have published whole songbooks of their own (as, for example, the blessed Paul Gerhardt's splendid spiritual songs in particular, which have been printed more than once), to compile a complete songbook is absolutely impossible, and that the completeness of a songbook is not found primarily in the quantity, but rather in the quality of the songs themselves. Thus, if the Christian reader has attained the gift of discernment in this task, he will find here no slight matter about faith and liturgy which is not brought out in one or more songs of a lovely, edifying, and powerful kind.

. . .

The order of the subject headings has been arranged according to the requirements and products of the economy of our salvation. Thus, first have been placed the subject headings containing essential matters that deal with Christ, the ground of our salvation, with his gifts and kindnesses, which is presented in a lovely way (this encompasses the first seventeen subject headings). After that follows the subject heading of the gentleness of God and Christ, as the origin and fountainhead from which flows all our salvation and happiness. Then follow those that present the means by which God will bring us again into communion with him, dealing with his guiding hand in the work of creation and the divine providence and kingdom, but especially the so-called means of grace of the Word and Sacraments, as baptism and the Lord's Supper. After that come those that give the order by which you must be guided if you would take part in Christ and gain happiness from him. The requirement of this order serves as a warning to you, dear man of the congregation, as well as to false Christianity, to be instructed by true and righteous Christianity. In particular, the distress and ruin of humanity is introduced, thereby to bring true atonement, conversion, and true faith in Jesus, the Savior of the world, to you. This faith, if it is a true faith, not only brings justification in the blood of Christ, but also the Christian life and godly behavior that inevitably bears fruit and result. If you want to know what practice and virtue is contained in the Christian life and godly behavior, you must devoutly consider that in these Christian songs is communicated prayer, spiritual vigilance, spiritual struggle and victory, desire for God and Christ, love to Jesus, brotherly and universal love, the following of Christ, the mystery of the cross which is ordained for you; Christian peace, patience, and steadfastness which you must demonstrate; and the surrender of the heart to God. Now if you will be true in all these things, in this life you will have the reward of divine peace, joy in the Holy Spirit, and true joyfulness in the faith. Indeed, your heart and mouth will daily overflow with the love of God, and childlike wisdom will keep you.

But there is more! Your bridegroom will marry himself to you, that you may be able to share in the highest nobility of all believers, who overcome forever all the height and glory of this world, in which is all the blessedness of the kingdom of grace and the powerful foretaste of the future life. But since you are still short of the goal and have not reached the treasure, you should remember that the life of the faithful remains hidden with Christ in God, and the spiritual Zion cannot yet do without songs of lament. However, hope is not hidden, through which one has strength and comfort through all laments in this vale of tears, that one may not become weary in spirit and give up. And this hope continues through death and the blessed resurrection in heaven and the heavenly Jerusalem, when final and complete happiness and excellence shall be revealed, and where all fullness of the divine riches will be poured out on his congregation from one eternity to another. Finally appear morning, evening, and mealtime songs, and those which otherwise deal with everyday needs and life; to which is added an appendix of songs which conform to the preceding materials, and a group of songs as a small supplement.

The Theology Faculty of the University of Wittenberg (1714)

As might be expected, Freylinghausen's *Geistreiches Gesangbuch* was considerably less popular in Orthodox Lutheran circles than it was among the Pietists. In 1713, the nobility of Waldeck asked the Orthodox theology faculty of the University of Wittenberg to examine Freylinghausen's hymnal with a view to its possible adoption in the territory. The faculty made its report in 1714 (published in 1716) in a document titled *Der Löblichen Theologischen Facultät zu Wittenberg Bedencken über das zu Glauche an Halle 1703, im Wäysen-Hause daselbst edirte Gesang-Buch* (The Honorable Wittenberg Theology Faculty's Deliberation over the Hymnal Published by the Halle *Waisenhaus* in 1703). The faculty censured in no uncertain terms Freylinghausen's treatment of old hymns, the theology of the new hymns, the editorial procedures, and the "luxurious" melodies to be found within the book. Pietist poets were described as "fanatic" and the motives of those who compiled and published the hymnal were brought into question. The preface to Freylinghausen's *Geistreiches Gesangbuch* and the review by the Wittenberg faculty reveal that, despite the differences between them, both sides in the dispute considered hymnody to be of vital importance in religious life.

29   From *Der Löblichen Theologischen Facultät zu Wittenberg Bedencken über das zu Glauche an Halle 1703, im Wäysen-Hause daselbst edirte Gesang-Buch* (1716). *Source*: Translated by Dianne Marie McMullen in "The *Geistreiches Gesangbuch* of Johann Anastasius Freylinghausen (1670-1739): A German Pietist Hymnal" (Ph.D. dissertation, The University of Michigan, 1987), pp. 568, 572-574, 594, 596, and 599.

Most Honorable Sirs:

Last year you sent us the hymnal edited in 1703 at the _Waisenhaus_ in Glaucha near Halle and asked for our opinion from a theological point of view. You asked whether the hymnal could be introduced to the public and used by everyone without scandal, on account of the new hymns that it contains. These hymns are not found yet in other Lutheran hymnals, not to mention being sung in the churches. We have studied this hymnal, and after perusal and precise deliberation undertaken in the fear of the Lord, we can answer this question only in the negative.

. . .

1. We cannot help observing what it is in the preface. There it is alleged that hitherto God has put a new song into the mouths and hearts of his children and servants, in order that they may praise Him and in order to promote both the present and future mercy. We agree with this statement to this point. On the other hand, under this description, that which afflicted and caused disorder in God's church several years ago (and still does), namely the Pietist disruption, is praised as a wonderful kindness. One observes this by the fact that so many hymns by fanatic poets are included in the hymnal indiscriminately. Furthermore, these hymns are recommended to be truly spiritual, pleasing, devotional, and powerful. It is a distressing sign of the times that the intent behind this hymnal is perhaps nothing more than to bring the Pietist ferment among the people and eventually to introduce it into their hearts. The editors were so indiscriminate that hymns were printed in this hymnal, in spite of the fact that several well-meaning teachers had already issued admonitions about them. They will be a source of confusion to the people. Meanwhile, it is also apparent that the editors wanted to keep a number of old hymns in the hymnal, so it would not be called or seem to be frivolously new. Instead, by means of the old hymns, the new hymns would simultaneously come into the hands of the people. In actuality the editors were merely seeking to promote the new hymns. It would have been much better and more straightforward if they had left our traditional hymns alone in their dignity and issued a special hymnal for the new fanatic hymns. When both types of hymns appear together, not every reader can tell them apart.

2. We also find that the old hymns are not always handled without distortion; rather, they are either left out or truncated and

altered. This is permissible when it happens for the spirit and with a purpose. An example of the omission of an old hymn is "Erhalt uns Herr bei deinem Wort." It is not to be found in this Halle hymnal, which leads one to believe that it is no longer necessary to pray for the preservation of true doctrine. If one left out hymns of this type for the sake of our adversaries, in order to recommend such a book to them, we leave it to the judgment of the important Judge and the One who knows hearts how He will view this manifestation of Protestant ministers in the days to come. The hymn "Das alte Jahr vergangen ist" is an example of a hymn that has been altered. The editors have substituted the words "false doctrine" for the author's words "Pope's doctrine." We accept this substitution, for, perhaps this hymn was reproduced from a copy in which the words "false doctrine" already stood. Such copies exist. In this case, nothing was deliberately altered.

3. We find that the authors' names of old, as well as of new, hymns have been left out. These are cited in almost all hymnals. As far as we can see, this omission was caused neither by lack of space nor for any other reason. The reason is probably that the editors wanted to confuse the reader and singer about which was an old or new hymn, in order, with time, to lend the new, absurd hymns the appearance of antiquity and in order to canonize them, in a manner of speaking. In fact, it is important to know what a poet wrote, as well as who wrote a hymn.

4. We also notice in this hymnal many hymns filled with false doctrine or offensive and highly questionable phrases. These are not to be tolerated either as a whole or in isolated passages, even though the writer could provide a reasonable explanation, if he were asked. Not even in the preface is it concealed that innovation is the primary goal. For, what is the description of eternal life supposed to mean? Does it mean that the entire abundance of divine riches will overflow from one eternity into the other in His congregation? And what are these eternities supposed to be that flow from one to the other, if they are not specific periods and eternities that consist of limited durations? This is not to mention other things found in this preface. Certain hymns are full of enthusiastic and fanatic doctrine.

. . .

5. We have also observed that a type of chorale-hymn is introduced in this hymnal that appears to be translated from

another language and that consists of prose, rather than of poetry.
. . .

    6. Finally, and sixth of all, in this hymnal we find a large
number of hopping, leaping, dactylic texts, that for the most part
have unsacred and almost luxuriant melodies. These do not agree
in the least with the seriousness of the lofty secrets that they ought
to contain. Certainly, a poet can also exercise his scholarship in this
respect and construct verse about divine matters from whatever
type. But, to make hymns out of these and to offer them to an
entire Christian congregation, indeed to the entire Protestant
church, to sing, is not appropriate, in our opinion. The same is true
with those phrases in which the love of Christ and of the devout
souls was described. Here, of course, much care must be taken that
no concept is presented that is more objectionable and vexatious
than edifying. When a luxurious melody is added to that, one
cannot easily identify where the devotion and practice in devotion
remains or from whence it should arise. One finds such leaping
hymns now and again, made in a totally new way, especially under
the rubrics: "Longing for Christ," "Love for Jesus," "Brotherly and
Universal Love," "Joy in the Holy Spirit," "Spiritual Marriage with
Christ," and similar titles. Certainly the matter is not improved
with such titles. It is imprudent to set hymns of this type in
congregational hymnals. . . .

    . . . One cannot be too distressed about the misfortune of our
times, not that such trash is scribbled, but that it is held to be divine
enlightenments and equivalent to God's Word and that it should be
respected as secrets. The editors of the Halle hymnal have the
impudence to draw from the very same muddy wells and then to
distribute what they drew as a core of hymns, disregarding the false
doctrines and phrases that we have noted above and that are to be
found in large numbers. We maintain for this and other reasons
explained above, that this hymnal can neither be introduced without
soliciting irritation nor be recommended and given to the people.

    However, may God, who is rich in mercy, view His poor
Protestant church, which is the aim of so many piercing attacks,
with merciful eyes and protect it mightily, as well as keep it with the
old truth. May He effectively bring to a standstill the novices who
today seek to confuse under the pretext of a special devotion, so
that we are at liberty to extol and to praise Him forever for His
kindness.

We submit our high and most honorable men to his almighty protection and continue, willingly, to pray and to serve constantly. Written in Wittenberg on the 17th of September 1714.

Senior Deacon

And the rest of the Doctors and Professors

Of the theology faculty at Wittenberg.

6
Swiss Reformed

Huldreich Zwingli (1484-1531)

HULDREICH Zwingli, leader of the Swiss Reformation, made his final break with the Roman church in 1522. A militant activist, Zwingli convinced the people and authorities of Zürich to adopt his program of church reform, and ultimately died in a battle against the Catholic cantons of Switzerland.

Zwingli was an ardent lover of music, probably the best musician among the principal reformers of the sixteenth century, and a firm believer in extra-liturgical devotional song. Nevertheless, he rejected any use of music or singing in the corporate worship of the church, arriving at this conclusion by regarding singing as a form of prayer.

In his *Auslegen und Gründe der Schlussreden* (Explanation and Foundation of the Conclusions, 1523), a set of articles he proposed for public debate, he pointed out that prayer is a private matter between the believer and God. Thus, public prayer—and, by extension, public singing—is hypocritical.

Zwingli even turned Colossians 3:16, a passage often cited in support of church song, into an argument against ecclesiastical singing, noting that believers are admonished to sing to the Lord "not with the voice, like the Jewish singers, but with the hearts." Zwingli's views were adopted quickly in Zürich, and by 1525 all the churches in the city were songless, a state of affairs that lasted until near the end of the sixteenth century.

30   From *Auslegen und Gründe der Schlussreden* (1523). *Source*: *Huldreich Zwinglis Sämtliche Werke*, ed. by Emil Egli and Georg Finsler. Vol LXXXIX of Corpus

Reformatorum (München: Kraus Reprint, n.d.), vol.
2, pp. 348-350.

On Prayer.
The Forty-Fourth Article.
The true worshipper calls upon God in spirit
and truth, without the clamor of men.

Now is the time for this article, that secret prayer is pleasing to
God, as is the one who truly knows God and truly calls with a heart
free from doubt, without hypocrisy, but with righteousness, true
confession, and knowledge. For example, in Exodus 14, Moses
anxiously calls to God in his heart without moving his lips. Hannah
did the same thing without loud clamor (1 Kings 1). Also, Christ
has forbidden much prattle (Matt. 6) and taught that true worship
is in spirit and in truth (John 4). In the latter passage he also
delivers us from appointed places for worship. God does not want
to be called upon from one place more than another, but from any
place where God is called upon in spirit and truth he says: Here
am I.

The Forty-Fifth Article.
Hypocrites do their work that they may be seen of men,
thus having the reward in this life.

In order that one may recognize hypocrisy that passes for
devotion, I have placed this article with the others. The pure words
of Christ, which he speaks of the scribes and Pharisees in Matt. 23,
are: "They do all their work that they may be seen of men." Christ
paints them this color, not I. In Matt. 6, Christ commands that we
shall not be hypocrites in almsgiving, prayers, and fasts, who make
their prayer before crowds of people. Instead, we pray well when
we go into our closet, shut the door after us, and there call upon
our heavenly father in secret. Thus, it follows that they who do all
their prayer only in public, hypocrisy, which Christ rebukes, are
hypocrites. It also follows that the hypocrites have their reward
here, as he says: "Truly I say to you, they have had their reward."
Therefore, they who do their work for the world are hypocrites.
Since they are hypocrites, they do all their work that they may be
seen before men. Thus, their work is nothing other than hypocrisy,
and they also have their reward here.

None of the objections produced to this point in any way permits
the choral singing of the psalms, which one in a hundred do not
understand; I mention the singing fools, the nuns, who for all the

world do not understand a verse of the psalms which they stumble through. But, they say, does it not make sense that one should sing God's love before all men? Answer: Prove to me that it is good and I will believe you. God alone is good and the sole fountain of all good. If psalm mumbling is good, it must come from God. Show me where God has arranged such stumbling singing, indistinct speech, and mumbling. Thus, one jumps like the cat before the furrier; but you find the contrary, that God has commanded you to go into your closet and there in a secret place speak with your heavenly father, who will adequately see, hear, and know you. When you pray, you must be alone. Prayer is corrupted by the many, unless one explains to the many the word of God, or the few speak with one another of the understanding of God's word, of which manner Paul speaks in Col. 3:16: "The word of Christ shall richly remain or live in you in all wisdom, that you (understood: 'in order to') teach and admonish yourselves with psalms, hymns, and spiritual songs, which you sing with love in your hearts to the Lord." Here Paul teaches us not howling and mumbling in the temple, but he indicates the true song that is pleasing to God, that we sing the praise and glory of God not with the voice, like the Jewish singers, but with the hearts. This happens if we converse with one another of the psalms and praises of God, which the prophets have also sung in their hearts and closets in order to teach and admonish one another. Therefore, my serious advice would be that instead of psalm mumblings, one would read the psalm and explain it, and realize the beautiful meaning of the Holy Spirit that lies therein. I say the same also of the other scriptures. By this man will be daily nourished and so drawn to the office of preaching, according to the scripture, that they thus will not walk about with unwashed hands and feet.

Conrad Grebel (c. 1498-1526)

Conrad Grebel was born in Zürich, Switzerland. After pursuing humanist studies in Basel, Vienna, and Paris, he returned to Zürich (1520), where he came under the influence of Zwingli and was converted to evangelical beliefs. By 1524, however, Grebel had begun to question his mentor's views on infant baptism, separation of church and state, and the appropriateness of military service for Christians. In early 1525, Grebel rebaptized George Blaurock, thus initiating the group that became known variously as the Anabaptists, Swiss Brethren, and later the Mennonites.

While Grebel rejected some aspects of Zwingli's program of church reform, he did follow the latter's prohibition of singing in corporate worship. This is evident from a letter written by Grebel on behalf of himself and several of his colleagues to Thomas Müntzer, a radical German reformer and minister at Allstedt. Müntzer probably never received the letter, but the writing does show the extent of Zwingli's influence on Grebel's views of church song.

It should be noted that many Anabaptists did not share Grebel's position. About 1565, a significant collection of Anabaptist hymns, the *Ausbund*, was published; a later revision of this book is still in use among some groups.

31   From Letter to Thomas Müntzer (September 5, 1524).
           Source: *Thomas Müntzer: Schriften und Briefe, Kritische
           Gesamtausgabe*, ed. Günther Franz. Vol. 33 of *Quellen
           und Forschungen zur Reformationsgeschichte* (Gütersloh:
           Verlagshaus Gerd Mohn, 1968), p. 439.

We understand and have seen that you have a German version of the mass and have set up new German songs. This is not good, for we find no teaching or example about singing in the New Testament. Paul reproaches the learned Corinthians more than he praises them because they mumbled in the congregation as if singing, in the same manner as the Jews and Italians, pronouncing things in a singing manner. For another thing, since singing in the Latin language sprang up without divine teaching, apostolic example, or need, and has brought neither good nor edification, it will be even less edifying in German and will be an external appearance of faith. Third, Paul also clearly forbids singing in Ephesians 5 and Colossians 3, since he says and teaches that one shall persuade oneself and instruct another with psalms and spiritual songs, and if one wants to sing, he should sing and say thanks in the heart. Fourth, what we are not taught by clear language and examples shall also be forbidden to us, as if it stood written: do not do that, do not sing. Fifth, in the Old Testament Christ called his messengers only to preach the word, as he also did in the New Testament. Paul likewise said that the word of Christ, not songs, should live among us. The bad singer is displeased, the good singer is prideful. Sixth, we should not do what seems good to us, or replace what is in the word. Seventh, if you would dispose of the mass, you must not replace it with German songs, which is perhaps your idea or that of Luther. Eighth, it must be rooted out with the word and essay of Christ. Ninth, for it was not planted by God.

7
Genevan Psalmody

Martin Bucer (1491-1551)

MARTIN Bucer was born near Strasbourg. He became a Dominican monk and subsequently a priest, but the influence of Luther induced him to leave his order and the Catholic church in 1521. In 1523, he became a minister in Strassburg, where he labored for twenty-five years. A widely respected church leader and theologian, he served as an intermediary in disputes between Luther and Zwingli. He also exercised considerable influence over John Calvin during the latter's sojourn in Strasbourg (1538-1541). In 1549, Bucer traveled to England to assist Thomas Cranmer in the Reformation movement there. Thus, Bucer played a significant role in each of the major reform movements of the sixteenth century.

In 1539, Bucer published a vernacular liturgy that gave congregational singing an important place. In his earlier *Grund und Ursach auss gotlicher schifft* (Foundation and reason from the divine scripture, 1524) he observed that psalms sung in the vernacular are the most suitable material for church singing. The influence of Bucer on Calvin's views of congregational singing is evident from a comparison of the following extract with the writing by Calvin given later in this volume.

32   From *Grund und ursach auss gotlicher schifft* (1524).
Source: *Martin Bucer's Deutsche Schriften* (Gütersloh: Verlagshaus Gerd Mohn, 1960), vol. 1, pp. 274-276.

Man has arranged many songs and prayers in the Masses and other times, heretofore propelled by the love of money, and still driven by

such, which Christians still do not recognize. Contrary to many
places in the Scripture, these are drawn out of fables as collects and
prayers of Saints Barbara, Katherine, Christopher, Margaret,
George, and many others, in order to sing and read them in Latin,
which the people of the congregation do not understand at all, and
of which they themselves also often understand little. Furthermore,
they have also bound these by time, custom, and number, contrary
to the manner of prayers and praises of God, which ought to be
spontaneous.

Now because we know that the divine thing may be known only
by the spirit of God (1 Cor. 2) and that God's Scripture is
completely good (2 Tim. 3), we use no songs or prayers that are not
drawn out of divine Scripture in God's congregation, and because
what is performed in God's congregation ought to improve everyone
in the congregation, we do not pray or sing in the congregation
except in the German language, that the common laity may say
"amen," as is taught by the spirit of God in 1 Cor. 14.

The Latin language,[1] which throughout contains nothing good
or useful that is not more stylistically and better written in Hebrew
and Greek, be it equally divine or natural—and, as with the old
Romans, so much more with the new Papists—has exceedingly
served to deceive other nations and bring them into bondage and
hold them in it. We know not to pay it any honor, with which the
congregation of God will be hindered and only apart from it to
interpret what is better for the laity to know.

Further, because it is an insult to God not to pray or sing with
our hearts, let us at no time be bound to such by a written statute,
but spontaneously on Sunday, as Christ's supper is observed, some
short prayers and songs should be chosen, all taken out of the
superior reason of the scripture. Likewise at vesper time, the
period of corporate celebration ought to be used for the
improvement of the spirit, singing but one, two, or three psalms
with a sermon, perhaps an explanation of a chapter out of divine
scripture. The whole congregation should also sing a psalm before
and after the daily sermon.

The above should not be undertaken in the assembled
congregation without the common sermon, but each one adapting
every spirit and prayer for himself, to pray and praise God without

---

[1]Latin language has harmed much and never been of great use.

ceasing in the heart. Thus, we give no offense to the teaching of Christ by making many words in prayer (Matt. 6) or insulting God with pretense and hypocrisy instead of praise, which happens when the heart is not involved.

And in this we know that we follow the teaching of God's spirit (1 Cor. 14 and many other places). In Colossians 3 Paul also writes: _Let the word of God richly live in you in all wisdom, teaching and admonishing yourselves with psalms and hymns and spiritual songs in grace, and sing to the Lord in your hearts._ He says the same in Ephesians 5. We are to love God with all our might. Why shall we not also then sing to him, as all the saints of the Old and New Testaments have done? Just make sure that such song happens not only with the mouth, but also in the heart, that it flows and originates out of the heart. This is what the Apostle means when he says "_and sing to the Lord in your hearts._" His meaning is not to sing without the voice; how else could others be admonished and made better, or we speak with one another, as he writes to the Ephesians?

Therefore know that to thus reject song in God's congregation contains little either of the scripture or the custom of the first and apostolic churches and congregations, who also praised the eternal God with song.[2] For this purpose the psalms are particularly useful, which we gather not only from Paul's writings and our histories, but also from the written testimony of pagans such as Pliny the Younger. Christ himself concluded his supper and last sermon with a hymn (Matt. 26). But there are some who have such a love for it that is not well pleasing, thus they err. Therefore we have revealed the foundation and reason for the degradation of prayer and song, so that the godly might be sure to produce no displeasure. God helps the others, that he himself is pleasing to you and that his word will well endure with us.

Clement Marot (1496-1544)
Clement Marot was the son of a court poet who served in the retinues of Anne of Brittany and the French king Francis I. Clement followed in his father's footsteps, becoming court poet to Marguerite of Alençon, then _valet de chambre_ to the

---

[2]The ancient Christians always sang commonly in the congregation.

king. Marot began versifying psalms in 1532, and these and
others of his poems caused his popularity to soar until 1534,
when suspicions that he harbored Protestant sympathies
forced him to flee to Italy. He returned to France in 1537
under a royal amnesty, and in 1541 published the thirty
psalms he had versified to that time.

In 1542 Marot was again compelled to leave France. This
time he settled in Geneva, where he was welcomed by John
Calvin. Calvin encouraged Marot to continue versifying the
psalms, and in 1543 the thirty psalms previously published
were issued in a revised version, together with nineteen new
ones and several canticles, as _Cinquante Pseaumes en francois
par Clem. Marot_. Marot was unhappy in Geneva and left the
city before the end of 1543, traveling to Italy, where he died
the following year.

Marot's earlier psalms were written mainly for the
entertainment of the king and his court. In his poetic epistle
"To the Ladies of France" from _Cinquante Pseaumes_, Marot
expressed his wish that "the plowman at his plow, the carter
in the street, and the craftsman in his shop" would sing
psalms for their own comfort. Nevertheless, his essentially
aristocratic outlook is evident in his urging of the "Ladies of
France" to take the lead in singing songs of love—not the
love symbolized by "that little God/whom the painters make
with wings" (Cupid), but that of "the True God of invariable
Love."

33   "To the Ladies of France Touching These Psalms" from
        Cinquante Pseaumes (1543). _Source: Oeuvres complètes
        de Clément Marot_, ed. Abel Grenier (Paris: Librairie
        Garnier Frères, n.d.), vol. 2, pp. 308-309.

When will the golden age come
When one will see God alone adored,
Praised, sung, as he ordained it,
Without giving his glory to another?
When no more will there be either currency or place
For the songs of that little God
Whom the painters make with wings?
O you, ladies and young ladies,

Whom God makes to be his temple,
And who reject the evil example of making
Both rooms and halls resound
With worldly or indecent songs,
I want to here present you
With something inoffensive to sing;
And knowing that you are not pleased
By songs that are silent about love,
Those that I here venture to present
Speak not indeed of any other thing.
This only is love: Love even to him;
For his supreme wisdom
Composed them, and vain man
Has not been their author.

    Love, whose speaking I see
Has given you speech and voice
In order to sing his high praises,
Not those of strange gods,
Who are neither able nor willing
To create a single of your hairs.

    The Love which I want to sing
Will not return to torment your hearts
As will the other; but, without doubt,
It will supply you with all the love
Of that comforting pleasure
That the angels in the heavens feel;
Because his spirit will give you grace
In order to come into your hearts
And convert and change them,
Making your lips stir
And your fingers on the spinets
To speak holy songs.

    O blessed ones who will be able to see
The time flower when one will hear
The plowman at his plow,
The carter in the street,
And the craftsman in his shop,
With a psalm or canticle
Succor himself in his labor!
Happy ones, who will hear the shepherd

And the shepherdess in the forest
Make rocks and ponds
Sing in response the eminence
Of the holy name of their Creator!
    Will you allow God to call them
To such joy before you?
Begin, ladies, begin,
Bring forth the golden age
By singing with an acceptable heart
From this holy songbook,
To the end that the world flees,
This fickle God of silly love,
Amicably making place
For the True God of invariable Love.

John Calvin (1509-1564)

John Calvin was the chief figure in the development of
Reformed Protestantism. Born in France, Calvin initially
studied for service in the Roman Catholic church, then
turned to the study of law and classical humanism. In 1533
or 1534 he was converted to Protestant views. After sojourns
in Basel, Geneva, and Strasbourg, he settled in Geneva
(1541) and remained there the rest of his life. Calvin was an
important theologian who is best known for his *Institutes of
the Christian Religion* (1536 and later eds.) and his views on
predestination and the supreme authority of Scripture.

In his liturgical views, Calvin was heavily influenced by
Martin Bucer. In 1542, Calvin wrote a preface to the
Genevan Psalter. A year later, he published an expanded
version of the preface. This expanded preface, translated
below, reveals several of Calvin's beliefs about congregational
song: It is a form of prayer and so must be in a language
understood by the people; music in the church must be
carefully regulated so that it does not do more harm than
good; humans cannot worthily offer anything to God but
God's own words themselves; the psalms provide the most
suitable material for the people to sing, not only at church
but also in "houses and fields." Calvin's strictures had
considerable impact not only on the European continent, but

also in England, Scotland, and North America, where psalm-singing was to hold sway until long after Calvin's death.

34   "Epistle to the Reader" from *Cinquante Pseaumes en francois par Clem. Marot* (1543). *Source: Ioannis Calvini, Opera quae Supersunt Omnia*, Vol. VI, ed. Guillelmus Baum, Eduardus Cunitz, and Eduardus Reuss, eds.; Vol. VI. Vol. XXXIV of Corpus Reformatorum (Brunsvigae: C. A. Schwetschke et Filium, 1867), pp. [165]-[172].

John Calvin to all Christians and lovers of God's word.

As it is a very proper thing in Christendom, and most necessary, that each of the faithful observe and maintain the communion of the Church in his place, frequenting the assemblies which occur on Sunday and other days for the purpose of honoring and serving God, it is also expedient and reasonable that all know and understand what is said and done at the Temple, to receive fruit and edification from it. For our Lord has not instituted the order that we must maintain when we agree in his name only to amuse the world as it watches and considers, but rather has desired that all his people should profit from it. As Saint Paul testifies, commanding that all that is done in the Church may be for the common edification of all. The servant would not command this unless it was the intention of the Master. But this may not be done until we may be instructed in order to understand all that has been ordained for our use. For to say that we can have devotion in prayers and ceremonies with no understanding of them is a great mockery, however much this is commonly said. Proper affection toward God is not a dead or carnal thing, but is a living change, coming from the holy Spirit when the heart is rightly touched and the understanding illuminated. And, in fact, if one could be edified by the things which one sees, without knowing what they signify, Saint Paul would not so vigorously prohibit speaking in an unknown tongue and would not give as his reason that there is no edification without doctrine. However, if we want to properly honor the holy ordinances of our Lord, who makes use of us in the Church, it is most important to know their contents, meaning, and in what direction they lead, in order that their use may be beneficial and advantageous, and therefore rightly directed. Now there are in sum three things which our Lord has commanded us to observe in our spiritual assemblies. Namely, the preaching of his word, public and solemn prayers, and the administration of the sacraments. I refrain from speaking of preaching at this time, since it is not in question. Touching the two remaining parts we have the express commandment of the holy Spirit that prayers be made in the common language and understanding of the people. And, as the Apostle says, the people cannot respond with "Amen" to prayer that has been made in a strange tongue. Now it is thus since one does it in the name and person of all in which each must be a participant. This has been an exceedingly great impudence on the part of those who introduced the Latin language into the Church, where it was not commonly understood. And no subtlety nor trivial objection may be able to excuse them, that this ceremony may not be perverse and disagreeable to God. For it presumes that it may be acceptable, though it goes directly against his will and in spite of him. Now, one would not know how to vex him more than by thus going contrary to his justification and glorifying himself in this rebellion, as if it were a holy and very praiseworthy thing. As for the Sacraments, if we examine well their nature, we shall know that it is a perverse custom for them to celebrate in such a manner that the people may have nothing of it except the sight without an exposition of the mysteries which are contained in it. For if these are visible words, as Saint Augustine called them, it is not necessary that there may be only an exterior show, but doctrine may be joined with it to give understanding. And also our Lord, in instituting it, has well demonstrated that. For he says that these are testimonies of his union with us, which he has confirmed by his death. Therefore, it is most necessary for them to give reason that we may know and understand what is said there. Otherwise, what our Lord would open his mouth to speak would be in vain if there were no ears to hear. This is not a matter for further dispute. For when the thing shall be judged by calm reason there shall not be one who does not confess that it is pure stupidity to amuse the people by signs through which the meaning may not be exposed. It is easy to see that one profanes the Sacraments of Jesus Christ by administering them in such a way that the people may not understand the words that are spoken there. And, in fact, one sees the superstitions which have come of it. For it is commonly thought that the consecration of the water of Baptism, as well as of the bread and wine in the Supper of our Lord, may be like a kind of enchantment. That is, when one's mouth has whispered and pronounced the words so that the creatures are insensible of perceiving the virtue or that the men understand nothing. Now the true consecration is the one that is done by the word of Faith when it is proclaimed and received, as Saint Augustine says. This is expressly understood by the words of Jesus Christ. For he did not speak to the bread, that it might be made his body, but he addressed his word to the company of the faithful, saying: "Take, eat," etc. If then we want to celebrate the Sacrament well, it is necessary for us to have the doctrine by which what is therein meant may be declared to us. I well know that this seems to be very strange advice to those who are not accustomed to it, as happens with all new things. But if we are disciples of Jesus Christ, it makes good sense that we prefer his institution to our custom. And that which he has instituted from the beginning should not seem to us to be new advice.

If that cannot again be understood by each one, it is useless for us to pray God that he may be pleased to illuminate the ignorant so they can understand, though he is wiser than all the men of earth, in order that they may learn to pause no longer at their proper sense, nor at the stupid and mad wisdom of their leaders, who are blind men. However, for the use of our Church, it has seemed good advice to publish a formulation of the prayers and Sacraments in order that each may recognize what he may have to say and do in the Christian assembly. Further, this Book shall profit not only the people of this Church, but also all those who shall desire to know what form the faithful should hold and follow when they agree in the Name of Jesus Christ. Thus, we have gathered in a summary the manner of celebrating the Sacraments and sanctifying marriage: likewise the prayers and praises which we use. We will speak later of the Sacraments. As for public prayers, there are two kinds. Some are made through simple words, others with singing. And this is not a thing invented in recent times. For history shows that it has been from the earliest origin of the Church. And Saint Paul says the same not only of prayer of the mouth, but also of singing. And in truth, we know through experience that song has great power and strength to move and inflame the heart of men to invoke and praise God with a more vehement and ardent zeal. It is always necessary to give heed that the song may not be light and vulgar, but may have poise and majesty, as Saint Augustine says. And thus there may be great difference between the music that one makes for entertaining men at table and in their house, and the psalms which are sung in the Church in the presence of God and his angels. Now when one would judge rightly of the form that is here presented we hope that it shall be found holy and pure, seeing that it is simply ordered for the edification of which we have spoken, no matter how far the use of singing extends itself. Even in houses and fields this may be an incentive to us and a means to praise God and raise our hearts to him, to comfort us in meditating on his virtue, goodness, wisdom, and justice. What is more necessary than that one would not be able to say. First, it is not without reason that the Holy Spirit exhorts us so carefully through the holy scriptures to rejoice in God and that all our joy may be there reduced to its true end. For he knows how we are inclined to rejoice ourselves in vanity. Thus, all our nature pulls and induces us to seek for every means of foolish and wrong rejoicing: but on the contrary, to separate and redeem us from temptations of the flesh and the world, our Lord presents us all means by which it is possible for us to live in this spiritual joy which he so much recommends to us. Now of the other things which are proper to recreate man and give him delight, Music is either the first or one of the principal: and we must consider that it is a gift of God given for our use. Therefore, we ought all the more to take care not to abuse it, lest we stain or contaminate it, changing it to our condemnation when it was designed for our profit and salvation. For if there would not be any other motive than this alone, we must be moved to regulate the use of music to make it serve all uprightness and not be an opportunity for us to slacken the bridle on dissolution, or of making us effeminate in disorderly pleasures and not be an instrument of defilement nor shamelessness. But yet it is advantageous. For there is scarcely anything in this world that can more greatly turn or bend in any direction the morals of men, as Plato has prudently considered. And in fact we experience that it has a secret and almost incredible faculty to move hearts in one way or another.

Thus, we must be all the more diligent in regulating it in such a way that it may be useful and not injurious to us. For this reason the ancient Doctors of the Church often complain that the people of their time were devoted to disgraceful and impudent songs, which not without reason they call fatal and Satanic poison for the corruption of the world. But in speaking now of Music I include two parts, namely the letter or subject and substance, secondly the song or melody. It is true that every evil word (as Saint Paul says) corrupts good morals, but when melody is with it, this stabs the heart much more strongly and enters within. Just as wine is poured inside a vessel through a funnel, so poison and corruption is distilled down to the depths of the heart through the melody. Now what is it that should be done? It is to have songs that are not only upright, but also holy, which may be like spurs to us, to incite us to prayer and to praise God, to meditate on his works, in order to love, fear, honor, and glorify him. Now what St. Augustine says is true, that no one can sing things worthy of God, except what he may have received from him: when we shall have moved all around to search here and there, we shall find no better nor more proper songs to do this than the Psalms of David, which the holy Spirit has spoken and made through him. And thus, when we sing them, we are certain that God puts on our mouth the words, as if he himself were singing with us to exalt his glory. Chrysostom exhorts men as well as women and little children to get used to singing them, that this may be like a meditation to unite themselves with the company of the Angels. For the rest, we must recall what St. Paul says, that spiritual songs themselves cannot be sung better than with the heart. Now the heart requires the mind. And in this (Saint Augustine says) lies the difference between the song of men and that of birds. For a Linnet, a Nightingale, a Parrot sing well, but without understanding. But the proper gift of man is to sing knowing what he says: the heart and the affection must follow after the mind, which cannot be when we do not have the song imprinted in our memory in order to never cease to sing.

For these reasons the present book even for this cause, beyond the rest that has been said, ought to be in singular recommendation to each who desires to rejoice himself honestly and according to God, even for his salvation and the profit of his neighbors. And so the matter does not have to be much recommended by me, seeing that it carries its value and its praise in itself: but that the world may be advised that in the place of songs that are in part vain and frivolous, in part foolish and clumsy, in part coarse and ugly, and therefore evil and harmful, which it has used before now, it may accustom itself after this to sing these divine and heavenly Songs with the good King David. Concerning the melody, it has seemed the best advice for it to be restrained in the way that we have set it, to carry the weight and majesty appropriate to the subject and to make it proper to sing in the Church, according to what has been said.

Theodore de Beza (1519-1605)

Upon the death of Clement Marot, John Calvin secured the services of Theodore de Beza to complete the French psalter. Beza had led a rather dissolute life until 1548 when, after a serious illness, he came under the influence of Calvin. Beginning in 1549, Beza taught Greek at Lausanne and (after 1558) at Geneva. When Calvin died in 1564, Beza succeeded him as administrative head of the Genevan church and wrote a biography of his illustrious predecessor.

Beza's first significant publication of metrical psalms was in *Pseaumes octante trois de Dauid* (1551), which included the forty-nine psalms of Marot and thirty-four by Beza. The 1553 edition of this publication included a poetic epistle "To the Church of our Savior" in which Beza lamented the fact that Marot had completed "only a third of the work begun" (i.e., forty-nine of the 150 psalms) and gave his reasons for seeking to complete Marot's work.

In the following year, Guillaume Guéroult, a poet and printer who lived alternately in Lyon and Geneva, also undertook to finish the psalter by printing his own version of the psalms not translated by Marot, together with an epistle criticizing the work of Beza. No copy of Guéroult's book is now extant, but what appears to have been his epistle, a ten-line French poem, has been preserved in a manuscript addition Beza made to a copy of his *Poemata* (1597).

In his epistle, Guéroult suggests that Marot's psalms are worthy of the "laurel of glory," but that Beza deserves only "the ears of Midas" (donkey ears). Beza's answer to the criticism of Guéroult is strongly stated in his "Response . . . to the Envious Ass."

Guéroult's attack on Beza was obviously motivated largely by self-interest, but there were undoubtedly others who also considered Beza an unworthy successor to Marot. Nevertheless, it was Beza who ultimately completed Marot's work, resulting in the 1562 publication of the complete Genevan Psalter.

35   From "Theodore de Beza to the Church of our Savior," *Pseaumes octante trois de Dauid* (1553). *Source*: *Correspondance de Théodore de Bèze*, Vol. I., ed. Hippolyte Aubert. Vol. XL of *Travaux d'Humanisme et Renaissance* (Geneva: Librairie E. Droz, 1960), p. 210.

But then at last, so that no one has excuse
Not to praise God, Marot with his Muse
Formerly sang up to a third of the songs
Of the great David, who first made
His harp speak to the Hebrews
And then chose the pen of Clement,
So that God was praised
By the French people with both heart and voice.
Alas, you are dead, without having advanced
Past only a third of the work begun,
And what is worse, not having left to the world,
Learned poet, a man to take your place.
That is why, when death carried you away,
David also fell silent:
All the best minds feared, as it were,
To try their hand at the work you undertook.
To the one who follows you, some brave person will say,
Why undertake such a serious work?
Listen friend, I well know, thanks to God,
What I undertake, and also who I am.
I very well know that my rank
Follows far behind my good affection;
But yet a good heart too often deserves better,
Even when power fails,
When a great power and desire too often falls short.
But if someone is offended while reading me,
He is far from thereby offending me.
On the contrary, rather than be tedious to him,
I would rather that, whoever he may be,
It may stimulate him to do a better.

36   Guillaume Guéroult, "Sonnet of a Certain Envious Fool"
and "Response of Th. de Beza to the Envious Ass"
(1554). *Source*: Ibid., p. 213.

Sonnet of a Certain Envious Fool.
Whoever will listen to the verse
Of Marot and of Beza to choose the better,
Understanding the long and short of it,
Will be able to tell by listening to them read.
Marot's are of Amphion's lyre,
Or of the god Pan's pleasing flageolet:
But Beza's are a defective French,
Rough, ostentatious, and marvellously forced.
Give to Marot the laurel of glory.
What to Beza? The ears of Midas.

Response of Th. de Beza to the Envious Ass
A certain eccentric wit
Finds my verses rough and harsh,
Ostentatious, and marvellously forced,
Giving the precious laurel
To sweet and pleasing Marot,
To me the ears of Midas.
Envious ass, I have well learned
To give the prize to Marot,
But as for the changing of my ears
It is not necessary
To seek so far for a Midas.
Do you not know where yours are?

8
English and Scottish Psalmody

Thomas Sternhold (d. 1549)

LITTLE is known about the life of Thomas Sternhold, except
that he served as "grome of ye Kynges Maiesties Roobes" for
both Henry VIII and Edward VI. Sometime between 1547
and 1549 Sternhold published a collection of nineteen
English metrical psalms under the title *Certayne Psalmes
chosen out of the Psalter of Dauid*. This was enlarged after
Sternhold's death by John Hopkins (d. 1570), who included
a number of previously unpublished psalms by Sternhold, as
well as several of his own. Reprinted and expanded in
successive editions, the collection initiated by Sternhold
culminated in the 1562 publication of *The Whole Book of
Psalms*. In this form, the "Old Version" or "Sternhold and
Hopkins," as it was nicknamed, became the dominant force
in English congregational song for the next 150 years. The
preface to Sternhold's original publication, which was
dedicated to Edward VI, indicates that the young king had
taken "pleasure to heare" these psalms "song sometimes" by
the author before their publication. Sternhold also promised
that if his publication was well received by the king, he would
versify "the residue" of the psalms, a promise he was
prevented from keeping by his death in 1549.

37 Preface to *Certayne Psalmes chosen out of the Psalter of
Dauid* (London, c. 1549).

Although, most noble Soueraigne, the grossenesse of my witte doth
not suffice to searche out the secret misteries hydden in the booke
of Psalmes, which by the opinion of many learned menne,
comprehendeth theffecte of the whole Byble: yet trustying to ye

goodnes of God, which hath in hys hand ye keye thereof, whiche shutteth and no man openeth, openeth & no man shutteth, albeit I cannot geue to your Maiestie great loaues therof, or bring into the lordes barne, full handfulles, yet to thintente I woulde not appeare in the haruest utterly ydle and barraine, beyng warned with the example of the drye fyggtree, I am bolde to presente unto youre Maiestie, a few crummes whiche I haue pyked up frome under the lordes bord, and am glad with the pore woman Ruth, the Moabite, to come behynde and gather a fewe eares of corne after the reapers, rendrynge thankes to almyghtye God, that hath appoynted us suche a Kynge and gouernour, that forbyddeth not laye men to gather and leaze in the lordes haruest, but rather commaundeth the reapers to cast out of their handfulles among us, that we maye boldly gather wythout rebuke: perceyuyng also that your maiestie hath so searched ye fountaines of the scriptures, that yet being young you understande theym better then manye elders, the verye meane to attayne to the perfyte gouernement of this your realme, to goddes glory, the prosperitie of the publique wealthe, & to the comforte of all your maiesties subiectes: Seeynge furdre that youre tender and Godly zeale doethe more delyghte in the holye songes of veritie than in anye fayned rimes of vanitie, I am encouraged to trauayle furdre in the sayed boke of psalmes, trustyng that as your grace taketh pleasure to heare them song sometimes of me, so ye wyll also delyghte not onlye to see and reade them your selfe, but also to commaunde them to be song to you of others: yt as ye haue ye psalme it selfe in youre mynde, so ye maye iudge myne endeuoure by your eare. And yf I maye perceyue your maiestie wyllynglye to accepte my wyll herein, where my doyng is no thanke wurthy, & to sauour so this my begynnyng yt my labor be acceptable, in perfourming the residue, I shall endeuoure my selfe wyth diligence, not onelye to enterpryse that which better learned ought more iustlye to doe, but also to perfourme that without fault, which youre maiestie will receyue with iuste thanke.   The Lorde of earthly kynges, geue your grace, dayly increase of honour and vertue, and fulfyll all your godly requestes in him, without whose gifte we haue or can obtayne nothyng. Amen.

William Whittingham (1524-1579)

The coronation of King Edward VI's half sister Mary as Queen of England in 1553 led to severe persecution of

English Protestants, many of whom fled to the Continent.
One band of exiles settled in Frankfurt, but dissension over
whether to follow the Prayer Book or Calvinist form of
worship led to a split in the group. Adherents of the
Calvinist model moved to Geneva in 1555 and, in 1556,
published _The Forme of Prayers and Ministration of the
Sacraments_. The work had been prepared in Frankfurt by
John Knox, William Whittingham, Anthony Gilby, John Foxe,
and Thomas Cole. Knox (c. 1515-1572) subsequently became
the leader of the Scottish Reformation, while Whittingham,
an Englishman, later served as Dean of Durham (1563-1579).
A number of Whittingham's psalm versifications were
published in the Anglo-Genevan Psalter (1556, 1558, 1561)
and several were transferred to the 1562 _Whole Book of
Psalms_ ("Old Version").

The preface to _The Forme of Prayers_, though unsigned, is
often attributed to Whittingham. The philosophy of
congregational song espoused in this document obviously
reflects the influence of Calvin in its endorsement of metrical
psalmody. It is also representative of the views of John Knox
and the future direction of congregational song in the
churches of the Scottish Reformation. The last paragraph of
the present extract points out that several of the psalm
versions by Thomas Sternhold included in the accompanying
Anglo-Genevan Psalter (1556) had been altered to make
them accord better with the sense of the Hebrew. These
alterations have also been attributed to Whittingham.

38   From Preface to _The forme of prayers and ministration of
the Sacraments, &c. vsed in the Englishe Congregation at
Geneua: and approued, by the famous and godly learned
man, Iohn Caluyn_ (1556). _Source_: _The Works of John
Knox_, collected and edited by David Laing (Edinburgh:
Johnstone and Hunter, 1855), vol. 4, pp. 165-167.

But as ther is no gift of God so precious or excellent, that Satan
hath not after a sort drawen to himself and corrupt, so hath he
most impudentlye abused this notable gifte of singinge, chieflye by
the Papistes his ministers, in disfiguring it, partly by strange
language, that can not edifie, and partly by a curious wanton sort,

hyringe men to tickle the eares and flatter the phantasies, not esteminge it as a gifte approved by the Worde of God, profitable for the Churche, and confirmed by all Antiquitie. As, besides other places, is most manifest by the wordes of Plinius,[1] called the younger, who, when he was depute in Asia unto the Emperour Trajan, and had receyved charge to enquire out the Christians to put them to deathe, writ emongs other thinges, touchinge the Christians, "That their maners were to singe verses or psalmes early in the morninge to Christ their God." Yf any, paradventure, wolde doute, when, or by whom these churches or assembles were institute, it is likewise evident, that S. John the Apostle[2] who, althogh in Domitian's tyme he was banished in the Ile Pathmos; yet when Nerva his successor, and next before Trajan raigned, retourned to Ephesus, and so planted the churches, as the stories report. Seinge therfore God's Woorde dothe approve it, antiquitie beareth witenes therof, and best reformed Churches have receyved the same, no man can reprove it, except he will contemne God's Worde, despice Antiquitie, and utterlie condemne the godlie reformed Churches.

And there are no songes more meete then the Psalmes of the Prophet David, which the Holy Ghoste hath framed to the same use, and commended to the Churche, as conteininge the effect of the whole Scriptures, that hereby our heartes might be more lyvelie touched, as appereth by Moses, Ezechias, Judith, Debora, Marie, Zacharie, and others,[3] who by songes and metre, rather then in their commune speache and prose, gave thankes to God for suche comfort as he sent them.

Here it were to longe to intreate of the metre; but for asmuche

---

[1]Epist. lib. 10.

[2]Eccle. Hist. lib. 3. cap. 22.

[3]Exo. 15. a.
Esa. 38. c.
Jud. 16. a.
Jug. 5. a.
Luk. 1. f.
Luk. 1. c.

as the learned doubt not therof, and it is playnly proven that the Psalmes are not only metre, and conteyne juste Cesures, but also have grace and majestie in the verse more then any other places of the Scriptures, we nede not to enter into any probation. For they that are skilfull in the Hebrews tounge,[4] by comparinge the Psalmes with the reste of the Scriptures, easelie may perceyve the metre. And to whome is it not knowen, how the Holy Ghoste by all means soght to helpe our memorie, when he facioned many Psalmes accordinge to the letters of the alphabet; so that every verse beginneth with the lettres therof in ordre. Sometimes A. beginneth the halfe verse, and B. the other halfe; and in an other place, thre verses, yea and eight verses with one letter, even the Psalme throughout; as if all men shulde be inflamed with the love therof, bothe for varietie of matter, and also briefenes, easines, and delectation.

Nowe, to make you privie also why we altered the ryme in certeyne places of hym, whome for the gyftes that God had gevyn him, we estemed and reverenced, thys may suffice: that in this entreprise, we did onely set God before our eyes, and therfore wayed the wordes and sense of the Prophete, rather consideringe the meanyng therof then what any man had wrytt. And chiefly beinge in this place, where as moste perfite and godly judgement dyd assure us, and exhortations to the same encorage us, we thoght it better to frame the ryme to the Hebrewe sense, then to bynde that sense to the Englishe meter: and so either altered for the better, in such places as he had not attayned unto, or els where he had escaped parte of the verse, or some tymes the whole, we added the same, not as men desyrous to finde fautes, but onely as suche which covvete to hyde theym, as the learned can judge.

Thomas Est (c. 1540-1609)
Thomas Est, whose last name appeared in a variety of forms including East, Easte, and Este, was an important London music publisher, printing works by William Byrd, Thomas Morley, John Dowland, and other late sixteenth- and early seventeenth-century English composers. In 1592 he issued a

---

[4]Reade Moses Chabib, in his bookes called, מ ד פא לש ו ך
דרב י נ ו ו ם

collection of harmonized tunes for Sternhold and Hopkins's *Whole Book of Psalms*. This was among the first music publications to be printed in score format, rather than in individual parts; it was also the first psalter to give names to individual tunes. In the dedication and preface, Est commented on the power of the psalms and of music, as well as detailing some of the procedures he used in putting the book together.

39   Dedication and Preface to *The Whole Booke of Psalmes; with their wonted Tunes* (London, 1592), pp. [i]-[iii].

To the Right Honorable Sir Iohn Puckering Knight Lord keeper of the great seale of England.

The woord of God (Right honorable) delighteth those which are spiritually mynded: the Art of Musick recreateth such, as are not sensually affected: wher zeal in the one, and skill in the other doe meet, the whole man is reuiued. The mercies of God are great, prouoking unto thankfulnesse: the necessities of man are daily, enforcing unto praier: the state of us all is such, that the publishing of Gods glory for the edifying one of an other cannot be overslipped: In all these the hart must be the workmaster, the tongue the instrument, & a sanctified knowledge as the hand to pullish the work. The Psalmes of David are a Paraphrasis of the Scriptures: they teach us thankefulnesse, praier, & all the duties of a christian whatsoever: they haue such comfort in them, that such as will bee conversant in the same, cannot possibly loose their labour. Blessed is that man, which delighteth therein, & meditateth in the same continually. He that is heauy, hath the Psalmes to help his prayer: He that is merry, hath the Psalms to guide his affections: and he, that hath a desire to be seriously employed in either of these duties, hath this excellent gift of God the knowledge of Musicke offered him for his further help: that the hart reioycing in the word, & the eares delighting in the Notes & Tunes, both these might ioyne together unto the praise of God. Some haue pleased themselues with Pastoralls, others with Madrigalls, but such as are endued with Dauids hart, desire with Dauid to sing unto God Psalmes & Hymnes, and spirituall songs. For whose sake I haue set foorth this woorke, that they may busie themselves in the Psalmes of this holy man, beeing by men of skill put into foure parts, that ech man may sing that part, which best may serue his uoice.

In this booke the Church Tunes are carefully corrected, & other short Tunes added, which are song in London, & other places of this Realme. And regarding chiefely to help the simple, curiositie is shunned. The profit is theirs that will use this booke, the paynes theirs that have compyled it, the charges his, who setting it foorth, respecteth a publique benefit, not his priuate gaine. Now hauing finished it, in most humble manner I present it unto your Honour, as to a maintainer of godlines, a friend to Vertue, & a louer of Musick: hoping of your Lordships fauorable acceptance, crauing your honorable Patronage & countenance, and praying unto God long to continue your Lordstip, a protectour of the iust, and the same God to bee a protectour of your Lordships welfare for euer.

         Your good L. most humbly
           at command
           Thomas Est.

The Preface

Although I might haue vsed the skill of some one learned Musition, in the setting of these Psalmes in 4. parts, yet for varieties sake, I haue intreated the help of many: beeing such as I know to be expert in the Arte, & sufficient to answere such curious carping Musitions, whose skill hath not bene employed to the furthering of this work. And I haue not onely set downe in this booke all the Tunes vsually printed heretofore, with as much truth as I could possibly gather among diuers of our ordinary Psalme bookes, but also haue added those, which are commonly song now adayes, and not printed in our common Psalme books with the rest. And all this haue I so orderly cast, that the 4. parts lye alwayes together in open sight. The which my trauayle as it hath bene to the furtherance of Musicke, in all godly sort, & to the comfort of all good Christians: so I pray thee to take it in good part, & vse it to the glory of God.

           T. E.

The Westminster Assembly (1645)

The first half of the seventeenth century saw increasingly deteriorating relationships between the Puritan-dominated English Parliament and kings James I (1566-1625) and Charles I (1600-1649). After ruling without Parliament for eleven years, Charles was finally forced to recall the assembly in November 1640. However, when he tried to seize several members of this so-called "Long Parliament" in 1642, civil war broke out, resulting in the defeat and eventual beheading of Charles (1649), and the establishment of the Commonwealth and Protectorate under Oliver Cromwell (1599-1658).

The Westminster Assembly was called by the Long Parliament in 1643 and met off and on for the next ten years. Composed primarily of Presbyterian sympathizers, the Assembly was charged with imposing Puritan ideals on the Church of England. Among the important documents produced by the Assembly were the Westminster Confession, the Larger and Shorter Catechisms, and the Westminster *Directory for the Publique Worship of God.* An important feature of the Directory was its recognition and endorsement of lining-out (the leader reading each line of text before it was sung by the congregation) as a stopgap measure "where many in the Congregation cannot reade." However, lining-out became ingrained as custom, and continued to be an important feature of English and American congregational singing for the next century and a half.

40   From *A Directory for the Publique Worship of God, Throughout the Three Kingdoms of England, Scotland, and Ireland* (London, 1645), p. 40.

Of Singing of Psalmes

It is the duty of Christians to praise God publiquely by singing of Psames together in the Congregation, and also privately in the Family.

In singing of Psalms, the voice is to be tunable and gravely ordered: But the chief care must be, to sing with understanding, and with Grace in the heart, making melody unto the Lord.

That the whole Congregation may join herein, every one that can read is to have a Psalm-book, and all others, not disabled by age or otherwise, are to be exhorted to learn to reade. But for the present, where many in the Congregation cannot reade, it is convenient that the Minister, or some other fit person appointed by him and the other Ruling Officers, do reade the Psalme, line by line, before the singing thereof.

Nahum Tate and Nicholas Brady (17th-18th centuries)

After more than 130 years of monopolizing English and American congregational song, the Sternhold and Hopkins _Whole Book of Psalms_ (1562) met its first serious rival in the _New Version of the Psalms of David_ (1696). This collection was compiled by two Irishmen, Nahum Tate (c. 1652-1715) and Nicholas Brady (1659-1726). Tate, the son of a Puritan minister, was poet laureate of Great Britain and an associate of such prominent English composers as John Blow and Henry Purcell (he wrote the libretto for Purcell's _Dido and Aeneas_). Brady was a clergyman and something of a poet himself. The _New Version_ represented a freer approach than the Old Version in its handling of the Scriptures and was also more literary in style. While Tate and Brady never completely replaced Sternhold and Hopkins, many eighteenth-century congregations in both England and America adopted the _New Version_ as a preliminary step along the road to the use of "hymns of human composure." The "Advertisement" to the first edition describes some of the procedures used in arranging the psalms for the collection.

41   "Advertisement" from _A New Version of the Psalms of David_ (London, 1696), pp. [319]-[320].

Advertisement.

Having design'd to make such a Version of the Psalms _as may be fit for Common Use we have enceavour'd it by the following Methods,_

1. By keeping strictly to the Text, and where the Sense was doubtful, determining it by the Scope and Occasion of the Psalm.

2. By taking care to make the whole Version easie and intelligible.

3. By endeavouring to express the Spirit and Genius of every Psalm, and suiting our Style to the several Passions of the Author.

4. By retaining the Connexion throughout each Psalm, which does not always appear in the Prose Translation.

5. By rendring the Hebraisms in their plain Sense and Meaning, as agreed upon by the best Commentators.

6. By adapting our Measures to the Tunes that are best received, turning several Psalms to those that are most Musical, such as that of 100, 113, 148, _and others._

N. T. N. B.

9

American Psalmody

Francis Fletcher (16th-17th centuries)

IN 1577, the English admiral Sir Francis Drake set sail in the *Pelican* (later renamed the *Golden Hind*) with four other ships for a voyage around the world. While this was ostensibly a voyage of discovery, one of Drake's unstated purposes was probably the plundering of Spanish ships and possessions. Drake's mission was completed in a little less than three years, when he sailed into Plymouth in September 1580.

One of the members of Drake's party was Francis Fletcher, who served as chaplain for the voyage. In 1628, *The World Encompassed by Sir Francis Drake* was published, having been "carefully collected out of the notes of Master Francis Fletcher . . . and diuers others" (title page). According to Fletcher's account, in June 1579 the *Golden Hind* dropped anchor in a "conuenient and fit harborough" located in the San Francisco Bay area (p. 64). Six days later, a group of natives attempted to worship the newcomers as gods, the women tearing the flesh from their cheeks with their nails and dashing themselves on the ground. As an example to the Indians, Drake and his crew "fell to prayers," not neglecting the "singing of Psalmes," which seems to have stirred considerable interest in the natives. The Englishmen never quite convinced the inhabitants that they were not gods, and when the explorers prepared to sail a month later, they again had to resort to "prayers and singing of Psalmes." These "Psalmes" were undoubtedly those of the Old Version. Fletcher's account is the earliest known reference to the singing of metrical psalms on the west coast of what was later to become the United States of America.

42   From *The World Encompassed by Sir Francis Drake*
           (London: Nicholas Bourne, 1628), pp. 72, 81.

This bloudie sacrifice (against our wils) beeing thus performed, our
Generall with his companie in the presence of those strangers fell
to prayers: and by signes in lifting vp our eyes and hands to
heauen, signified vnto them, that that God whom we did serue, and
whom they ought to worship, was aboue: Beseeching God if it were
his good pleasure to open by some meanes their blinded eyes; that
they might in due time be called to the knowledge of him the true
and euerliuing God, and of Iesus Christ whom he hath sent, the
saluation of the Gentiles. In the time of which prayers, singing of
Psalmes, and reading of certaine Chapters in the Bible, they sate
very attentiuely: and obseruing the end at euery pause, with one
voice still cryed, Oh, greatly reioycing in our exercises. Yea they
tooke such pleasure in our singing of Psalmes, that whensoeuer they
resorted to vs, their first request was commonly this, *Gnaáh*, by
which they intreated that we would sing.

   . . .

   Howbeit seeing they could not still enioy our presence, they
(supposing vs to be gods indeed) thought it their duties to intreate
vs that being absent, we would yet be mindfull of them, and making
signes of their desires, that in time to come wee would see them
againe, they stole vpon vs a sacrifice, and set it on fire erre we were
aware; burning therein a chaine and a bunch of feathers. We
laboured by all meanes possible to withhold or withdraw them but
could not preuaile, till at last we fell to prayers and singing of
Psalmes, whereby they were allured immediatly to forget their folly,
and leaue their sacrifice vnconsumed, suffering the fire to go out,
and imitating vs in all our actions; they fell a lifting vp their eyes
and hands to heauen as they saw vs do.

The Bay Psalm Book (1640)

   Less than ten years after the arrival of the *Mayflower* Pilgrims
   in the New World (1620), a group of English Puritans
   founded the Massachusetts Bay Colony. Within a decade,
   these new settlers had established a college (Harvard
   College, now Harvard University) and laid plans for
   publishing their own metrical psalter. This collection, *The
   Whole Booke of Psalmes Faithfully Translated into English*

Metre, was issued in 1640, the first book-length production
from an American press. Familiarly known today as the
"Bay Psalm Book," the collection received a major revision
in 1651, and in this form dominated congregational song in
New England for nearly a century.

The preface to the first edition, though unsigned, has
been convincingly shown by Zoltán Haraszti to have been the
work of John Cotton (1584-1652), pastor of the First Church
in Boston (_The Enigma of the Bay Psalm Book_, Chicago:
University of Chicago Press, 1956, pp. 19-27). The preface
serves as an apologia for the exclusive singing of scriptural
versifications and the literalness of the translations.

43   Preface to _The Whole Booke of Psalmes Faithfully
         Translated into English Metre_ ([Cambridge: Stephen
         Daye], 1640).

The singing of Psalmes, though it breath forth nothing but holy
harmony, and melody: yet such is the subtilty of the enemie, and
the enmity of our nature against the Lord, & his wayes, that our
hearts can finde matter of discord in this harmony, and crotchets of
division in this holy melody -for- There have been three questions
especially stirring concerning singing. First. what psalmes are to be
sung in churches? whether Davids and other scripture psalmes, or
the psalmes invented by the gifts of godly men in every age of the
church.   Secondly, if scripture psalmes, whether in their owne
words, or in such meter as english poetry is wont to run in?
Thirdly. by whom are they to be sung? whether by the whole
churches together with their voices? or by one man singing alone
and the rest joyning in silence, & in the close saying amen.

Touching the first, certainly the singing of Davids psalmes was
an acceptable worship of God, not only in his owne, but in
succeeding times. as in Solomons time 2 _Chron_. 5. 13. in
Jehosaphats time 2 _chron_. 20. 21. in Ezra his time _Ezra_ 3. 10, 11.
and the text is evident in Hezekiahs time they are commanded to
sing praise in the words of David and Asaph, 2 _chron_. 29, 30. which
one place may serve to resolve two of the questions (the first and
the last at once, for this commandement was it cerimoniall or
morall? some things in it indeed were cerimoniall, as their musicall
instruments &c but what cerimony was there in singing prayse with

the words of David and Asaph? what if David was a type of Christ, was Asaph also? was every thing of David typicall? are his words (which are of morall, universall, and perpetuall authority in all nations and ages) are they typicall? what type can be imagined in making use of his songs to prayse the Lord? If they were typicall because the cerimony of musicall instruments was joyned with them, then their prayers were also typicall, because they had that ceremony of incense admixt with them: but wee know that prayer then was a morall duty, notwithstanding the incense; and soe singing those psalmes notwithstanding their musicall instruments. Beside, that which was typicall (as that they were sung with musicall instruments, by the twenty-foure orders of Priests and Levites. 1 *chron.* 25. 9.) must have the morall and spirituall accomplishment in the new Testament, in all the Churches of the Saints principally, who are made kings & priests *Reu.* 1. 6. and are the first fruits unto God. *Reu.* 14 4. as the Levites were *Num.* 3. 45. with hearts & lippes, in stead of musicall instruments, to prayse the Lord; who are set forth (as some iudiciously thinke) *Reu.* 4. 4. by twenty foure Elders, in the ripe age of the Church, *Gal.* 4. 1, 2, 3. answering to the twenty foure orders of Priests and Levites 1. *chron.* 25. 9. Therefore not some select members, but the whole Church is commaunded to teach one another in all the severall sorts of Davids psalmes, some being called by himselfe מ ז מ ו ר י ם : psalms, some ת ה י ל ל י ם : Hymns some שׁ י ר י ם : spirituall songs. soe that if the singing Davids psalmes be a morall duty & therfore perpetuall; then wee under the new Testament are bound to sing them as well as they under the old: and if wee are expresly commanded to sing Psalmes, Hymnes, and spirituall songs, then either wee must sing Davids psalmes, or else may affirm they are not spirituall songs: which being penned by an extraordinary gift of the Spirit, for the sake especially of Gods spirtuall Israell; not to be read and preached only (as other parts of holy writ) but to be sung also, they are therefore most spirituall, and still to be sung of all the Israell of God: and verily as their sin is exceeding great, who will allow Davids psalmes (as other scriptures) to be read in churches (which is one end) but not to be preached also, (which is another end[)] soe their sin is crying before God, who will allow them to be read and preached, but seeke to deprive the Lord of the glory of the third end of them, which is to sing them in christian churches.

obj. 1 If it be sayd that the Saints in the primitive Church did compile spirituall songs of their owne inditing, and sing them before the Church. 1 Cor. 14, 15, 16.

Ans. We answer first, that those Saints compiled these spirituall songs by the extraordinary gifts of the spirit (common in those dayes) whereby they were inabled to praise the Lord in strange tongues, wherin learned _Paraeus_ proves those psalmes were uttered, in his Comment on that place _uers_ 14 which extraordinary gifts, if they were still in the Churches, wee should allow them the like liberty now. Secondly, suppose those psalmes were sung by an ordinary gift (which wee suppose cannot be evicted) doth it therefore follow that they did not, & that we ought not to sing Davids psalmes? must the ordinary gifts of a private man quench the spirit still speaking to us by the extraordinary gifts of his servant David? there is not the least foot-step of example, or precept, or colour reason for such a bold practise.

obj. 2. Ministers are allowed to pray conceived prayers, and why not to sing conceived psalmes? must wee not sing in the spirit as well as pray in the spirit?

Ans. First because every good minister hath not a gift of spirituall poetry to compose extemporary psalmes as he hath of prayer. Secondly. Suppose he had, yet seeing psalmes are to be sung by a joynt consent and harmony of all the Church in heart and voyce (as wee shall prove) this cannot be done except he that composeth a psalme, bringeth into the Church set formes of psalmes of his owne invention; for which wee finde no warrant or president in any ordinary officers of the Church throughout the scriptures. Thirdly. Because the booke of psalmes is so compleat a System of psalmes, which the Holy-Ghost himselfe in infinite wisdome hath made to suit all the conditions, necessityes, temptations, affections, &c. of men in all ages; (as most of all our interpreters on the psalmes have fully and perticularly cleared) therefore by this the Lord seemeth to stoppe all mens mouths and mindes ordinarily to compile or sing any other psalmes (under colour that the ocasions and conditions of the Church are new) &c. for the publick use of the Church, seing, let our condition be what it will, the Lord himselfe hath supplyed us with farre better; and therefore in Hezekiahs time, though doubtlesse there were among them those which had extraoridnary gifts to compile new songs on those new ocasions, as Isaiah and Micah &c. yet wee read that they are commanded to sing in the words of David and Asaph, which were ordinarily to be used in the publick worship of God: and wee doubt not but those that are wise will easily see; that those set formes of psalmes of Gods owne appoyntment not of mans conceived gift or humane imposition were sung in the Spirit by those holy Levites, as well as their prayers were in the spirit which themselves conceived, the Lord not then binding them therin to any set formes; and shall set formes of psalmes appoynted of God not be sung in the spirit now, which others did then?

Question. But why may not one compose a psalme & sing it alone with a loud voice & the rest joyne with him in silence and in the end say Amen?

Ans. If such a practise was found in the Church of Corinth, when any had a psalme suggested by an extraordinary gift; yet in singing ordinary psalmes the whole Church is to ioyne together in heart and voyce to prayse the Lord. -for-

First. Davids psalmes as hath beene shewed, were sung in heart and voyce together by the twenty foure orders of the musicians of the Temple, who typed out the twenty foure Elders all the members especially of christian Churches *Reu* 5. 8. who are made Kings and Priests to God to prayse him as they did: for if there were any other order of singing Choristers beside the body of the people to succeed those, the Lord would doubtlesse have given direction in the gospell for their quallification, election, maintainance &c. as he did for the musicians of the Temple, and as his faithfullnes hath done for all other church officers in the new Testament.

Secondly. Others beside the Levites (the chiefe Singers) in the Jewish Church did also sing the Lords songs; else why are they commanded frequently to sing: as in ps. 100, 1, 2, 3. ps. 95, 1, 2, 3. ps. 102. title. with vers 18. & Ex. 15. 1. not only Moses but all Israell sang that song, they spake saying (as it is in the *orig.*) all as well as Moses, the women also as well as the men. v. 20 21. and *deut.* 32. (whereto some thinke, Iohn had reference as well as to Ex. 15. 1. when he brings in the protestant Churches getting the victory over the Beast with harps in their hands and singing the song of Moses. *Reu.* 15. 3.) this song Moses is commanded not only to put it into their hearts but into their mouthes also: *deut.* 31. 19. which argues, they were with their mouthes to sing it together as well as with their hearts.

Thirdly. Isaiah foretells in the dayes of the new-Testament that Gods watchmen and desolate lost soules, (signified by wast places) should with their voices sing together, Isa. 52. 8, 9. and _Reu_-7. 9, 10. the song of the Lamb was by many together, and the Apostle expresly commands the singing of Psalmes, Himnes, &c. not to any select christians, but to the whole Church Eph. 5. 19 _coll._ 3. 16. Paule & Silas sang together in private _Acts_. 16. 25. and must the publick heare only one man sing? to all these wee may adde the practise of the primitive Churches; the testimony of ancient and holy _Basil_ is in stead of many _Epist._ 63 When one of us (saith he) hath begun a psalme, the rest of us set in to sing with him, all of us with one heart and one voyce; and this saith he is the common practise of the Churches in Egypt, Lybia, Thebes, Palestina, Syria and those that dwell on Euphrates, and generally every where, where singing of psalmes is of any account. To the same purpose also _Eusebius_ gives witnes, _Eccles. Hist. lib._ 2. _cap._ 17. The objections made against this doe most of them plead against joyning to sing in heart as well as in voyce, as that by this meanes others out of the Church will sing as also that wee are not alway in a sutable estate to the matter sung, & likewise that all cannot sing with understanding; shall not therefore all that have understanding ioyne in heart and voyce together? are not all the creatures in heaven, earth, seas: men, beasts, fishes, foules &c. commanded to praise the Lord, and yet none of these but men, and godly men too, can doe it with spirituall understanding?

As for the scruple that some take at the translation of the book of psalmes into meeter, because Davids psalmes were sung in his owne words without meeter: wee answer- First. There are many verses together in several psalmes of David which run in rithmes (as those that know the hebrew and as Buxtorf shews _Thesau._ pa. 629.) which shews at least the lawfullnes of singing psalmes in english rithmes.

Secondly. The psalmes are penned in such verses as are sutable to the poetry of the hebrew language, and not in the common style of such other bookes of the old Testament as are not poeticall; now no protestant doubteth but that all the bookes of the scripture should by Gods ordinance be extant in the mother tongue of each nation, that they may be understood of all, hence the psalmes are to be translated into our english tongue; and if in our english tongue wee are to sing them, then as all our english songs (according to the course of our english poetry) do run in metre, soe ought Davids psalmes to be translated into meeter, that soe wee

may sing the Lords songs, as in our english tongue soe in such
verses as are familiar to an english eare which are commonly
metricall: and as it can be no just offence to any good conscience
to sing Davids hebrew songs in english words, soe neither to sing his
poeticall verses in english poeticall metre: men might as well
stumble at singing the hebrew psalmes in our english tunes (and not
in the hebrew tunes) as at singing them in english meeter, (which
are our verses) and not in such verses as are generally used by
David according to the poetry of the hebrew language: but the
truth is, as the Lord hath hid from us the hebrew tunes, lest wee
should think our selves bound to imitate them; soe also the course
and frame (for the most part) of their hebrew poetry, that wee
might not think our selves bound to imitate that, but that every
nation without scruple might follow as the graver sort of tunes of
their owne country songs, soe the graver sort of verses of their owne
country poetry.

Neither let any think, that for the meetre sake wee have taken
liberty or poeticall licence to depart from the true and proper sence
of the Davids words in the hebrew verses, noe; but it hath beene
one part of our religious care and faithfull indeavour, to keepe close
to the originall text.

As for other objections taken from the difficulty of *Ainsworths*
tunes, and the corruptions in our common psalme books, wee hope
they are answered in this new edition of psalmes which wee here
present to God and his Churches. For although wee have cause to
blesse God in many respects for the religious indeavours of the
translaters of the psalmes into meetre usually annexed to our
Bibles, yet it is not unknowne to the godly learned that they have
rather presented a paraphrase then the words of David translated
according to the rule 2 *chron.* 29. 30. and that their addition to the
words, detractions from the words are not seldome and rare, but
very frequent and many times needles, (which we suppose would
not be approved of if the psalmes were so translated into prose)
and that their variations of the sense, and alterations of the sacred
text too frequently, may iustly minister matter of offence to them
that are able to compare the translation with the text; of which
failings, some iudicious have oft complained, others have been
grieved, wherupon it hath bin generally desired, that as wee doe
inioye other, soe (if it were the Lords will) wee might inioye this
ordinance also in its native purity: wee have therefore done our

indeavour to make a plaine and familiar translation of the psalmes and words of David into english metre, and have not soe much as presumed to paraphrase to give the sense of his meaning in other words; we have therefore attended heerin as our chief guide the originall, shunning all additions, except such as even the best translators of them in prose supply, avoiding all materiall detractions from words or sence. The word ו . which wee translate _and_ as it is redundant sometime in the Hebrew, soe somtime (though not very often) it hath been left out, and yet not then, if the sence were not faire without it.

As for our translations, wee have with our english Bibles (to which next to the Originall wee have had respect) used the Idioms of our owne tongue in stead of Hebraismes, lest they might seeme english barbarismes.

Synonimaes wee use indifferently: as _folk_ for _people_, and _Lord_ for _Iehovah_, and sometime (though seldome) _God_ for _Iehovah_; for which (as for some other interpretations of places cited in the new Testament) we have the scriptures authority ps. 14. with 53. Heb. 1. 6. with psalme 97. 7.   Where a phrase is doubtfull wee have followed that which (in our owne apprehension) is most genuine & edifying:

Somtime wee have contracted, somtime dilated the same hebrew word, both for the sence and the verse sake: which dilatation wee conceive to be no paraphrasticall addition no more then the contraction of a true and full translation to be any unfaithfull detraction or diminution: as when wee dilate _who healeth_ and say _he it is who healeth_; soe when wee contract, _those that stand in awe of God_ and say _Gods fearers_.

Lastly.   Because some hebrew words have a more full and emphaticall signification then any one english word can or doth somtime expresse, hence wee have done that somtime which faithfull translators may doe, _viz._ not only to translate the word but the emphasis of it; as ל א _mighty God_, for _God_. ך ר ב _humbly blesse_ for _blesse_; _rise to stand_, psalm 1. for _stand_; _truth and faithfullnes_ for _truth_.   Howbeit, for the verse sake wee doe not alway thus, yet wee render the word truly though not fully; as when wee somtime say _reioyce_ for _shout for ioye_.

As for all other changes of numbers, tenses, and characters of speech, they are such as either the hebrew will unforcedly beare, or our english forceably calls for, or they no way change the sence; and such are printed usually in an other character.

If therefore the verses are not alwayes so smooth and elegant as some may desire or expect; let them consider that Gods Altar needs not our pollishings: Ex. 20. for wee have respected rather a plaine translation, then to smooth our verses with the sweetnes of any paraphrase, and soe have attended Conscience rather then Elegance, fidelity rather then poetry, in translating the hebrew words into english language, and Davids poetry into english meetre;

that soe wee may sing in Sion the Lords
songs of prayse according to his owne
will; untill hee take us from hence,
and wipe away all our teares, &
bid us enter into our masters
ioye to sing eternall
Halleluiahs.

Cotton Mather (1663-1728)

Cotton Mather was the son of Increase Mather, a prominent Massachusetts Puritan divine, and the grandson of Richard Mather and John Cotton, both of whom were involved in the compiling of the 1640 Bay Psalm Book. Upholding the family tradition, Cotton Mather also entered the ministry, ultimately becoming the most significant New England Puritan of his time, writing more than 400 books and maintaining an extensive correspondence with many important figures, including Isaac Watts. His most important historical work, *Magnalia Christi Americana* (1702), though sketchy in some areas and poorly organized in others, remains a prime source of information on the early Puritans of New England. In the following extract, Mather discusses the role of Henry Dunster in the 1651 revision of the Bay Psalm Book, and provides information about the original 1640 publication. The Latin poem that concludes the passage may be translated as follows: "A herald, I have sounded the holy with my voice; a father, I have encouraged students with rigor; a servant, I have followed Christ with faithfulness. Virtue has extended my fame with praise; Christ has restored my soul with salvation; earth has resigned my body to its bosom."

44   From _Magnalia Christi Americana_ (1702). _Source_: Cotton
            Mather, _Magnalia Christi Americana; or, The Ecclesiastical
            History of New-England_ (Hartford: Silas Andrus and Son,
            1855), vol. 1, pp. 405-408.

Psaltes. The Life of Mr. Henry Dunster.

Notwithstanding the veneration which we pay to the _names_ and
works of those reverend men, whom we call _the fathers_, yet even the
Roman Catholicks themselves confess, that those fathers were not
infallible. Andradius, among others, in his defence of the Council
of Trent, has this passage: "there can be nothing devised more
superstitious, than to count all things delivered by the fathers _divine
oracles_." And, indeed, it is plain enough that those excellent men
were not without _errors_ and _frailties_, of which, I hope, it will not be
the part of a _cham_ to take some little notice. Thus, Jerom had his
erroneous opinion of Peter's being unjustly reprehended; and was
fearfully _asleep_ in the other matters, wherein he opposed
Vigilantius. Augustine was for admitting the _infants_ of Christians
unto the Lord's Supper: and, alas! how much of Babylon is there
in his best book, "_De Civitate Dei_." Hilary denied the _soul-sorrows_
of our Lord in his passion, if you will believe the report of
Bellarmine. Clemens Alexandrinus affirmed that our Lord neither
eat nor _drank_ from the necessities of human life; and that he and
his apostles, after their death, preached unto the _damned_ in hell, of
whom there were many converted. Origen taught many things
contrary unto the _true faith_, and frequently confounded the
Scriptures with false expositions. Tertullian fell into Montanism,
and forbad all _second marriages_. How little agreement was there
between Epiphanius and Chrysostom, Irenaeus and Victor,
Cornelius and Cyprian? And, indeed, that I may draw near to my
present purpose, the erroneous opinion of _rebaptism_ in Cyprian, is
well known to the world.

Wherefore it may not be wondred at if, among the first _fathers_
of New-England, there were some things not altogether so
agreeable to the _principles_ whereupon the country was in the main
established. But among those of our fathers who differed somewhat
from his brethren, was that learned and worthy man Mr. Henry
Dunster.

He was the president of our Harvard College in Cambridge, and
an able man: [as we may give some account, when the history of

that college comes to be offered.]

But wonderfully falling into the errors of Antipaedobaptism, the *overseers* of the college became solicitous that the students there might not be unawares ensnared in the errors of their president. Wherefore they laboured with an extreme agony, either to rescue the good man from his *own mistakes*, or to restrain him from imposing them upon *the hope of the flock*, of both which, finding themselves to despair, they did, as quietly as they could, procure his *removal*, and provide him a successor, in Mr. Charles Chauncey.

He was a very good Hebrician, and for that cause he bore a great part in the metrical version of the Psalms, now used in our churches. But after some short retirement and secession from all publick business, at Scituate, in the year 1659, he went thither, where he bears his part in everlasting and caelestial *hallelujahs*. It was justly counted an instance of an *excellent spirit*, in Margaret Meering, that though she had been excommunicated by the congregation of Protestants, whereof Mr. Rough was pastor, and she seemed to have hard measure also in her excommunication; yet when Mr. Rough was imprisoned for the truth, she was very serviceable to him, and at length suffered martyrdom for the truth with him. Something that was not altogether unlike this "excellent spirit" was instanced by our Dunster. For he died in such *harmony* of affection with the good men who had been the authors of his removal from Cambridge, that he, by his will, ordered his body to be carried into Cambridge for its burial, and bequeathed *legacies* to those very persons.

Now, I know not where, better than here, to insert that article of our church-history, which concerns our *metrical translation* of the Psalms now sung in our churches.

About the year 1639, the New-English reformers, considering that their churches enjoyed the other ordinances of Heaven in their scriptural purity, were willing that the ordinance of "The singing of psalms," should be restored among them unto a share in that *purity*. Though they blessed God for the religious endeavours of them who translated the Psalms into the *meetre* usually annexed at the end of the Bible, yet they beheld in the translation so many *detractions* from, *additions* to, and *variations* of, not only the text, but the very *sense* of the psalmist, that it was an offence unto them. Resolving then upon a new translation, the chief divines in the country took each of them a portion to be translated: among whom were Mr.

Welds and Mr. Eliot of Roxbury, and Mr. Mather of Dorchester. These, like the rest, were of so different a *genius* for their poetry, that Mr. Shepard, of Cambridge, on the occasion addressed them to this purpose:

> You Roxb'ry poets, keep clear of the crime
> Of missing to give us very good rhime.
> And you of Dorchester, your verses lengthen,
> But with the text's own words, you will them strengthen.

The Psalms thus turned into *meetre* were printed at Cambridge, in the year 1640. But, afterwards, it was thought that a little more of art was to be employed upon them: and for that cause, they were committed unto Mr. Dunster, who revised and refined this translation; and (with some assistance from one Mr. Richard Lyon, who being sent over by Sir Henry Mildmay, as an attendant unto his son, then a student in Harvard College, now resided in Mr. Dunster's house:) he brought it into the condition wherein our churches ever since have used it.

Now, though I heartily join with those gentlemen who wish that the *poetry* hereof were mended; yet I must confess, that the Psalms have never yet seen such a *translation*, that I know of, nearer to the Hebrew *original*; and I am willing to receive the excuse which our translators themselves do offer us, when they say:

> "If the verses are not always so elegant as some desire or expect, let them consider that God's altar needs not our polishings; we have respected rather a plain translation, than to smooth our verses with the sweetness of any paraphrase. We have attended conscience rather than elegance, fidelity rather than ingenuity; so that we may sing in Zion the Lord's songs of praise, according unto his own will, until he bid us enter into our Master's joy, to sing eternal hallelujahs."

Reader, when the Reformation in France began, Clement Marot and Theodore Beza turned the Psalms into French *meetre*, and Lewis Guadimel set melodious tunes unto them. The singing hereof charmed the souls of court and city, town and country. They were sung in the Lovre it self, as well as in the Protestant churches: ladies, nobles, princes—yea, King Henry himself—sang them. This one thing mightily contributed unto the downfal of Popery, and the progress of the gospel. All ranks of men practised it; a gentleman of the reformed religion would not eat a meal without it. The popish clergy raging hereat, the cardinal of Lorrain got the profane and obscene *odes* of the pagan poets to be turned into French, and sang at the court: and the Divine Psalms were thus banished from that wicked court.

Behold, the reformation pursued in the churches of New-England by the Psalms in a new *meetre*: God grant the reformation may never be lost while the Psalms are sung in our churches!

But in this matter, Mr. Dunster is to be acknowledged. And if unto the Christian, while singing of Psalms on earth, Chrysostom could well say, Μετ' 'Αγγελων 'αδεις, μετ' 'Αγγελων 'υμνεῖς —*Thou art in a consort with angels!*—how much more may that *now* be said of our Dunster?

From the epitaph of Henricus Rentzius, we will now furnish our Henry Dunster with an

Epitaph.

Praeco, Pater, Servus; Sonui, Fovi, Coluique;
Sacra, Scholam, Christum; Voce, Rigore, Fide;
Famam, Animam, Corpus; Dispergit, Recreat, Abdit;
Virtus, Christus, Humus; Laude, Salute, Sinu.

Samuel Sewall (1652-1730)

Samuel Sewall was born in England and immigrated to America with his family in 1661. He graduated from Harvard College (now Harvard University) and became a leading participant in the political, civic, social, and religious life of Puritan Boston. Sewall served as chief justice of the Massachusetts Superior Court and was one of the judges at the famous Salem witch trials, though he later regretted his role in this event. In 1673, he began a diary, which he kept faithfully until near the end of his life. This document preserves a remarkable record of people, events, and customs of the time.

In addition to his other activities, Sewall served for many years as precentor of the Old South Church in Boston. The duties of the precentor included "setting the psalm"—singing a portion or all of the tune to help the congregation remember it—and leading the group with his own voice (no instruments were permitted in Puritan churches).

This procedure seems simple enough, but the extracts from Sewall's diary given below reveal that there were numerous pitfalls for the unwary precentor. In the course of describing these events, Sewall mentions several popular psalm tunes by name. The "Mr. Franklin" referred to on February 23, 1718, was Josiah Franklin, father of Benjamin Franklin.

45 From the diary of Samuel Sewall. _Source: The Diary of Samuel Sewall 1674-1729_, ed. by M. Halsey Thomas, 2 vols. (New York: Farrar, Straus and Giroux, 1973), pp. 283, 720, 881, 885-887.

Sabbath, Oct. 25 [1691]. Capt. Frary's voice failing him in his own Essay, by reason of his Palsie, he calls to me to set the Tune, which accordingly I doe; 17, 18, 19, 20, verses 68th Psalm, Windsor Tune; After the Lord's Supper, 6, 7, 8, 9, verses 16th Low-Dutch. P.M. 2 1/2 staves of 141. Ps. St. Davids, Jehova, I upon Thee call. After Evening Exercise, 2d part 84th Ps. Litchfield; I knew not that had the Tune till got to the 2d Line, being somewhat surprized, though design'd that Tune. I would have assisted Capt. Frary but scarce knew what Tune he design'd; and the Tune I guess'd at, was in so high a Key that I could not reach it.

. . .

July, 5 [1713]. Thunder and Rain at Noon. Mr. Stoddard preaches p. m. Prays for my Son that God would prepare him, and that he might live long to be a Rich Blessing. At the close appoint 1 1/2 staff in the first part 40th PS. I try'd to set Low-Dutch Tune and fail'd. Try'd again and fell into the tune of 119th Psalm, so Capt. Williams read the whole first part, that he might have Psalm to the Tune. Partial Rainbow in the evening.

. . .

Febr. 2. [1718] _Lord's Day_. In the Morning I set York Tune, and in the 2d going over, the Gallery carried it irresistibly to St David's, which discouraged me very much. I spake earnestly to Mr. White to set it in the Afternoon, but he declines it. p. m. The Tune went well. Madam Winthrop went out before the Admissions.

. . .

Lord's Day, Feb. 23. [1718] Mr. Foxcroft preaches. I set York Tune, and the Congregation went out of it into St. David's in the very 2d going over. They did the same 3 weeks before. This is the 2d Sign. I think they began in the last Line of the first going over. This seems to me an intimation and call for me to resign the

Praecentor's Place to a better Voice. I have through the divine Long-suffering and Favour done it for 24. years, and now God by his Providence seems to call me off; my voice being enfeebled. I spake to Mr. White earnestly to set it in the Afternoon; but he declin'd it. After the Exercises, I went to Mr. Sewall's, Thank'd Mr. Prince for his very good Discourse: and laid this matter before them, told them how long I had set the Tune; Mr. Prince said, Do it Six years longer. I persisted and said that Mr. White or Franklin might do it very well. The Return of the Gallery where Mr. Franklin sat was a place very Convenient for it.

. . .

Feb. 27 [1718]. I told Mr. White Next Sabbath was in a Spring Moneth, he must then set the Tune. I set now Litchfield Tune to a good Key.

Feb. 28. I told Mr. Nathanl Williams My voice was much Enfeebled; He said twas apparently so. I bid him tell Mr. White of it. . . .

March, 2 [1718]. I told Mr. White the elders desired him, he must Set the Tune, he disabled himself, as if he had a Cold. But when the Psalm was appointed, I forbore to do it, and rose up and turn'd to him, and he set York Tune to a very good Key. I thank'd him for restoring York Tune to its Station with so much Authority and Honor. I was glad; I saw twas Convenient that I had resign'd, being for the benefit of the Congregation. P. m. Madam Winthrop's Essex is baptised, she undertaking for the Child's education.

Part III

English Hymnody

10
The Sixteenth Century

Myles Coverdale (c. 1488-1569)

MYLES Coverdale, an Augustinian monk, left the cloister in 1525 and in 1528 joined a group of English Protestants who were in exile on the Continent. Coverdale returned to England in 1534, but the unstable political and religious climate of the country led to two more periods of exile before he was able to return permanently in 1559. Coverdale is best known as the translator of the first complete version of the Bible in English (1535). He also had a hand in the Great Bible (1539) and the Geneva Bible (1560).

Another of Coverdale's firsts was his publication of the first hymnal in English, *Goostly Psalmes and Spirituall Songes*, issued about 1535. This collection was heavily influenced by contemporary Lutheran hymnody in both its texts and its music, though it also contained a number of metrical psalms. In the preface to the volume, Coverdale echoed Luther in expressing his desire to provide youth with something worthwhile to sing in place of "foule & corrupte balettes." His reference to "carters & plow men" whistling "Psalmes, hymnes, and soch godly songes as Dauid is occupied with all" recalls the similar phrase used later in Clement Marot's "To the Ladies of France" (see above). Unfortunately for Coverdale, both his English Bible and *Goostly Psalmes* were eventually banned by Henry VIII, and when the Reformation finally took root in England it was not the hymnody of the Lutherans, but Genevan psalmody that served as the model for congregational song.

46   "To the boke" and Preface from *Goostly psalmes and spirituall songes drawen out of the holy Scripture* (c. 1535), pp. [i]-[viii].

To the boke.

Go lytle boke, get the acquaintaunce
Among the louers of Gods worde
Geue them occasyon the same to auaunce
And to make theyr songes of the Lorde
That they may thrust under the borde
All other balettes of fylthynes
And that we all with one accorde
May geue ensample of godlynes

Go lytle boke amonge mens chyldren
And get the to theyr companye
Teach them to synge ye commaundements ten
And other balettes of Gods glorye
Be not ashamed I warande the
Though thou be rude in songe and ryme
Thou shalt to youth some occasion be
In godly sportes to passe theyr tyme.

Myles Couerdale Unto the Christen reader.

It greueth me (most deare Reader) whan I consydre the unthankfulnesse of men, notwithstondynge the great abundaunt mercy and kyndnesse of almyghty God, whiche so plenteously is heaped upon us on euery syde. For though Christe oure Sauioure goeth now aboute from place to place, as diligently as euer he dyd, teachynge in euery countre, and preachynge[1] the Gospell of the kyngdome, healyng al maner of sicknesses and diseases both of body and conscience amonge the people: Yet is the unthankfulnesse of the worlde so great, that where ten are clensed, and haue remission of theyr synnes, there is scarse one that commeth agayne unto Christ, & sayeth: Lorde gramercy, As ye poore Samaritane dyd in ye gospell of Luke.[2] which whan he sawe that he was clensed, turned back agayne, and with a loude voyce praysed God, & fell downe upon his face at Christes fete, & gaue hym thankes.

---

[1]Math. 4. c.
Mar. 1. c.

[2]Luc. 17. b.

And by this we maye preceave what causeth us to be so unthankfull as we are: namely, because we do not call to mynde, nether consydre yt we are clensed (as this man dyd). For yf we wold open oure eyes, and remembre well what kyndnesse it is that the father of mercy hathe shewed us in Christe, and what great benefites he hath done and daylye doth for us in hym and for his sake, we wolde not onely fall downe upon oure faces & geue hym thankes, but with loude voyces wolde we prayse hym, and in the myddes of the congregacyon wolde we extolle his name, as Dauid & Asaph do almost in euery Psalme. For doutles who so beleueth yt God loueth hym and feleth by his fayth that he hath forgeuen him all his synnes, and careth for hym, and delyuereth hym from all euell, who so euer he be (I saye) that feleth this in his hert, shalbe compelled by the sprete of God to breake out in to prayse and thankesgeuynge therfore: yee he shall not be content, nor fully satisfied in his mynde, tyll other men knowe also what God hath done for hym, but shall crye and call upon them, as Dauid doth, sayenge:[3] O prayse the Lorde with me, & let us magnyfie his name together. I sought the Lorde, and he herde me, yee he delyuered me out of all my feare. And in the same Psalme: O taist and se how frendly the Lorde is: blessed is the man that trusteth in hym. And in another place:[4] O come hither and harken (all ye that feare God) I wyll tell you what he hath done for my soule. &c.

O that men wolde pryase ye goodnesse of the Lorde, and the wonders that he doth for ye chyldren of men. O that we wolde remembre what great thinges ye father of mercy hath done, doth dayly, and is euer ready to do for oure soules. O that mens[5] lippes were so opened, that theyr mouthes myght shewe the prayse of God. Yee wolde God that oure mynstrels had none other thynge to playe upon, nether oure carters & plow men other thynge to whistle upon, saue Psalmes, hymnes, and soch godly songes as Dauid is occupied with all. And yf women syttynge at theyr rockes, or spynnynge at the wheles, had none other songes to passe theyr

---

[3]Psal. 33. a.

[4]Psal. 65. b.

[5]Psal. 50. b.

tyme withall, that soch as Moses sister, Elchanas wife, Debora, and Mary the mother of Christ haue song before them, they shulde be better occupied, then with hey nony nony, hey troly loly, & soch lyke fantasies.

If yonge men also that haue the gyfte of syngynge, toke theyr pleasure in soch wholsome balettes, as[6] the thre chyldren synge in the fyre, & as Jesus the sonne of Syrac doth in his last chaper, it were a token, both that they felt some sparke of Gods loue in theyr hertes, and yt they also had some loue unto hymn, For truly as we loue, so synge we: and where oure affeccyon is, thence commeth oure myrth and ioye. Whan oure hertes are tangled with the vaine lustes of this corrupte worlde, than, yf we be mery and are desposed to gladnesse, our myrth is nothynge but wantonesse and inordinate pastyme, And when we are sad, oure heuyness is ether desperacyon, or els some carefulnes of this uayne worlde.

Contrary wyse, yf oure myndes be fyxed upon God, and we subdued to the holy desyres of his sprete, then, lyke as oure hertes are occupied in the meditacyon of his goodnes & loue whiche he beareth towarde us, Euen so are our tonges exercysed in the prayse of his holy name: So yt when we are mery, oure pastyme and pleasure, oure ioye, myrth and gladnesse is all of hym. And as for oure heuines, when we are sad (as euery thyng muste have a tyme)[7] it is eyther pacience in trouble, repentaunce for offences done in tyme past, compassyon upon other men, or els mournynge for oure owne infirmities, because oure body of synne prouoketh us so oft to do the wyll of the fleshe. And thus God causeth both the myrth and sorowe of them yet loue hymn, to worke for theyr profite,[8] as all other thynges turne to theyr best.

Seynge then that ([9]as the prophete Dauid sayeth) it is so good and pleasaunt a thynge to prayse ye Lorde, & so expedient for us

---

[6]Dan. 3
Eccle., 51. a.

[7]Eccle. 3. a.

[8]Ro. 8. d

[9]Psal. 148. a.

to be thankfull, Therefore to geue oure youth of Englonde some occasion to chaunge theyr foule & corrupte balettes into swete songes and spirituall Hymnes of Gods honoure, and for theyr owne consolacion in hym, I haue here (good reader) set out certayne comfortable songes grounded on Gods worde, and taken some out of the holy scripture specyally out of the Psalmes of Dauid, At whom wolde God that oure Musicians wolde lerne to make theyr songes: & yt they which are disposed to be mery, wolde in theyr myrth folowe the councell of saynt Paule and saynt James,[10] and not to passe theyr tyme in naughty songes of fleshly love and wantonesse, but with syngynge of Psalmes and soch songes as edifye, & corruppe not mens conuersacyon.

As for the comen sorte of balettes which now are used in ye world, I reporte me to euery good mans conscience what wycked frutes they brynge. Corruppe they not the maners of yonge persones? Do they not tangel them in the snares of unclennesse? Yes truly, and blynde so the eyes of theyr understondynge, that they can nether thynke wel in theyr hertes, nor outwardly entre into the waye of godly and vertuous lyuynge. I nede not rehearce what euell ensamples of ydelnesse, corrupte talkynge (and all soch vyces as folowe the same) are geuen to yonge people thorowe soch unchristen songes. Alas the worlde is all to full of vicious and euell lyuers alredy. It is no nede to cast oyle in ye fyre.[11] Oure owne nature prouoketh us to uyces (God knoweth) all to sore. No man nedeth entysynge therto.

Seyng then that we are[12] commaunded not to loue this worlde nether ye lustes therof: seyng (I saye) that all the pleasures and ioyes that ye worlde can imagyn,[13] are but vanite, & vanyshe awaye as doth the smoke: what cause haue we then to reioyse so moch therin? why do we not rather take these worldy lustes for oure very

---

[10]Coll. 3.
  Jac. 5.

[11]Gen. 6.

[12]1. Jo. 2.

[13]Psal. 61. b.

enemyes, that stoppe the waye betwixte us & that euerlasting ioye which is prepared for us in heauen? why do we not rather seke ye thynges that are aboue, where Christe is at the ryght hande of God[14] as saynt Paule sayeth?

Wherfore[15] Let not the wyseman reioyse in his wysedome, nor the stronge man in his strength nether the ryche man in his ryches (yee I dare be bolde to warne them that wyll be counceled) let not ye courtyer reioyce in his balettes, let not youth take theyr lust and pastyme in wantones & ignoraunce of God, or in myspendynge ye frutes of theyr fathers laboure: but let us altogether (from the most unto ye least) be glad, reioyce and be mery euen from our herte rotes, that we haue gotten the knowledge of the Lorde among us, that we are sure of his loue and fauoure, & that oure names are written in heauen.

The chyldren of Israel in the olde tyme[16] whan God had delyuered them from theyr enemyes, gaue thankes unto hym, and made theyr songe of hym, as thou seist by Moses, Barac, Dauid, and other mo.[17] why shulde not we then make oure songes and myrth of God as well as they? Hath he not done as moche for us as for them? Hath he not delyuered us from as great troubles as them? Yes doubtless, why shulde he not then be our pastyme as well as theyrs?

As for soche Psalmes as the scripture descrybeth, (besyde the great consolacyon yt they brynge into the herte of the spiritual synger) they do not only cause hym to spende his tyme well by exercysynge him selfe in the swete worde of God. but thorow soch ensamples they prouoke other men also unto the prayse of God and vertuous lyuynge. And this is ye very ryght use wherfore Psalmes shulde be songe: Namely, to conforte a mans herte in God, to

---

[14]Col. 3.

[15]Jer. 9.

[16]Luc. 10
Exo. 15

[17]Judi. 5
2 Reg. 22. a.

make hym thankfull, & to exercyse hym in his worde, to corage hym in the waye of godlynesse, and to prouoke other men unto the same.   By this thou mayest perceaue, what spirituall edifienge commeth of godly Psalmes and songes of Gods worde: and what inconuenience foloweth the corrupte ballettes of this uayne worlde.

Now (beloued Reader) thou seist the occasyon of this my small laboure. wherefore yf thou perceauest, that the very worde of God is ye master therof, I praye the accept it, use it, and prouoke youth unto ye same. And yf thou felest in thine hert, that all the lordes dealynge is uery mercy & kyndness, cease not then to be thankfull unto hymn therefore: but in thy myrth be alwaye syngyng of him, that his blessed name may be praysed now and ever. Amen.

11
The Seventeenth Century

George Wither (1588-1667)

GEORGE Wither was a well-known literary figure in late sixteenth- and early seventeenth-century England. He possessed a satirical bent that often got him in trouble with the authorities, and for which he was several times imprisoned. Wither also published several collections of religious poetry, including *Hymnes and Songs of the Chvrch* (1623) and *Hallelujah, or Britain's Second Remembrancer* (1641). King James I granted Wither a patent for the *Hymnes and Songs of the Chvrch*, ordering that it be bound up with every metrical psalter printed in England. Unfortunately for Wither, the Stationer's Company opposed the patent, and it was generally ignored. The texts of the *Hymnes and Songs of the Chvrch* were based on various lyrical scripture passages, but marked an important step away from metrical psalmody in the freedom of their style. Wither's "hymns and songs" have largely been forgotten, but several of the fifteen tunes written by Orlando Gibbons to accompany these texts are in common use.

47   Dedication to *The Hymnes and Songs of the Chvrch* (London: Printed by the Assignees of George Wither, [1623]).

To the High and Mighty prince, Iames, by the Grace of *God, King of Great Britain, France, and Ireland, Defender of the Faith, &c: Grace, Mercy and Peace, through Iesus Christ our Lord.*

These *Hymnes* (Dread Soueraign) hauing diuers waies receiued life from your Maiestie (as well as that approbation which the *Church* alloweth) are now imprinted according to your Royall Priuiledge, to come abroad vnder your Gracious Protection. And what I deliuered vnto your Princely view at seuerall times, I here present again, incorporated into one Volume. The first Part wherof comprehends those Canonicall *Hymnes*, which were written, and left for our instruction, by the Holy Ghost. And those are not only plainely and briefly expressed in *Lyrick verse*: but by their short *Prefaces*, properly applied also to the *Churches* particular occasions in these times. Insomuch, that (howeuer some neglect them as impertinent) it is thereby apparant, that they appertaine no lesse to vs, then vnto those, in whose times they were first composed. And (if the coniecture of many good and learned men deceiue them not) the latter Part, containing *Spirituall Songs*, appropriated to the seuerall times and occasions obseruable in the *Church* of *England* (together with briefe Arguments, declaring the purpose of those *Obseruations*) shall become a meanes both of encreasing Knowledge, and Christian Conformitie within your Dominions; Which, no doubt, your Maiestie wisely foresawe, when you pleased to graunt and command, that these *Hymnes* should be annexed to all *Psalme-Bookes* in English Meeter. And I hope, you shall thereby encrease both the honour of God, and of your Maiestie: For, these *Hymnes*, and the knowledge which they offer, could no other way, with such certainety, and so little inconuenience, be conueied to the common people, as by that meanes which your Maiestie hath graciously prouided.

And now (maugre their malice, who labour to disparage & suppresse these *Helps to Deuotion*) they shall, I trust, haue free scope to worke that effect which is desired; and to which end I was encouraged to translate and compose them. For, how meanly soeuer some men may thinke of this endeauour; I trust the successe shall make it appeare, that the *Spirit* of *God* was the first moouer of the worke. Wherein, as I haue endeuored to make my Expressions such as may not bee contemptible to men of best vnderstandings: So I haue also labored to sute them to the nature of the Subiect, and the common Peoples capacities, without regard of catching the vaine blasts of Opinion. The same also hath beene the ayme of Master *Orlando Gibbons* (your Maiesties seruant, and one of the Gentlemen of your Honourable Chapell) in fitting them with tunes. For, he hath chosen to make his musicke agreeable to the matter, and what the common apprehension can best admit; rather then to the curious Fancies of the Time: Which path both of vs could more easily haue troden. Not caring therfore, what any of those shall censure, who are more apt to controule, then to consider; I commit this to Gods blessing, and Your fauourable Protection: Humbly beseeching your Maiestie to accept of these our Endeuours; and praying God to sanctifie both vs and this Worke to his glory: Wishing also (most vnfainedly) euerlasting consolations to your Maiestie, for those temporall Comforts you haue vouchsafed me, and that felicity here, which may aduance your happinesse in the life to come. Amen.

Benjamin Keach (1640-1704)

Benjamin Keach was the pastor of a Particular Baptist church in Horsley-down, Southwark. Particular Baptists followed the Calvinistic doctrine of a limited atonement, while their near relatives, the General Baptists, emphasized the free will of the individual in salvation. Most General Baptists and a few Particular Baptists objected to the use of "prelimited forms" in praising God; this restriction applied not only to "hymns of human composure" but to metrical psalmody as well, thus effectively eliminating congregational singing altogether.

In 1690 one Isaac Marlow, a member of Keach's church, attacked his pastor's increasing use of congregational singing in a pamphlet titled _A Brief Discourse Concerning Singing._ Keach responded by publishing _The Breach Repaired in God's Worship_ (1691), which, if not always logical in its arguments, is nevertheless a classic document in defense of congregational singing. These two books touched off a pamphlet war among the Baptists that lasted off and on for the next ten years. In _The Breach Repaired_, Keach not only took a stand in favor of metrical psalmody, but anticipated Watts in advocating the use of hymns. Keach's endorsement of hymnody was further emphasized with the publication of his hymnal, _Spiritual Melody_, also in 1691.

48   From _The Breach Repaired in God's Worship_ (London: Printed for the Author, 1691), pp. vi-x, 127-131.

I have been provoked by our Brother, who wrote against Singing, to set Pen to Paper, and not only by him and his Book, but I have been induced by Multitudes, for several Months, to give him an Answer, so that I hope you will not be offended with me in what I have done. I have much Peace in the doing of it, and truly, Brethren, the loss of this Ordinance doth, I am afraid, more obstruct the increase of our Churches than many are aware of. What a Multitude are convinced of Christ's true Baptism, and yet refuse to have Communion with our Churches when baptized, because they say, if they should, they must lose this Ordinance of Singing, which they have an equal Esteem for: And how doth it open the Mouths of our Godly Brethren of other Perswasions, to speak against us, for being so zealous for one Gospel-Ordinance, and so careless about another, that very few Christians, who have had the greatest Light, Zeal and Piety in any Age of the Church, ever doubted of? It grieves me to think there should be a Breach made in God's Worship among you, to whom God hath given so much Light in other Cases. And, O that what is here said, might through the Blessing of God prove a Means to repair it.

In a Word, Singing is injoyned; Some thing it is: If we have it not (but 'tis with you) we would willingly know what your Singing is, or what you call Singing: For we do say and testify, we believe you are wholly without Singing in any proper Sense at all. The Lord give us Moderation; don't let us be bitter one against another.

I shall beg a part in your Prayers, and intreat you to look over what Weakness you may see in this small Tract, for I am, you know, but a Babe in Christ's School, and know but in part.

And now to you, my Beloved Brethren and Sisters, (who meet on *Horselydown*) whom I hope I may say are my Joy and my Crown, whose Souls are most dear to me, and whom I can say I truly love and long after; it rejoices my Spirit to see how generally you are inlightned into this Gospel-duty; but 'tis no small grief to me to see (since the Church in such a solemn manner agreed to sing the Praises of God on the Lord's Day) to find some of you so much offended; I am perswaded 'tis for want of Consideration, for you have no new thing brought in among you. Hath not the Church sung at breaking of Bread always for 16 or 18 Years last past, and could not, nor would omit it in the time of the late Persecution? And have not many of the honest Hearers (who have stayed to see that Holy Administration) sung with you, at that time, and yet none of you ever signified the least trouble? And have we not for this 12 or 14 Years sung in *mixt Assemblies, on Days of Thanksgiving,* and never any offended at it, as ever I heard? What is done more now? 'tis only practised oftner: and sure if it be God's Ordinance, the often practising of it, by such who find their Hearts draw out so to do, cannot be sinful.

And on that Solemn Day, when the Church would have it put up, to see how the Members stood affected about Singing, almost every ones Hand was up for it, or to give Liberty to the Church at such times to sing. And when put up in the Negative, but about 5 or 6 at most (as I remember) were against it. Did any one of you, at that time say, if we did proceed to sing at such times, you could not have Communion with us? which if you had, I perceive the Church, nay every one of us who had born our Burden for many Years, would have born it a little longer? Besides, did not the Church agree to sing only after Sermon, and when Prayer was ended? And if those few Brethren and Sisters who were not satisfied, could not stay whilst we sung, they might freely go forth, and we would not be offended with them; so far was the Church, or my self, from imposing on the Consciences of any. But is it not hard that some of us should so long be laid under a Burden, when the Church generally was against Singing at that time, and you cannot bear it now it is come to be your Lot? I am afraid the noise of these things are misrepresented abroad, and therefore I thought it might not be amiss to rectify Mistakes in you, or any other Brethren. The matter of Difference that is at present between the Church and some few of our dear and beloved Brethren and Sisters, is not about Singing it self, nor singing with others, for that has been all along the practise of the Church for many Years (as before I hinted) but only about singing on the Lords Day, unless it be one Member, except the Judgments of any other are lately changed.

. . .

II. *Of* David's *Psalms.*

1. You say, *There was no Institution of Singing before* David's *Time.*

Answ. We have proved Singing the Praises of God is a part of natural Religion, and so a moral Duty in its own Nature, as Prayer is; and that the Heathen sang the Praises of God for his goodness in Creation, that have no written Word: And what is this then to the purpose, if we should grant that Singing was not brought under an Institution till *David*'s Time?

As touching what you say about the *Israelites* in the Wilderness, how in trouble they did not sing, 'tis more than you know, for I think you will find they were not far from the Wilderness when *Moses* and the Congregation sang, *Exod.* 15. However our Lord Jesus and his Disciples sang when it was a sad Wilderness-time with them, it was just the Night before our Blessed Saviour was betrayed. And *Paul* and *Silas* sung in the Wilderness of a Prison; and though the Saints are always sorrowful, yet they are required ever-more to rejoice. All outward Comforts of this World, are not the thousand part such cause of Joy and Singing, as our spiritual Deliverance and Salvation by Christ is. Do you think that outward Blessings here will better tend to tune our Spirits and Tongues to sing the Praises of God, than the Love of God in Jesus Christ, Pardon of Sin, Justification, Union, Communion, Adoption? &c. No, no, here is the spring of Joy, and cause of true spiritual Singing, and none can learn *David*'s Psalms, nor any other Scripture-Hymns or Songs thus to sing them, but the 144000; none but such who have that *new Name*, that *new Nature*, can learn this Song as thus to sing it, *Rev.* 14. 3. And let me tell you, this Singing of the hundred and forty four thousand spoken of, was under the Reign of Antichrist, for the seven Angels with their seven Vials came out of the Temple afterwards, who destroy *Babylon*.

Take what our late Annotators speak on the place. "The New Song here spoken of, is probably the same with that we met with before, *chap.* 5. 11. sang by the Voice of many Angels round about the Throne, and the Beasts, and the Elders; called a new Song, either for the excellency of it, or because sung unto God after Christ was manifested in the Flesh. The design of it was, to declare the worthiness of Christ, to receive *Power, and Riches, and Wisdom, and Strength, and Honour, and Blessing. A new Song,* signifies a Song which praises God for new benefits received from him. During the Reign of Antichrist, none could learn this Song, to give Power, Riches, Wisdom, Strength, Honour, Glory, and Blessing, but a small number redeemed through the Blood of Christ." *Annot.* on *Rev.* 14. 3.[1]

Secondly, You say, *The singing of* David's *Psalms, were suitable*

---

[1] *This shews other Spiritual Songs may be sung besides* David's *Psalms in Gospel-days; this was none of those.*

to all the rest of the Levitical Ceremonies, and Temple-Worship, pag. 12, 13.

Answ. There is no doubt but the Singing of *David*'s Psalms with Instruments of Musick, was suited to the order of the *Levites* and to the Temple-worship. What then, must not we sing Psalms in the Gospel-days, with Grace in our Hearts to the Lord? We know no Psalms, but *David*'s *Psalms*, or those called the *Book of Psalms*, and the holy Ghost doth injoin the Gospel-Churches to sing *Psalms*, as well as *Hymns, and spiritual Songs*. Will you take upon you to countermand God's holy Precept? Will you say we must not sing Psalms, when the Churches are exhorted so to do? Pray, when you write again, tell us what psalms they are the Holy Ghost here speaks of, if not them, or some of them called the *Psalms of* David.

True, all *Types, Shadows, and Ceremonies*, are removed and done away; but Singing the Praise of God was no Ceremony, but a Moral Duty, and performed by the Children of *Israel*, before the Law of Shadows and Ceremonies was given forth, *Exod*. 15. 1, 2. You may as well say Prayer was a Ceremony, because there were divers ceremonial Rites used in the performance of it, particularly that of Incense.

2. Did not Christ sing an Hymn after the Supper? Would he have left that as a Pattern to us, and annexed it to such a pure Gospel-Ordinance, had it been a Ceremony, and only belonging to the Jewish Worship? Or, would the Apostle *Paul* have given, by the Authority of the Holy Ghost, such a Precept to the Church of *Coloss* to sing Psalms, *&c.* whom he strives so much to take off from Jewish Rites, Days, and Ceremonies? Had singing of Psalms, Hymns, and spiritual Songs been a Jewish Ceremony, he would not have done thus. This is sufficient to convince any sober and unbiassed Person, *i.e.* that Singing the Praises of God is a Gospel-Duty, and that it did not belong only to the Jews, in the Days of the Old Testament. But you contradict this your self; for afterwards you grant that the Saints, when the extraordinary Gifts are given, as you suppose they will in the thousand Years Reign, you intimate then they shall sing as we do; or else I know not what you mean.

How shall they use a legal and Typical Rite, that only appertained to the *Jews and Levites*, in that glorious state of the Church? Doubtless their Singing of Old, with musical Instruments, was a Figure of that sweet spiritual Melody the Saints should make from a well-tuned gracious Heart, and with united and melodious

Tongues together in the Gospel-days, as I have again and again
shewed, and this therefore is not mixing Law and Gospel together,
but continuing a Gospel-Ordinance in the Church that is of Gospel-
Authority, both from Precepts and Examples, as I have proved in
this Treatise: so that I have answered your second, and third, and
part of your fourth Thesis together.

12
The Eighteenth Century

Isaac Watts (1674-1748)

ISAAC Watts, an Independent pastor, theologian, and writer, has been called the "Father of English hymnody" because of his key role in the transition from metrical psalmody to hymnody. The high quality, simplicity, and evangelical flavor of his verse led many churches in both England and America to abandon metrical psalmody and accept the singing of hymns, or at least paraphrased (rather than versified) scripture. Watts's most significant hymnic publications, *Hymns and Spiritual Songs* (1707) and *The Psalms of David Imitated in the Language of the New Testament* (1719), received numerous reprintings on both sides of the Atlantic, ultimately achieving a monopoly in many churches similar to that enjoyed by metrical psalmody during the sixteenth and seventeenth centuries. In the prefaces of these two books, reprinted below, Watts gives his defense of hymnody and paraphrased psalmody, as well as describing his method of work, the contents of the collections, and his suggestions for the improvement of congregational singing.

49　　Preface to *Hymns and Spiritual Songs* (London:　J. Humphreys, for John Lawrence, 1707), pp. iii-xiv.

The Preface.

While we sing the Praises of our God in his Church, we are employ'd in that part of Worship which of all others is the nearest a-kin to Heaven; and 'tis pity that this of all others should be perform'd the worst upon Earth. The Gospel brings us nearer to the heavenly State than all the former Dispensations of God amongst Men: And in these very last Days of the Gospel we are brought almost within sight of the Kingdom of our Lord; yet we are

115

very much unacquainted with the Songs of the *New Jerusalem*, and unpractis'd in the Work of Praise. To see the dull Indifference, the negligent and the thoughtless Air that sits upon the Faces of a whole Assembly, while the Psalm is on their Lips, might tempt even a charitable Observer to suspect the Fervency of inward Religion; and 'tis much to be fear'd that the Minds of most of the Worshippers are absent or unconcern'd. Perhaps the Modes of Preaching in the best Churches still want some Degrees of Reformation, nor are the Methods of Prayer so perfect as to stand in need of no Correction or Improvement: But of all our Religious Solemnities *Psalmodie* is the most unhappily manag'd. That very Action which should elevate us to the most delightful and divine Sensations, doth not only flat our Devotion, but too often awakens our Regret, and touches all the Springs of Uneasiness within us.

I have been long convinc'd, that one great Occasion of this Evil arises from the Matter and Words to which we confine all our Songs. Some of 'em are almost opposite to the Spirit of the Gospel: Many of them foreign to the State of the New-Testament, and widely different from the present Circumstances of Christians. Hence it comes to pass, that when spiritual Affections are excited within us, and our Souls are raised a little above this Earth in the beginning of a Psalm, we are check'd on a sudden in our Ascent toward Heaven by some Expressions that are more suited to the Days of *Carnal Ordinances*, and fit only to be sung in the *Worldly Sanctuary*. When we are just entring into an Evangelic Frame by some of the Glories of the Gospel presented in the brightest Figures of *Judaism*, yet the very next Line perhaps which the Clerk parcels out unto us, hath something in it so extremely *Jewish* and cloudy, that darkens our Sight of God the Saviour: Thus by keeping too close to *David* in the House of God, the Vail of *Moses* is thrown over our Hearts. While we are kindling into Divine Love by the Meditations of the *loving Kindness of God, and the Multitude of his tender Mercies*, within a few Verses some dreadful Curse against Men is propos'd to our Lips; That *God would add Iniquity unto their Iniquity, not let 'em come into his Righteousness, but blot 'em out of the Book of the Living*, Psal. 69. 16, 27, 28. which is so contrary to the New Commandment, *of loving our Enemies*. Some Sentences of the *Psalmist* that are expressive of the Temper of our own Hearts and the Circumstances of our Lives may compose our Spirits to Seriousness, and allure us to a sweet Retirement within our selves; but we meet with a following Line which so peculiarly belongs but to one Action or Hour of the Life of *David* or *Asaph*, that breaks off our Song in the midst; our Consciences are affrighted lest we should speak a Falshood unto God: Thus the Powers of our Souls are shock'd on a sudden, and our Spirits ruffled before we have time to reflect that this may be sung only as a History of antient Saints: And perhaps in some Instances that *Salvo* is hardly sufficient neither.

Many Ministers and many private Christians have long groan'd under this Inconvenience, and have wish'd rather than attempted a Reformation: At their importunate and repeated Requests I have for some Years past devoted many Hours of leisure to this Service. Far be it from my Thoughts to lay aside the Psalms of *David* in public Worship; few can pretend so great a Value for 'em as my self: It is the most artful, most devotional and Divine Collection of Poesy; and nothing can be suppos'd more proper to raise a pious Soul to Heaven than some parts of that Book; never was a piece of Experimental Divinity so nobly written, and so justly reverenced and admired: But it must be acknowledged still, that there are a thousand Lines in it which were not made for a Saint in our Day, to assume as his own; There are also many deficiencies of Light and Glory which our Lord *Jesus* and his Apostles have supply'd in the Writings of the New Testament; and with this Advantage I have compos'd these spiritual Songs which are now presented to the World. Nor is the Attempt vain-glorious or presuming; for in respect of clear Evangelic Knowledge, *The least in the Kingdom of Heav'n is greater than all the Jewish Prophets*, Mat. 11. 11.

Now let me give a short Account of the following Composures.

The greatest Part of 'em are suited to the General State of the Gospel, and the most common Affairs of Christians: I hope there will be very few found but what may properly be used in a religious Assembly, and not one of 'em but may well be adapted to some Seasons, either of private or of public Worship. The most frequent Tempers and Changes of our Spirit, and Conditions of our Life are here copied, and the Breathings of our Piety exprest according to the variety of our Passions; our Love, our Fear, our Hope, our Desire, our Sorrow, our Wonder and our Joy, all refin'd into Devotion, and acting under the Influence and Conduct of the Blessed Spirit; all conversing with God the Father by the new and living Way of Access to the Throne, even the Person and the

Mediation of our Lord *Jesus Christ*. To him also, even to the *Lamb that was slain and now lives*, I have addrest many a Song; for thus doth the Holy Scripture instruct and teach us to Worship in the various short Patterns of Christian Psalmodie described in the Revelations. I have avoided the more obscure and controverted Points of Christianity, that we might all obey the Direction of the Word of God, and *sing his Praises with Understanding*, Psal. 47. 7. The Contentions and distinguishing Words of Sects and Parties are secluded, that whole Assemblies might assist at the Harmony, and different Churches join in the same Worship without Offence.

The whole Book is confin'd to three Sorts of Metre, and fitted to the most common Tunes. I have seldom permitted a Stop in the middle of a Line, and seldom left the end of a Line without one, to comport a little with the unhappy Mixture of Reading and Singing, which cannot presently be reformed. The Metaphors are generally sunk to the Level of vulgar Capacities. I have aimed at ease of Numbers and Smoothness of Sound, and endeavour'd to make the Sense plain and obvious; if the Verse appears so gentle and flowing as to incure the Censure of Feebleness, I may honestly affirm, that sometimes it cost me labour to make it so: Some of the Beauties of Poesy are neglected, and some wilfully defac'd: I have thrown out the Lines that were too sonorous, and giv'n an Allay to the Verse, lest a more exalted Turn of Thought or Language should darken or disturb the Devotion of the plainest Souls. But hence it comes to pass, that I have been forc'd to lay aside many Hymns after they were finished, and utterly exclude 'em from this Volume, because of the Bolder Figures of Speech that crowded themselves into the Verse, and a more unconfin'd Variety of Number which I could not easily restrain. Perhaps these may e'er long appear as an Additional Part to the Poems already Published under the Title of *Horae Lyricae*.

I have divided the whole into three Books.

In the *first* I have borrow'd the Sense, and much of the Form of the Song from some particular Portions of Scripture, and have paraphras'd most of the Doxologies in the New Testament that contain any thing in 'em peculiarly Evangelical, and many parts of the Old Testament also that have a reference to the Times of the *Messiah*. In these I expect to be often censur'd for a too religious Observance of the Words of Scripture, whereby the Verse is weakned and debas'd according to the Judgment of the Criticks:

But as my whole Design was to aid the Devotion of Christians, so more Especially this part was written for the meanest of them, and I am satisfied I shall hereby attain two Ends, (_viz._) Assist the Worship of all serious Minds to whom the Expressions of Scripture are ever dear and delightful; and gratify the Taste and Inclination of those who think nothing must be sung unto God but the Translations of his own Word. Yet you will always find in this Paraphrase dark Expressions enlighten'd, and the Levitical Ceremonies, and Hebrew Forms of Speech chang'd into the Worship of the Gospel, and explain'd in the Language of our Time and Nation; and what would not bear such an Alteration is omitted and laid aside. After this manner should I rejoice to see a good part of the Book of Psalms fitted for the use of our Churches, and _David_ converted into a Christian. In the first, second and third Psalms especially, I have attempted a Specimen of what I desire and hope some more capable Genius will undertake.

The _Second_ Part consists of Hymns whose Form is of meer humane Composure, but I hope the Sense and Materials will always appear Divine. I might have brought some Text or other, and applied it to the Margin of every Verse if this method had been as Useful as it was easy. If there be Poems in the Book that are capable of giving Delight to Persons of a more refin'd Taste and polite Education, they must be sought for only in this Part; but except they lay aside the humour of Criticism, and enter into a devout Frame, every Ode here already despairs of pleasing. I confess my self to have been too often tempted away from the more Spiritual Designs I propos'd, by some gay and flowry Expressions that gratify'd the Fancy; the bright Images too often prevail'd above the Fire of Divine Affection; and the Light exceeded the Heat: Yet I hope, in many of them the Reader will find that Devotion dictated the Song, and the Head and Hand were nothing but Interpreters and Secretaries to the Heart: Nor is the Magnificence or Boldness of the Figures comparable to that Divine License, which is found in the Eighteenth, and Sixty eighth Psalms, several Chapters of _Job_, and other Poetical Parts of Scripture: And in this respect, I may hope to escape the reproof of those who pay a Sacred Reverence to the Holy Bible.

I have prepar'd the _Third_ Part only for the Celebration of the Lord's Supper, that in imitation of our Blessed Saviour we might sing an Hymn after we have partaken of the Bread and Wine. Here you will find some Paraphrases of Scripture, and some other Compositions. There are almost an hundred Hymns in the two former Parts that may very properly be used in this Ordinance, and sometimes perhaps appear more suitable than any of these last: But there are Expressions used in all these, which confine 'em only to the Table of the Lord, and therefore I have distinguish'd and set 'em by themselves.

Since there are some Christians who are not yet perswaded that it is lawful to sing any thing in Divine Worship, but a meer Version of some part of the Word of God, I have subjoyned a Discourse for the satisfaction of their Consciences; wherein I indeavour to prove, that the Duty of Singing under the Gospel is not confin'd to the _Jewish_ Psalms, or any other Scriptural Songs; but that Hymns of human Composure suited to the clearer _Revelations_ of the New Testament, are incouraged by the Word of God, and almost necessary for Christian Churches, that desire to worship Christ in the Beauty of Holiness, and praise him for the Wonders of redeeming Grace. I earnestly intreat such Persons to read this Discourse over without prejudice or prepossession, and seriously to inquire whether it be not possible for 'em to have ty'd themselves up too much to Legal Forms, and whether they find no ground to release their Consciences from those Bands, and worship their Redeemer according to the more glorious Liberty of the Gospel.

If the Lord who inhabits the Praises of _Israel_, shall refuse to smile upon this Attempt for the Reformation of Psalmodie amongst the Churches, yet I humbly hope that his Blessed Spirit will make these Composures useful to private Christians; and if they may but attain the honour of being esteem'd pious Meditations to assist the devout and the retir'd Soul in the Exercises of Love, Faith and Joy, 'twill be a valuable Compensation of my Labours; my Heart shall rejoyce at the Notice of it, and my God shall receive the Glory.

50   Preface to _The Psalms of David Imitated in the Language of the New Testament_ (London: Printed for J. Clark, R. Ford, and R. Cruttenden, 1719), pp. [iii]-xxxii.

The Preface or,
An Enquiry into the right Way of fitting the Book of
Psalms for Christian Worship.
Tho' the _Psalms of David_ are a work of admirable and divine

Composure, tho' they contain the noblest Sentiments of Piety, and breathe a most exalted Spirit of Devotion, yet when the best of Christians attempt to sing many of them in our common Translations, that Spirit of Devotion vanishes and is lost, the Psalm dies upon their Lips, and they feel scarce any thing of the holy Pleasure.

If I were to render the Reasons of it, I would give this for one of the chief, (viz.) that the *Royal Psalmist* here expresses his own Concerns in Words exactly suited to his own Thoughts, agreeable to his own personal Character, and in the Language of his own Religion: This keeps all the Springs of pious Passion awake, when every Line and Syllable so nearly affects himself: This naturally raises in a devout Mind a more transporting and sublime Worship. But when we sing the same Lines, we express nothing but the Character, the Concerns, and the Religion of the *Jewish King*, while our own Circumstances and our own Religion (which are so widely different from his) have little to do in the sacred Song; and our Affections want something of Property or Interest in the Words, to awaken them at first, and to keep them lively.

If this *Attempt* of mine, thro' the divine Blessing, become so happy as to remove this great inconvenience, and to introduce warm Devotion into this Part of divine Worship, I shall esteem it an honourable Service done to the *Church of Christ*.

'Tis necessary therefore that I should here inform my Readers at large what the Title Page expresseth in a shorter Way, and assure them that they are not to expect in this book an exact Translation of the *Psalms of David*; for if I had not conceived a different Design from all that have gone before me in this Work, I had never attempted a Service so full of Labour, tho' I must confess it has not wanted its Pleasure too.

In order to give a plain Account of my present Undertaking I shall first represent the Methods that my Predecessors have followed in their Versions: In the next place I hope to make it evident that those Methods can never attain the noblest and highest Ends of *Christian Psalmody*; and then describe the Course that I have taken, different from them all, together with some brief Hints of the Reasons that induced me to it.

First, I will represent *the Methods that my Predecessors have followed*. I have seen above twenty Versions of the *Psalter* by Persons of richer and meaner Talents; and how various soever their

Professions and their Prefaces are, yet in the Performance they all seem to aim at this one Point, (viz.) to make the *Hebrew Psalmist* only speak *English*, and keep all his own Characters still. Wheresoever the Psalm introduces him as a Soldier or a Prophet, as a Shepherd or a great Musician, as a King on the Throne or as a Fugitive in the Wilderness, the Translators ever represent him in the same Circumstances: Some of them lead an Assembly of common *Christians* to worship God as near as possible in those very Words; and they generally agree also to perform and repeat that Worship in the ancient *Jewish* Forms, wherever the *Psalmist* uses them.

There are several Psalms indeed which have scarce any thing in them personal or peculiar to *David* or the *Jews*, such as *Ps.* i. xix. xxv. xxxvii. lxvii. c. &c. and these if translated into the plain national Language are very proper Materials for Psalmody in all Times and Places; but there are but a few of this Kind in Comparison of the great Number which have something of *Personal Concerns*, *Prophetical Darknesses*, *Hebraisms*, or *Jewish Affairs* mingled with them.

I confess *Mr. Milbourn and Mr. Darby* in very different Verse have now and then given an Evangelic Turn to the *Hebrew* Sense; and Dr. *Patrick* hath gone much beyond them in this Respect, that he hath made use of the present Language of *Christians* in several Psalms, and left out many of the *Judaisms*. This is the Thing that hath introduced him into the Favour of so many religious Assemblies. Even those very Persons that have an Aversion to sing any thing in Worship but *David*'s Psalms have been led insensibly to fall in with Dr. *Patrick*'s Performance by a Relish of pious Pleasure; never considering that his Work is by no means a just Translation, but a Paraphrase; and there are scarce any that have departed farther from the inspired *Words of Scripture* than he hath often done, in order to suit his Thoughts to the State and Worship of *Christianity*. This I esteem his peculiar Excellency in those Psalms wherein he has practis'd it. This I have made my chief Care and Business in every Psalm, and have attempted at least to exceed him in this as well as in the Art of Verse; and yet I have often kept nearer to the Text.

But after all, this good Man hath suffer'd himself so far to be carried away by Custom, as to make all the other personal Characters and Circumstances of *David* appear strong and plain, except that of a _Jew_; and many of them he has represented in stronger and plainer Terms than the Original. This will appear to any one that compares these following Texts in Dr. _Patrick_ with the Bible, (_viz._) Psal. iv. 2. and ix. 4, 5. and xviii. 43. and li. 4. and lx. 6, 7. and ci. 1. and cxli. 6. and cxliii. 3. and several others: So that 'tis hard to find even in his Version six or eight Stanza's together in any Psalm (that has personal or national Affairs in it) fit to be assumed by a _vulgar Christian_, or proper to be sung by a _whole Congregation_. This renders the due Performance of Psalmody every where difficult to him that appoints the Verses: But 'tis extremely troublesome in those Assemblies where the Psalm is sung without reading it Line by Line, which yet is, beyond all Exception, the truest and the best Method; for here there can be no Omission of a Verse, tho' it be never so improper; but the whole Church must run down to the next Division of the Psalm, and sing all that comes next to their Lips, till the Clerk puts them to Silence. Or to remedy this inconvenience, if a wise Man leads the Song, he dwells always upon four or five and twenty Pieces of some select Psalms, tho' the whole 150 lie before him; and he is forced to run that narrow Round still for want of larger Provision suited to our present Circumstances.

I might here also remark to what a hard Shift the Minister is put to find proper Hymns at the _Celebration of the Lord's-Supper_, where the People will sing nothing but out of _David_'s Psalm-Book: How perpetually do they repeat some part of the xxiiid or the cxviiith Psalm? And confine all the glorious Joy and Melody of that Ordinance to a few obscure Lines, because the Translators have not indulg'd an Evangelical Turn to the Words of _David_; no not in those very Places where the _Jewish Psalmist_ seems to mean the Gospel; but he was not able to speak it plain by reason of the Infancy of that Dispensation, and longs for the Aid of a _Christian Poet_. Tho', to speak my own Sense freely, I do not think _David_ ever wrote a Psalm of sufficient Glory and Sweetness to represent the Blessings of this holy Institution of _Christ_, even tho' it were explain'd by a copious Commentator; therefore 'tis my Opinion, that other _Spiritual Songs_ should sometimes be us'd to render _Christian Psalmody_ compleat. But this is not my present Business, and I have written on this Subject elsewhere.

To proceed to the _Second_ Part of my Preface, which is to shew _how insufficient a strict Translation of the Psalms is to attain the design'd End._

There are several Songs of this *Royal Author* that seem improper for any Person besides himself; so that I cannot believe that the *Whole Book of Psalms* (even in the Original) was appointed by God for the ordinary and constant Worship of the *Jewish Sanctuary or the Synagogues*, tho' several of them might be often sung; much less are they all proper for a *Christian Church*: Yet the Way of a close Translation of this whole Book of *Hebrew Psalms* for *English Psalmody* has generally obtain'd among us.

Some pretend, *'tis but a just Respect to the holy Scriptures*; for they have imbib'd a fond Opinion from their very Childhood, that nothing is to be sung at Church but the inspir'd Writings, how different soever the Sense is from our present State. But this Opinion has been taken upon Trust by the most part of its Advocates, and borrow'd chiefly from Education, Custom, and the Authority of others; which, if duly examin'd, will appear to have been built upon too slight and feeble Foundations; the Weakness of it I shall shew more at large in another Place: but it appears of itself more eminently inconsistent in those Persons that scruple to address God in Prose in any precompos'd Forms whatsoever, and they give this Reason, Because they cannot be fitted to all our Occasions; and yet in Verse they confine their Addresses to such Forms as were fitted chiefly for *Jewish* Worshippers, and for the special Occasions of *David* the King.

Others maintain that a strict and scrupulous Confinement to the Sense of the Original is *necessary to do Justice to the Royal Author*; but in my Judgment the Royal Author is most honour'd when he is made most intelligible; and when his admirable Composures are copy'd in such Language as gives Light and Joy to the Saints that live two thousand Years after him; whereas such a meer Translation of all his Verse into *English* to be sung in our Worship seems to darken our Religion, to damp our Delight, and forbid the *Christian Worshipper* to pursue the Song. How can we assume all his Words in our personal or publick Addresses to God, when our Condition of Life, our Time, Place and Religion are so vastly different from those of *David*?

I grant 'tis necessary and proper, that in translating every Part of Scripture for our *Reading* or *Hearing*, the Sense of the Original should be exactly and faithfully represented; for there we learn what God says to us in his Word: But in *Singing* for the most part the Case is alter'd: For as the greatest Number of the Psalms are devotional, and there the Psalmists express their own personal or national Concerns; so we are taught by their Example what is the chief Design of Psalmody, (_viz._) that we should represent our own sense of things in Singing, and address ourselves to God expressing our own Case; therefore the Words should be so far adapted to the general State of the Worshippers, as that we might seldom sing those Expressions in which we have no Concern: Or at least our Translators of the Psalms should observe this Rule, that when the peculiar Circumstances of antient Saints are form'd into a Song for our present and publick Use, they should be related in an historical Manner; and not retain the personal Pronouns _I_ and _We_, where the Transactions cannot belong to any of us, nor be apply'd to our Persons, Churches or Nation.

Moses, _Deborah_ and the Princes of _Israel_, _David_, _Asaph_ and _Habakkuk_, and all the Saints under the _Jewish_ State, sung their own Joys and Victories, their own Hopes and Fears and Deliverances, as I hinted before; and why must we under the Gospel sing nothing else but the Joys, Hopes and Fears of _Asaph_ and _David_? Why must _Christians_ be forbid all other Melody, but what arises from the Victories and Deliverances of the _Jews_? _David_ would have thought it very hard to have been confin'd to the Words of _Moses_, and sung nothing else on all his Rejoycing-days but the _Drowning of_ Pharaoh _in the Fifteenth of_ Exodus. He might have suppos'd it a little unreasonable when he had peculiar Occasions of mournfull Musick, if he had been forced to keep close to _Moses's Prayer in the Ninetieth Psalm_, and always sung over the _Shortness of human Life_, especially if he were not permitted the Liberty of a Paraphrase; and yet the special Concerns of _David_ and _Moses_ were much more akin to each other than ours are to either of them, and they were both of the same Religion, but ours is very different.

It is true, that _David_ has left us a richer Variety of holy Songs than all that went before him; but rich as it is, 'tis still far short of the glorious Things that we _Christians_ have to sing before the Lord. We and our Churches have our own special Affairs as well as they: Now if by a little Turn of their Words, or by the Change of a short Sentence we may express our own Meditations, Joys and Desires in the Verse of those _antient Psalmists_, why should we be forbid this sweet Priviledge? Why should we be ty'd up to Forms more than the _Jews_ themselves were, and such as are much more improper for our Age and State too? Let us remember that the very Power of

Singing was given to human Nature chiefly for this purpose, that our warmest Affections of Soul might break out into natural or divine Melody, and the Tongue of the Worshipper express his own Heart.

I confess 'tis not unlawful nor absurd for a Person of knowledge and Skill in divine Things to sing any Part of the *Jewish Psalm-Book*, and consider it meerly as the *Word of God*; from which by wise Meditation he may draw some pious Inferences for his own Use: For Instruction is allow'd to be one End of Psalmody. But where the Words are obscure *Hebraisms*, or personate a *Jew*, a *Soldier*, or a *King* speaking to himself or to God, this Mode of Instruction in a Song seems not so natural or easy even to the most skilfull Christian, and 'tis almost impracticable to the greatest Part of Mankind: And both the Wise and the Weak must confess this, that it does by no means raise their own Devotion so well as if they were speaking in their own Persons and expressing their own Sense: Besides that, the weaker Christian is ready to chime in with the Words he sings, and use them as his own, tho' they are never so foreign to his Purpose.

Now tho' it cannot be, that a large Book of lively Devotions should be so framed as to have every Line perfectly suited to all the Circumstances of every Worshipper, but after the Writer's utmost Care there will still be room for Christian Wisdom to exercise the Thoughts aright in Singing when the Words seem improper to our particular Case; yet as far as possible every Difficulty of this Kind should be removed, and such Sentences should by no Means be chosen which can scarce be used in their proper Sense by any that are present.

I could never persuade myself that the best Way to raise a devout Frame in *plain Christians* was to bring *a King* or *a Captain* into their Churches, and let him lead and dictate the Worship in his own Style of Royalty, or in the Language of a Field of Battel. Does every menial Servant in the Assembly know how to use these Words devoutly, (*viz.*) *When I receive the Congregation I will judge uprightly*, Psalm lxxv. 2. *A Bow of Steel is broken by mine Arms,* —— *As soon as they hear of me they shall obey me*, Psalm xviii. 34, 44. Would I encourage a Parish Clerk to stand up in the midst of a Country Church, and bid all the People joyn with his Words and say, *I will praise thee upon a Psaltery*; or, *I will open my dark Saying upon the Harp*; when even our Cathedrals sing only to the Sound of an Organ, most of the meaner Churches can have no Music but the

Voice, and others will have none besides? Why then must all that will sing a Psalm at Church use such Words as if they were to play upon Harp and Psaltery, when Thousands never saw such an Instrument, and know nothing of the Art? You will tell me, perhaps, that when you take these Expressions upon your Lips, you mean only, *That you will worship God according to his Appointment now, even as* David *worshipped him in his Day according to God's Appointment then*. But why will ye confine yourselves to speak one thing and mean another? Why must we be bound up to such Words as can never be address'd to God in their own Sense? And since the Heart of a Christian cannot joyn herein with his Lips, Why may not his Lips be led to speak his Heart? Experience itself has often shewn that it interrupts the holy Melody and spoils the Devotion of many a sincere Good Man or Woman, when in the midst of the Song some Speeches of *David* have been almost impos'd upon their Tongues, where he relates his own Troubles, his Banishment, or peculiar Deliverances; where he speaks like a Prince, a Musician, or a Prophet; or where the Sense is so obscure that it cannot be understood without a learned Commentator.

Here I may with Courage address myself to the Heart and Conscience of many pious and observing Christians, and ask them, Whether they have not found a most divine Pleasure in Singing, when the Words of the Psalms have happily express'd their Frame of Soul? Have you not felt a new Joy spring within you when you could speak your own Desires and Hopes, your own Faith, Love and Zeal in the Language of the holy Psalmist? Have not your Spirits taken Wing, and mounted up near to God and Glory with the Song of *David* on your Tongue? But on a sudden the Clerk has proposed the next Line to your Lips with dark Sayings and Prophecies, with Burnt-Offerings or Hyssop, with New-Moons, and Trumpets and Timbrels in it, with *Confession of Sins* which you never committed, with *Complaints of Sorrows* such as you never felt, *cursing such Enemies* as you never had, giving *Thanks for such Victories* as you never obtained, or leading you to speak in your own Persons of *Things*, *Places* and *Actions*, that you never knew. And how have all your Souls been discomposed at once, and the Strings of Harmony all untuned! You could not proceed in the Song with your Hearts, and your Lips have sunk their Joy and faultered in the Tune; you have been baulked and ashamed, and knew not whether it were best to be silent or to follow on with the Clerk and the

Multitude, and sing with cold Devotion, and perhaps in Darkness too, without Thought or Meaning.

Let it be *reply'd* here, That to prevent this inconvenience, *such Psalms or Sentences may be always omitted by him that leads the Song*, or may *have a more useful Turn given in the Mind of those that sing*. But I *answer*, Since such Psalms or Sentences are not to be sung, *they may be as well omitted by the Translator*, or may *have a more usefull Turn given in the Verse* than it is possible for all the Singers to give on a sudden: And this is all that I contend for.

I come therefore to the *Third thing* I proposed, and that is to explain my own Design; which in short is this; (*viz.*) *To accommodate the Book of Psalms to Christian Worship*: And in order to this 'tis necessary to divest *David* and *Asaph*, &c. of every other Character but that of a *Psalmist* and a *Saint*, and *to make them always speak the common Sense and Language of a Christian.*

Attempting the Work with this View I have entirely omitted several whole Psalms, and large Pieces of many others; and have chosen out of all of them such Parts only as might easily and naturally be accommodated to the various Occasions of the Christian Life, or at least might afford us some beautifull Allusion to Christian Affairs: These I have copied and explained in the general Style of the Gospel; nor have I confined my Expressions to any particular Party or Opinion; that in Words prepared for public Worship and for the Lips of Multitudes, there might not be a Syllable offensive to sincere Christians whose Judgments may differ in the lesser Matters of Religion.

Where the Psalmist uses sharp Invectives against his personal Enemies, I have endeavored to turn the Edge of them against our spiritual Adversaries, *Sin, Satan* and *Temptation*. Where the Flights of his Faith and Love are sublime, I have often sunk the Expressions within the reach of an ordinary Christian. Where the Words imply some peculiar Wants or Distresses, Joys or Blessings, I have used Words of greater Latitude and Comprehension suited to the general Circumstances of Men.

Where the Original runs in the Form of Prophecy concerning *Christ* and his Salvation, I have given an Historical Turn to the Sense: There is no necessity that we should always sing in the obscure and doubtfull Style of Prediction, when the Things foretold are brought into open Light by a full Accomplishment. Where the Writers of the New Testament have cited or alluded to any part of the Psalms, I have often indulged the Liberty of Paraphrase according to the Words of _Christ_ or his Apostles. And surely this may be esteemed _the Word of God_ still, tho' borrowed from several parts of the Holy Scripture. Where the Psalmist describes Religion by the _Fear of God_, I have often joyn'd _Faith and Love_ to it. Where he speaks of the Pardon of Sin thro' the _Mercies of God_, I have added the _Merits of a Saviour_. Where he talks of sacrificing _Goats or Bullocks_, I rather chuse to mention the Sacrifice of _Christ the Lamb of God_. When he attends the _Ark with Shouting_ into _Zion_, I sing the _Ascension of my Saviour_ into Heaven, or his _Presence in his Church_ on Earth. Where he promises abundance of _Wealth, Honour_ and _long Life_, I have changed some of these _typical_ Blessings for _Grace, Glory_ and _Life Eternal_, which are brought to Light by the Gospel, and promised in the New Testament: And I am fully satisfied that more Honour is done to our blessed Saviour by speaking his Name, his Graces and Actions in his own Language, according to the brighter Discoveries he hath now made, than by going back again to the _Jewish_ Forms of Worship, and the Language of Types and Figures.

All Men will confess this is just and necessary in Preaching and Praying; and I cannot find a Reason why we should not sing Praises also in a manner agreeable to the present and more glorious Dispensation. No Man can be persuaded, that to read a Sermon of the Royal Preacher out of the Book of _Ecclesiastes_, or a Prayer out of _Ezra_ or _Daniel_ is so edifying to a Christian Church (tho' they were inspired) as a well-compos'd Prayer or Sermon deliver'd in the usual Language of the Gospel of _Christ_. And why should the very Words of the Sweet-Singer of _Israel_ be esteem'd so necessary to Christian Psalmody, and the _Jewish_ Style so much preferable to the _Evangelical_ in our religious Songs of Praise?

Now since it appears so plain that the _Hebrew Psalter_ is very improper to be the precise Matter and Style of our Songs in a _Christian Church_; and since there is very good Reason to believe that it is left us not only as a most valuable Part of the Word of God for our Faith and Practice, but as an admirable and divine Pattern of spiritual Songs and Hymns under the Gospel, I have chosen rather to _imitate_ than to _translate_; and thus to compose a _Psalm-book for Christians_ after the Manner of the _Jewish Psalter_.

If I could be perswaded that nothing ought to be sung in worship but what was of immediate Inspiration from God, surely I would recommend *Anthems* only, (viz.) the Psalms themselves as we read them in the Bible, set to Musick as they are sung by Choristers in our Cathedral Churches: For these are nearest to the Words of Inspiration; and we must depart from those Words if we turn them into Rhyme and Metre of any Sort. And upon the foot of this Argument even *The Scotch Version* which has been so much commended for its Approach to the Original, would be unlawful as well as others.

But since I believe that any *Divine Sentence* or *Christian Verse* agreeable to Scripture may be sung, tho' it be composed by Men uninspired, I have not been so curious and exact in striving every where to express the antient Sense and Meaning of *David*, but have rather exprest myself as I may suppose *David* would have done, had he lived in the Days of *Christianity*. And by this means perhaps I have sometimes hit upon the true Intent of the Spirit of God in those Verses, farther and clearer than *David* himself could ever discover, as St. *Peter* encourages me to hope. I *Pet*. i. 11, 12. In several other Places I hope my Reader will find a natural Exposition of many a dark and doubtfull Text, and some new Beauties and Connexions of Thought discovered in the *Jewish* Poet, tho' not in the Language of a *Jew*. In all Places I have kept my grand Design in View, and that is *to teach my Author to speak like a Christian*. For why should I now address God my Saviour in a Song *with burnt Sacrifices of Fatlings and with the Incense of Rams*? Why should I pray to be *sprinkled with Hyssop*, or recur to the *Blood of Bullocks and Goats*? Why should I *bind my Sacrifice with Cords to the Horns of an Altar*, or sing the Praises of God to *high sounding Cymbals*, when the Gospel has shewn me a nobler Atonement for Sin, and appointed a purer and more spiritual Worship? Why must I joyn with *David* in his Legal or Prophetic Language to curse my Enemies, when my Saviour in his Sermons has taught me to love and bless them? Why may not a *Christian* omit all those Passages of the *Jewish* Psalmist that tend to fill the Mind with overwhelming Sorrows, despairing Thoughts, or bitter personal Resentments, none of which are well suited to the Spirit of Christianity, which is a Dispensation of Hope and Joy and Love? What need is there that I should wrap up the shining Honours of my Redeemer in the dark and shadowy Language of a Religion that is now for ever abolished; especially when Christians are so vehemently warned in the Epistles of St. *Paul* against a Judaizing Spirit in their Worship as well as

Doctrine? And what Fault can there be in enlarging a little on the more usefull Subjects in the Style of the Gospel, where the Psalm gives any Occasion, since the Whole Religion of the _Jews_ is censur'd often in the New Testament as a defective and imperfect Thing?

Tho' I have aimed to provide for a Variety of Affairs in the _Christian_ Life by the different _Metres_, _Paraphrases_, and _Divisions_ of the Psalms, (of which I shall speak particularly) yet after all, there are a great many Circumstances that attend _Common Christians_, which cannot be agreeably exprest by any Paraphrase on the Words of _David_; and for these I have endeavoured to provide in my Book of _Hymns_, that Christians might have something to sing in Divine Worship answerable to most or all their Occasions: In the _Preface_ to that Book I have shewn the Insufficiency of the common Versions of the _Psalms_, and given further Reasons for my present Attempt.

I am not so vain as to expect that the few short Hints I have mentioned in that _Preface_ or in this should be sufficient to justify my Performances in the Judgment of all Men, nor to convince and satisfy those who have long maintained different Sentiments. All the Favour therefore that I desire of my Readers is this, that they would not censure this Work till they have read my _Discourse of Psalmody_, which I hope will shortly be publish'd; but let them read it with serious Attention, and bring with them a generous and sincere Soul, ready to be convinced and to receive Truth where soever it can be found. In that Treatise I have given a large and particular Account how the Psalms of _Jewish_ Composure ought to be translated for _Christian_ Worship, and justify'd the Rules I lay down by such Reasons as seem to carry in them most plentifull Evidence and a fair Conviction.

If I might presume so much, I would entreat them also to forget their younger Prejudices for a Season, so far as to make a few Experiments of these Songs; and try whether they are not suited thro' Divine Grace to kindle in them a Fire of Zeal and Love, and to exalt the willing Soul to an Evangelic Temper of Joy and Praise. And if they shall find by sweet Experience any devout Affections raised, and a holy Frame of Mind awakened within them by these Attempts of _Christian Psalmistry_, I persuade myself that I shall receive their Thanks, and be assisted by their Prayers towards the Recovery of my Health and my publick Labours in the Church of _Christ_. Whatsoever Sentiments they had formerly entertain'd, yet surely they will not suffer their old and doubtfull Opinions to prevail against their own inward Sensations of Piety and religious joy.

Before I conclude I must add a few Things concerning my Division of the Psalms and my Manner of Versifying.

Of the Division of the Psalms.

In many of these sacred Songs it is evident that the Psalmist had several distinct Cases in View at the same time. As *Psalm* lxv. the first four or five Verses describe the *Temple Worship of Prayer and Praise*: The following Verses represent the *Providence of God in the Seasons of the Year*. So in *Psalm* lxviii. the first six Verses declare *the Majesty and Mercy of God*, and from the 7th Verse to the 16th *Israel is brought from Egypt* to fix divine worship at *Jerusalem*. The 17th and 18th are a Prophecy of the *Ascension of Christ*. Verse 24, &c. describes a *Religious Procession*, &c. The like may be observed in many other Psalms; especially such as represent some complicated Sorrows or Joys of the Psalmist. Now it is not to be supposed that Christians should have all the same distinct Occasions of Meditation, Complaint or Praise; much less all at the same time to be mentioned before God. Therefore I have divided many Psalms into several Parts, and disposed them into distinct Hymns on those various Subjects that may be proper Matter for *Christian Psalmody*.

Besides, that excessive long Tone of Voice that stretches out every Syllable in our publick Singing allows us neither Time nor Spirits to sing above six or eight Stanza's at once; and sometimes we make use of but three or four: Therefore I have reduced almost all the Work into Hymns of such a Length as may suit the usual Custom of the Churches; that they may not sing broken Fragments of Sense, as is too often done, and spoil the Beauty of this Worship; but may finish a whole Song and Subject at once.

For this End I have been forced to transpose some of the Verses; and by this means (some will object) that I have left out some usefull and significant Lines. Perhaps so. But if I had not, the Clerk would have left 'em out, to save the Time for other Parts of Worship: And I desire but the same Liberty which he has to chuse which Verses shall be sung. Yet I think it will be seldom found that I have omitted any usefull Psalm or Verse whose Sense is not abundantly repeated in other Parts of the Book; and what I have left out in one Metre I have often inserted in another.

When the Occasion or Subject are much the same throughout a long Psalm, I have either abridged the Verses, or divided the Psalm by *Pauses* after the *French* Manner, (where the Sense would admit an Interruption) that the Worship may not be tiresome.

Of the Verse.

I resign to Sir *John Denham* the Honour of the best Poet, if he had given his Genius but a just Liberty; yet his Work will ever shine brightest among those that have confined themselves to a meer Translation. But that close Confinement has often forbid the Freedom and Glory of Verse, and by cramping his Sense has render'd it sometimes too obscure for a plain Reader and the publick Worship, even tho' we lived in the Days of *David* and *Judaism*. These Inconveniences he himself suspects and fears in the Preface.

I am content to yield to Mr. *Milbourne* the Preference of his Poesy in many Parts of his Psalms, and to Mr. *Tate* and Dr. *Brady* in some of theirs. But in those very Places their Turns of Thought and Language are too much raised above a vulgar Audience, and fit only for Persons of an higher Education.

I have not refused in some few Psalms to borrow a single Line or two from these three authors; yet I have taken the most Freedom of that sort with Dr. *Patrick*, for his Style best agrees with my Design, tho' his Verse be generally of a lower Strain. But where I have used three or four Lines together of any Author, I have acknowledged it in the *Notes*.

In some of the more elevated Psalms I have given a little indulgence to my *Genius*; and if it should appear that I have aimed at the *Sublime*, yet I have generally kept within the Reach of an unlearned Reader: I never thought the Art of sublime Writing consisted in flying out of Sight; nor am I of the Mind of the *Italian*, who said, *Obscurity begets Greatness*. I have always avoided the Language of the Poets where it did not suit the Language of the Gospel.

In many of these Composures I have just permitted my Verse to rise above a Flat and indolent Style; yet I hope it is every where supported above the just Contempt of the Criticks; tho' I am sensible that I have often subdu'd it below their Esteem; because I would neither indulge any bold Metaphors, nor admit of hard Words, nor tempt an ignorant Worshipper to sing without his Understanding.

Tho' I have attempted to imitate the sacred Beauties of my Author in some of the sprightly Psalms, such as *Psal.* 45, 46, 49, 65, 72, 90, 91, 104, 114, 115, 139, &c. yet if my youthfull Readers complain that they expected to find here more elegant and beautifull Descriptions with which the sacred Original abounds, let them consider that some of those Pieces of descriptive Poesy are the flowry Elegancies peculiar to *Eastern* Nations and antique Ages, and are much too large also to be brought into such short *Christian* Sonnets as are used in our present Worship; almost all those Psalms I have contracted and fitted to more spiritual Devotion, as *Ps.* 18, 68, 73, 78, 105, 106, 109, &c.

Of the Metre and Rhyme.

I have formed my Verse in the *three most usual Metres* to which our Psalm-Tunes are fitted, (viz,) The *Common Metre*, the Metre of the old 25th Psalm which I call *Short Metre*, and that of the old 100th Psalm which I call *Long Metre*. Besides these I have done some few Psalms in Stanza's of six, eight, or twelve Lines, to the best of the old Tunes. Many of them I have also cast into two or three Metres, not by leaving out or adding two Syllables in a Line, whereby others have cramped or stretched their Verse to the Destruction of all Poesy; but I have made an intire new Song, and oftentimes in the different Metres I have indulged those different Senses in which Commentators have explained the inspired Author: And if in one Metre I have given the Loose to a Paraphrase, I have confin'd myself to my Text in the other.

If I am charged by the Criticks for repeating the same Rhymes too often, let them consider, that the Words which continually recur in divine Poesy admit exceeding few Rhymes to them fit for sacred Use; these are, *God, World, Flesh, Soul, Life, Death, Faith, Hope, Heaven, Earth,* &c. which I think will make sufficient Apology; especially since I have coupled all my Lines by Rhymes much more than either Mr. *Tate* or Dr. *Patrick* have done, which is certainly most musical and agreeable to the Ear where Rhyme is used at all.

I must confess I have never yet seen any *Version* or *Paraphrase of the Psalms*, in their own *Jewish* Sense, so perfect as to discourage all further Attempts. But whoever undertakes the noble Work, let him bring with him a Soul devoted to Piety, an exalted Genius, and withal a studious Application. For *David*'s Harp abhors a prophane Finger, and disdains to answer to an unskilfull or a careless Touch. A meaner Pen may imitate at a Distance, but a compleat

Translation or a just Paraphrase demands a rich Treasury of Diction, an exalted Fancy, a quick Taste of devout Passion, together with a Judgment strict and severe to retrench every luxuriant Line, and to maintain a religious Sovereignty over the whole Work. Thus the *Psalmist of Israel* might arise in *Great Britain* in all his *Hebrew Glory*, and entertain the more knowing and polite *Christians* of our Age. But still I am bold to maintain the great *Principle* on which my present Work is founded; and that is, That if the brightest Genius on Earth or an Angel from Heaven should translate *David*, and keep close to the Sense and Style of the inspired Author, we should only obtain thereby a bright or heavenly Copy of the *Devotions of the Jewish King*; but it could never make the fittest *Psalm-Book for a Christian People*.

It was not my Design to exalt myself to the Rank and Glory of Poets; but I was ambitious to be a Servant to the Churches, and a Helper to the Joy of the meanest Christian. Tho' there are many gone before me that have taught the *Hebrew* Psalmist to speak *English*, yet I think I may assume this Pleasure of being the First who have brought down the Royal Author into the common Affairs of the Christian Life, and led the Psalmist of *Israel* into the Church of *Christ*, without any thing of a *Jew* about him. And whensoever there shall appear any *Paraphrase of the Book of Psalms* that hath more of the Savour of Piety, more of the Style and Spirit of the Gospel, with a superior Dignity of Verse, and yet the Lines as easy and flowing, and the Sense and Language as level to the lowest Capacity, I shall congratulate the World, and consent to say, *Let this Attempt of mine be buried in Silence*.

Till such a Work arise, I must attend these Evangelic Songs (which have been the Labour of so many Years) with a devout Wish.

May that God who has favour'd me with Life and Capacity to finish this Work for the Service of his Churches after so many Years of tiresome Sickness and Confinement, accept this humble Offering from a thankfull Heart. May the Lord who dwelt of old amidst the Praises of *Israel* encourage and bless this Essay to assist *Christians* in the Work of Praise! And may his Churches exalt him here on Earth in the Language of his Gospel and his Grace, till they shall be called up to Heaven and the noble Society above! There *David* and *Asaph* have chang'd their antient Style, and the Song of *Moses* and of the *Lamb* are one: There the *Jews* joyn with the *Nations* to exalt their God and Redeemer in the Language of Angels and in Strains of compleat Glory. *Amen.*

Advertisement to the Readers.

The chief Design of this Work was to improve Psalmody *or* Religious Singing, *and to encourage the frequent Practice of it in public Assemblies and private Families with more Honour and Delight; yet the Author hopes the Reading of it may also entertain the Parlour and the Closet with devout Pleasure and holy Meditations. Therefore he would request his Readers at proper Seasons to peruse it thro'; and among* 340 *sacred Hymns they may find out several that suit their own Case and Temper, or the Circumstances of their Families and Friends; they may teach their Children such as are proper for their Age, and by treasuring them in their Memory they may be furnish'd for pious Retirement, or may entertain their Friends with holy Melody.*

Of chusing or finding the Psalm.

The Perusal of the whole Book will acquaint every Reader with the Author's Method, and by consulting the Index *or* Table of Contents *at the End he may find Hymns very proper for many Occasions of the Christian Life and Worship, tho' no Copy of* David's Psalter *can provide for all.*

Or if he remember the first Line of any Psalm, the Table of the first Lines *will direct where to find it.*

Or if any shall think it best to sing all the Psalms in Order in Churches or Families, it may be done with profit; provided those Psalms be omitted that refer to special Occurrences of Nations, Churches or single Christians.

Of naming the Psalms.

Let the Number of the Psalm be named distinctly, together with the particular Metre, and particular Part of it: As for instance; Let us sing the 33d Psalm, 2d Part. Common Metre; *or*, Let us sing the 91st Psalm, 1st Part, beginning at the Pause, *or* ending at the Pause; *or*, Let us sing the 84th Psalm as the 148th Psalm, &c. *And then read over the first Stanza before you begin to sing, that the People may find it in their Books, whether you sing with or without reading Line by Line.*

Of Dividing the Psalm.

If the Psalm be too long for the Time or Custom of Singing, there _are_ Pauses _in many of 'em at which you may properly rest: Or you may leave out those Verses which are included in Crotchets_ [ ] _without disturbing the Sense: Or in some Places you may begin to sing at a_ Pause.

Do not always confine your selves to six Stanza's, _but sing seven or eight, rather than confound the Sense and abuse the Psalm in solemn Worship._

Of the Manner of Singing.

It were to be wish'd that all Congregations and private Families would sing as they do in foreign Protestant Countries without reading Line by Line. Tho' the Author has done what he could to make the Sense compleat in every Line or two, yet many Inconveniencies will always attend this unhappy Manner of Singing: But where it cannot be alter'd, these two things may give some Relief.

First, _Let as many as can do it bring_ Psalm-books _with them, and look on the Words while they sing so far as to make the Sense compleat._

Secondly, _Let the Clerk read the whole Psalm over aloud before he begins to parcel out the Lines, that the People may have some Notion of what they sing; and not be forced to drag on heavily thro' eight tedious Syllables without any Meaning, till the next Line come to give the Sense of them._

It were to be wish'd also that we might not dwell so long upon every single Note, and produce the Syllables to such a tiresome extent with a constant Uniformity of Time; which disgraces the Musick and puts the Congregation quite out of Breath in singing five or six Stanza's: whereas if the Method of Singing _were but reformed to a greater Speed of Pronunciation, we might often enjoy the Pleasure of a longer Psalm with less Expence of Time and Breath; and our Psalmody would be more agreeable to that of the antient Churches, more intelligible to others, and more delightfull to our selves._

The various Measures of the verse are fitted to the Tunes of the Old Psalm-Book.

To the Common Tunes _sing all entitled_ Common
    Metre.
To the Tunes of the 100th Psalm _sing all entitled_
    Long Metre.
To the Tune of the 25th Ps. _sing_ Short Metre.
To the 50th Ps. _sing one Metre of the_ 50th,
    93d.

To the 112th *or* 127th Psalm *sing one Metre of
    the* 104th *and* 148th.
To the 113th Psalm *sing one Metre of the* 19th,
    33d, 58th, 89th, *last Part*, 96th, 112th, 113th.
To the 122d Psalm *sing one of the Metres of
    the* 93d, 122d *and* 133d.
To the 148th Psalm *sing one Metre of the*
    84th, 121st, 136th *and* 148th.
To a New Tune *sing one Metre of the* 50th *and*
    115th.
Dec. 1st, 1718.

John Wesley (1703-1791)

John Wesley, the son of an Anglican clergyman, was the
chief figure in the development of the Methodist movement
in the eighteenth century. John and his brother, Charles
(1707-1788), served for a brief time as Church of England
missionaries in the American colony of Georgia, during
which time the older brother published the "Charlestown
Collection" of psalms and hymns (1737), the first hymnal
compiled in the colonies. After returning to England, the
brothers underwent separate spiritual renewals and spent the
remainder of their days traveling the length and breadth of
Great Britain preaching, founding and encouraging
Methodist societies, and writing.

From its very inception, the Methodist movement was
characterized by congregational singing. Charles Wesley
ranks with Isaac Watts as one of the great hymn writers of
English-speaking Christianity, but John's role as a translator
of hymns and collector/editor of his brother's works was
scarcely less important.

The following selections from the writings of John Wesley
reveal his concern for the materials and performance of
congregational singing among the Methodists, as well as his
distaste for those who published Wesleyan hymns in
unauthorized editions and altered forms.

51   Preface to *Select Hymns: With Tunes annext* (1761).
        Source: *WJW*, vol. 14, pp. 335-336.

1. Some years ago, a Collection of Tunes was published, under the title of _Harmonia Sacra_. I believe all unprejudiced persons who understand music allow, that it exceeds, beyond all degrees of comparison, anything of the kind which has appeared in England before; the tunes being admirably well chosen, and accurately engraven, not only for the voice, but likewise for the organ or harpsichord.

2. But this, though it is excellent in its kind, is not the thing which I want. I want the people called Methodists to sing true the tunes which are in common use among them. At the same time, I want them to have in one volume the best hymns which we have printed; and that in a small and portable volume, and one of an easy price.

3. I have been endeavouring for more than twenty years to procure such a book as this; but in vain. Masters of music were above following any direction but their own. And I was determined, whoever compiled this, should follow my direction; not mending our tunes, but setting them down, neither better nor worse than they were. At length I have prevailed. The following Collection contains all the tunes which are in common use among us. They are pricked true, exactly as I desire all our congregations may sing them; and here is prefixed to them a Collection of those Hymns which are, I think, some of the best we have published. The volume likewise is small, as well as the price. This therefore I recommend, preferable to all others.

JOHN WESLEY.

52 "Directions for Congregational Singing" from _Sacred Melody_ (1761). _Source_: _WJW_, vol. 14, p. 346.

That this part of divine worship may be more acceptable to God, as well as more profitable to yourself and others, be careful to observe the following directions:—

1. Sing _all_. See that you join with the congregation as frequently as you can. Let not a slight degree of weakness or weariness hinder you. If it is a cross to you, take it up, and you will find a blessing.

2. Sing _lustily_, and with a good courage. Beware of singing as if you were half dead, or half asleep; but lift up your voice with strength. Be no more afraid of your voice now, nor more ashamed

of its being heard, than when you sung the songs of Satan.

3. Sing *modestly*. Do not bawl, so as to be heard above, or distinct from, the rest of the congregation, that you may not destroy the harmony; but strive to unite your voices together, so as to make one clear melodious sound.

4. Sing *in time*. Whatever time is sung, be sure to keep with it. Do not run before, nor stay behind it; but attend closely to the leading voices, and move therewith as exactly as you can. And take care you sing not too slow. This drawling way naturally steals on all who are lazy; and it is high time to drive it out from among us, and sing all our tunes just as quick as we did at first.

5. Above all, sing *spiritually*. Have an eye to God in every word you sing. Aim at pleasing Him more than yourself, or any other creature. In order to this, attend strictly to the sense of what you sing; and see that your heart is not carried away with the sound, but offered to God continually; so shall your singing be such as the Lord will approve of here, and reward when he cometh in the clouds of heaven.

53   Letter to Thomas Rankin (September 11, 1765).
       Source: *The Letters of the Rev. John Wesley, A.M.*, ed.
       by John Telford (London: The Epworth Press, 1931),
       vol. 4, pp. 311-312.

Dear Tommy,—There is a good work in Cornwall. But where the great work goes on well we should take care to be exact in little things.

I will tell you several of these just as they occur to my mind. Grace Paddy at Redruth met in the select society, though she wore a large glittering necklace and met no band.

They sing all over Cornwall a tune so full of repetitions and flourishes that it can scarce be sung with devotion. It is to those words,
        Praise the Lord, ye blessed ones.
Away with it! Let it be heard no more.

They cannot sing our old common tunes.   Teach these everywhere. Take pains herein.

The Societies are not half supplied with books; not even with Jane Cooper's *Letters*, or the two or three Sermons which I printed last year; no, not with the shilling Hymn-Book or *Primitive Physick*.

They almost universally neglect fasting.

The preaching-houses are miserable, even the new ones. They have neither light nor air sufficient; and they are far, far too low and too small. Look at Yarm house.

Recommend the _Notes on the Old Testament_ in good earnest. Every Society as a Society should subscribe. Remind them everywhere that two, four, or six might join together for a copy, and bring the money to their leader weekly.

We have need to use all the common sense God has given us as well as all the grace.—I am, dear Tommy,

Your affectionate friend and brother.

54 Preface to _A Collection of Hymns for the Use of the People called Methodists_ (1780). _Source_: _WJW_, vol. 14, pp. 339-342.

1. For many years I have been importuned to publish such a Hymn Book as might be generally used in all our congregations throughout Great Britain and Ireland. I have hitherto withstood the importunity, as I believed such a publication was needless, considering the various Hymn Books which my brother and I have published within these forty years last past; so that it may be doubted whether any religious community in the world has a greater variety of them.

2. But it has been answered, "Such a publication is highly needful upon this very account; for the greater part of the people, being poor, are not able to purchase so many books. And those that have purchased them are, as it were, bewildered in the immense variety. There is therefore still wanting a proper Collection of Hymns for general use, carefully made out of all these books, and one comprised in so moderate a compass as neither to be cumbersome nor expensive."

3. It has been replied, "You have such a Collection already, (entitled Hymns and Spiritual Songs,) which I extracted several years ago from a variety of Hymn Books." But it is objected, "This is in the other extreme; it is abundantly too small. It does not, it cannot, in so narrow a compass, contain variety enough; not so much as we want, among whom singing makes so considerable a part of the public service. What we want is, a collection neither too

large, that it may be cheap and portable; nor too small, that it may contain a sufficient variety for all ordinary occasions."

4. Such a Hymn Book you have now before you. It is not so large as to be either cumbersome or expensive; and it is large enough to contain such a variety of hymns as will not soon be worn threadbare. It is large enough to contain all the important truths of our most holy religion, whether speculative or practical; yea, to illustrate them all, and to prove them both by Scripture and reason. And this is done in a regular order. The Hymns are not carelessly jumbled together, but carefully ranged under proper heads, according to the experience of real Christians. So that this book is, in effect, a little body of experimental and practical divinity.

5. As but a small part of these Hymns is of my own composing, I do not think it inconsistent with modesty to declare, that I am persuaded no such Hymn Book as this has yet been published in the English language. In what other publication of the kind have you so distinct and full an account of scriptural Christianity? such a declaration of the heights and depths of religion, speculative and practical? so strong cautions against the most plausible errors; particularly those that are now most prevalent? and so clear directions for making our calling and election sure; for perfecting holiness in the fear of God?

6. May I be permitted to add a few words with regard to the poetry? Then I will speak to those who are judges thereof with all freedom and unreserve. To these I may say, without offence, (1.) In these Hymns there is no doggerel, no botches, nothing put in to patch up the rhyme, no feeble expletives. (2.) Here is nothing turgid or bombast on the one hand, or low and creeping on the other. (3.) Here are no cant expressions, no words without meaning. Those who impute this to us know not what they say. We talk common sense, whether they understand it or not, both in verse and prose, and use no word but in a fixed and determinate sense. (4.) Here are, allow me to say, both the purity, the strength, and the elegance of the English language, and, at the same time, the utmost simplicity and plainness, suited to every capacity. Lastly, I desire men of taste to judge, (these are the only competent judges,) whether there be not in some of the following Hymns the true spirit of poetry, such as cannot be acquired by art and labour, but must be the gift of nature. By labour a man may become a tolerable imitator of Spenser, Shakspeare, or Milton, and may heap

together pretty compound epithets, as *pale-eyed, meek-eyed*, and the like; but unless he be born a poet, he will never attain the genuine spirit of poetry.

7. And here I beg leave to mention a thought which has been long upon my mind, and which I should long ago have inserted in the public papers, had I not been unwilling to stir up a nest of hornets. Many gentlemen have done my brother and me (though without naming us) the honour to reprint many of our Hymns. Now they are perfectly welcome so to do, provided they print them just as they are. But I desire they would not attempt to mend them; for they really are not able. None of them is able to mend either the sense or the verse. Therefore I must beg of them one of these two favours; either to let them stand as they are, to take them for better for worse, or to add the true reading in the margin, or at the bottom of the page; that we may no longer be accountable either for the nonsense or for the doggerel of other men.

8. But to return: That which is of infinitely more moment than the spirit of poetry, is the spirit of piety. And I trust, all persons of real judgment will find this breathing through the whole collection. It is in this view chiefly that I would recommend it to every truly pious reader as a means of raising or quickening the spirit of devotion, of confirming his faith, of enlivening his hope, and of kindling or increasing his love to God and man. When poetry thus keeps its place, as the handmaid of piety, it shall attain, not a poor perishable wreath, but a crown that fadeth not away.

London,
JOHN WESLEY
October 20, 1779.

55 Preface to *A Pocket Hymn Book for the Use of Christians of all Denominations* (1787). *Source: WJW,* vol. 14, pp. 343-345.

1. A few years ago I was desired by many of our Preachers to prepare and publish a small Hymn Book, to be used in common in our societies. This I promised to do as soon as I had finished some other business which was then on my hands. But before I could do this, a bookseller stepped in, and, without my consent or knowledge, extracted such a Hymn Book, chiefly from our works, and spread several editions of it throughout the kingdom.

2. Two years ago I published a Pocket Hymn Book, according to my promise: But most of our people were supplied already with the other Hymns. And these are circulated still. To cut off all pretence from the Methodists for buying them, our brethren in the late Conference, at Bristol, advised me to print the same Hymn Book which had been printed at York. This I have done in the present volume: Only with this difference:—

3. First. Out of those two hundred and thirty-two hymns, I have omitted seven-and-thirty. These I did not dare to palm upon the world, because fourteen of them appeared to me very flat and dull; fourteen more, mere prose, tagged with rhyme; and nine more to be grievous doggerel. But a friend tells me, "Some of these, especially those two that are doggerel double-distilled, namely, "The despised Nazarene," and that which begins,—

"A Christ I have; O what a Christ have I!"
are hugely admired, and continually echoed from Berwick-upon-Tweed to London." If they are, I am sorry for it: It will bring a deep reproach upon the judgment of the Methodists. But I dare not increase that reproach by countenancing, in any degree, such an insult both on religion and common sense. And I earnestly intreat all our Preachers, not only never to give them out, but to discountenance them by all prudent means, both in public and private.

4. Secondly. I have added a considerable number of the best hymns which we have ever published: Although I am sensible they will not suit the taste of the admirers of doggerel. But I advise them to keep their own counsel, and not betray their want of judgment.

5. Thirdly. Whereas in the other Hymn Book the hymns are strangely thrown out of their places, and all jumbled together; they are here carefully methodized again, and ranged in their proper order.

6. "But did not you, in a late preface, give any one leave to print your Hymns that pleased?" No, I never did; I never said, I never intended, any such thing. My words are, p. 6, "Many have . . . reprinted our Hymns. *They* are perfectly welcome so to do; provided they print them just as they are." *They are welcome.* Who? Why, Mr. Madan, Berridge, and those that have done it already, for the use of their several congregations. But could any one imagine I meant a bookseller? or that a Methodist bookseller

would undertake it? to take a whole book out of mine? only adding a few shreds out of other books for form's sake? And could I mean he was welcome to publish this among Methodists, just at the time when I had engaged to do it myself? Does not every one, unless he shuts his eyes, see, that every shilling he gains by it he takes out of my pocket? yet not so properly out of mine, as out of the pockets of the poor Preachers? For I lay up nothing: And I lay out no more upon myself than I did forty years ago: (My carriage is no expense to me; that expense being borne by a few friends:) But what I receive is for the poor, especially the poor Preachers.

7. Upon the whole: Although there are some hymns in this book which I should never have printed, but that I was desired to reprint *the whole book*, printed at York; yet I am bold to recommend this small-Hymn Book, as the best of the size that has ever been published among the Methodists. But it is still greatly inferior to the large Hymn Book; in which I believe the judicious and candid reader may find a clear explication of every branch both of speculative and practical divinity.

Highbury-Place,
JOHN WESLEY.
November 15, 1786.

John Newton (1725-1807)

John Newton, despite early religious training, lived a dissolute life until experiencing a dramatic conversion at sea. He began to preach in 1758, was appointed curate of the Anglican church in Olney, then became vicar at St. Mary Woolnoth, London. With his friend, William Cowper (1731-1800), he compiled *Olney Hymns* (1779), one of the most important English hymnals of the late eighteenth century and the source of such familiar texts as Newton's "Amazing grace! how sweet the sound" and Cowper's "God moves in a mysterious way." In the preface to the collection, Newton referred to the melancholy and depression suffered by Cowper, which forced Newton to complete the book by himself. He also noted that some of the hymns had already circulated in print—sometimes with misattributions—and defended the inclusion of hymns expressing his own views of Calvinist doctrine. Like Watts, Newton pointed out that these productions were intended for "the use of plain

people" and were not to be judged in the same manner as other
poetic writings, though he hoped he had not offended "persons of superior discernment."

56   Preface to *Olney Hymns* (1779). *Source: The Works of the Reverend John Newton* (London: Ball, Arnold, and Co., 1839), pp. 457-458.

Copies of a few of these Hymns have already appeared in periodical publications, and in some recent collections. I have observed one or two of them attributed to persons who certainly had no concern in them, but as transcribers. All that have been at different times parted with in manuscript are included in the present volume; and (if the information were of any great importance) the public may be assured, that the whole number were composed by two persons only. The original design would not admit of any other association. A desire of promoting the faith and comfort of sincere Christians, though the principal, was not the only motive to this undertaking. It was likewise intended as a monument, to perpetuate the remembrance of an intimate and endeared friendship. With this pleasing view, I entered upon my part, which would have been smaller than it is, and the book would have appeared much sooner, and in a very different form, if the wise, though mysterious, providence of God, had not seen fit to cross my wishes. We had not proceeded far upon our proposed plan, before my dear friend was prevented by a long and affecting indisposition, from affording me any further assistance. My grief and disappointment were great; I hung my harp upon the willows, and for some time thought myself determined to proceed no further without him. Yet my mind was afterwards led to resume the service. My progress in it, amidst a varity of other engagements, has been slow; yet, in a course of years, the Hymns amounted to a considerable number. And my deference to the judgment and desires of others, has at length overcome the reluctance I long felt to see them in print, while I had so few of my friend's hymns to insert in the collection. Though it is possible a good judge of composition might be able to distinguish those which are his, I have thought it proper to preclude a misapplication, by prefixing the letter C to each of them. For the rest I must be responsible.

There is a style and manner suited to the composition of hymns, which may be more successfully, or at least more easily, attained by a versifier, than by a poet. They should be _Hymns_, not _Odes_, if designed for public worship, and for the use of plain people. Perspicuity, simplicity, and ease, should be chiefly attended to; and the imagery and colouring of poetry, if admitted at all, should be indulged very sparingly, and with great judgment. The late Dr. Watts, many of whose hymns are admirable patterns in this species of writing, might, as a poet, have a right to say, that it cost him some labour to restrain his fire, and to accommodate himself to the capacities of common readers. But it would not become me to make such a declaration. It behoved me to do my best. But though I would not offend readers of taste by a wilful coarseness and negligence, I do not write professedly for them. If the Lord, whom I serve, has been pleased to favour me with that mediocrity of talent, which may qualify me for usefulness to the weak and the poor of his flock, without quite disgusting persons of superior discernment, I have reason to be satisfied.

As the workings of the heart of man, and of the Spirit of God, are in general the same in all who are the subjects of grace, I hope most of these hymns, being the fruit and expression of my own experience, will coincide with the views of real Christians of all denominations. But I cannot expect that every sentiment I have advanced will be universally approved. However, I am not conscious of having written a single line with an intention either to flatter or to offend any party or person upon earth. I have simply declared my own views and feelings, as I might have done if I had composed hymns in some of the newly-discovered islands in the South Sea, where no person had any knowledge of the name of Jesus, but myself. I am a friend of peace; and being deeply convinced that no one can profitably understand the great truths and doctrines of the gospel any further than he is taught of God, I have not a wish to obtrude my own tenets upon others, in a way of controversy; yet I do not think myself bound to conceal them. Many gracious persons, (for many such I am persuaded there are,) who differ from me, more or less, in those points which are called Calvinistic, appear desirous that the Calvinists should, for their sakes, studiously avoid every expression which they cannot approve. Yet few of them, I believe, impose a like restraint upon themselves, but think the importance of what they deem to be truth justifies them in speaking their sentiments plainly and strongly. May I not plead for an equal liberty? The views I have received of the doctrines of grace are essential to my peace; I could not live comfortably a day, or an hour, without them. I likewise believe, yea, so far as my poor attainments warrant me to speak, I know them to be friendly to holiness, and to have a direct influence in producing and maintaining a gospel conversation; and therefore I must not be ashamed of them.

The Hymns are distributed into three books. In the first I have classed those which are formed upon select passages of Scripture, and placed them in the order of the books of the Old and New Testament. The second contains Occasional Hymns, suited to particular seasons, or suggested by particular events or subjects. The third book is miscellaneous, comprising a variety of subjects relative to a life of faith in the Son of God, which have no express reference either to a single text of Scripture, or to any determinate season or incident. These are further subdivided into distinct heads. This arrangement is not so accurate but that several of the Hymns might have been differently disposed. Some attention to method may be found convenient; though a logical exactness was hardly practicable. As some subjects in the several books are nearly coincident, I have, under the divisions in the third book, pointed out those which are similar in the two former. And I have likewise here and there, in the first and second, made a reference to hymns of a like import in the third.

This publication, which, with my humble prayer to the Lord for his blessing upon it, I offer to the service and acceptance of all who love the Lord Jesus Christ in sincerity, of every name and in every place, into whose hands it may come, I more particularly dedicate to my dear friends in the parish and neighbourhood of Olney, for whose use the Hymns were originally composed; and as a testimony of the sincere love I bear them, and as a token of my gratitude to the Lord and to them, for the comfort and satisfaction with which the discharge of my ministry among them has been attended.

The hour is approaching, and, at my time of life, cannot be very distant, when my heart, my pen, and my tongue, will not longer be able to move in their service. But I trust, while my heart continues to beat, it will feel a warm desire for the prosperity of their souls; and while my hand can write, and my tongue speak, it will be the business and the pleasure of my life, to aim at promoting their growth and establishment in the grace of our God and Saviour. To this precious grace I commend them, and earnestly entreat them, and all who love his name, to strive mightily with their prayers to God for me, that I may be preserved faithful to the end, and enabled at last to finish my course with joy.

JOHN NEWTON.

Olney, Bucks, February 15, 1779.

13
The Nineteenth Century

Reginald Heber (1783-1826)

REGINALD Heber was ordained in the Church of England in 1807, and served as vicar at Hodnet, Shropshire (1807-1823) and Bishop of Calcutta, India (1823-1826). Even as a student, Heber was noted for the excellence of his poetry. A number of his hymns were published in a monthly magazine, the *Christian Observer*, between 1811 and 1816. Heber's collection of *Hymns Written and Adapted to the Weekly Church Service of the Year* was published posthumously in 1827. Among his best-known hymns are "Holy, holy, holy, Lord God almighty" and "From Greenland's icy mountains." Though signed "D. R.," the following letter to the editor of the *Christian Observer* refers to hymns written by Heber, since the texts accompanying the letter were all his work. The letter reveals Heber's interest in the liturgical use of hymns, as well as his distaste for the intimate imagery of some contemporary hymns.

57 Letter to the Editor of *The Christian Observer* (London, October, 1811). *Source: The Christian Observer, conducted by Members of the Established Church, for the year 1811. Being the tenth volume. From the London edition* (Boston: William Wells and T. B. Wait and Co., 1812), p. 630.

To the Editor of the Christian Observer.
The following hymns are part of an intended series, appropriate to the Sundays and principal holydays of the year; connected in some degree with their particular Collects and Gospels, and designed to be sung between the Nicene Creed and the Sermon.—The effect of an arrangement of this kind, though only partially adopted, is very

striking in the Romish liturgy; and its place should seem to be very imperfectly supplied by a few verses of a Psalm, entirely unconnected with the peculiar devotions of the day, and selected at the discretion of a clerk or organist. On the merits of the present imperfect essays, the author is unaffectedly diffident; and as his labours are intended for the use of his own congregation, he will be thankful for any suggestion which may advance or correct them. In one respect at least, he hopes that the following poems will not be found reprehensible;—no fulsome or indecorous language has been knowingly adopted: no erotic addresses to Him whom no unclean lip can approach; no allegory ill understood, and worse applied. It is not enough, in his opinion, to object to such expressions, that they are fanatical: they are positively profane. When our Saviour was on earth, and in great humility conversant with mankind; when he sat at the tables, and washed the feet, and healed the diseases of his creatures; yet did not his disciples give him any more familiar name than Master, or Lord. And now, at the right hand of his Father's Majesty, shall we address him with ditties of embraces and passion, or language which it would be disgraceful in an earthly sovereign to endure? Such expressions, it is said, are taken from Scripture: but even if the original application, which is often doubtful, were clearly and unequivocally ascertained, yet though the collective Christian church may very properly be personified as the spouse of Christ, an application of such language to individual believers is as dangerous as it is absurd and unauthorized. Nor is it going too far to assert, that the brutalities of a common swearer can hardly bring religion into more sure contempt, or more scandalously profane the Name which is above every name in heaven and earth, than certain epithets applied to Christ in our popular collections of religious poetry.

D. R.

Jonathan Gray (19th century)

In 1810, an English minister, Thomas Cotterill, published *A Selection of Psalms and Hymns for Public and Private Use*. The book ran through several editions and, in 1819, an enlarged eighth edition was published with the assistance of James Montgomery. The evangelical tenor of this edition and Cotterill's attempt to introduce it into his own congregation in Sheffield provoked considerable controversy, however, ultimately leading to a suit against the minister in the Consistory Court of the Archbishop of York. The basic premise of the suit was that the singing of hymns had never been duly authorized by the Church of England, and that only the metrical psalms of the Old and New Versions were permitted in worship. As indicated by Jonathan Gray's recounting of the proceedings, which includes a lengthy quotation of the decision handed down by the Chancellor of the Court, a compromise was reached in which Cotterill's book was withdrawn and a new one prepared and paid for by the Archbishop. While the compromise did not much benefit Cotterill, it did establish hymn singing as a legitimate activity in the Church of England and sounded the death knell for the "psalms only" approach to congregational singing among Anglicans.

58   Section VI from _An Inquiry into Historical Facts, Relative to Parochial Psalmody_ (York: J. Wolsten-holme, 1821), pp. 46-53.

PROCEEDINGS IN THE CONSISTORY COURT OF YORK, IN THE CAUSE OF HOLY AND WARD, _V._ THE REV. THOMAS COTTERILL.
The circumstances of this suit merit a detail, as immediately connected with our subject. In 1818, the Rev. Thomas Cotterill, Minister of St. Paul's Church, Sheffield, compiled a Selection of Psalms and Hymns for his Church. It is one of the most copious of modern selections; and contains a number of well-known and approved sacred hymns, and versions of psalms; besides several original compositions, by Mr. Montgomery. But an opposition was stirred up against its introduction, and a suit prosecuted against Mr. Cotterill on the subject. The Cause came on to be heard on the 6th July, 1820, in the Consistory Court of the Archbishop of York, before Granville Venables Vernon, Esq. Chancellor of the Church. It may here be proper to remark, that the Consistory Court of the Archbishop of York, is independent of any of the Courts of the province of Canterbury, and that there is no appeal from this Court, except to the King; in which event, the matter is referred to the Court of Delegates.

The fact of Mr. Cotterill's introduction of a Selection of Hymns into his Church, being admitted on his part, Counsel were heard on both sides, relative to the legality or illegality of their introduction.

Mr. Vernon then observed, that this was a very important question; and he should take time before he pronounced upon it.

There was, perhaps, not a Clergyman in the kingdom who had not violated the law, if Mr. Cotterill had done so. He presumed the prosecutors could have no universal objections to Hymns and Psalms, but only to some parts of this Selection. He was not called on to advert to the individual Selection; but, certainly it contained a great many extremely edifying and excellent Hymns and Psalms, to which there could, he conceived, be no reasonable objection. He had not himself noticed any of a different description.—He could much wish that some agreement might be come to. He could not conceive that the Clergyman would wish to press any particular parts of that Selection, which might be objected to by any individuals.

Mr. Vernon added, that the Archbishop would be happy to act as mediator between the parties; and he thought it much for the interests of religion that a compromise should take place. The Court then adjourned.

On the 28th of the same month, Mr. Vernon pronounced the Judgment of the Court in this important cause, as follows:—

"The question for my decision is upon the admissibility of articles, imputing to the Rev. Mr. Cotterill, the Minister of St. Paul's, Sheffield, irregularity in introducing and causing to be sung in his church, certain Hymns and a version of Psalms, not permitted by any lawful authority.

"This question, as I before intimated, is of so much importance, as it bears on the practice adopted by a majority of the Established Clergy, that I think it due to them to discuss it with some minuteness. So much advantage accrues from the prevalent usage of introducing into the church service Hymns and versions of Psalms, more edifying and acceptable to the congregations than any compositions which have obtained the sanction of competent authority, that I should have gladly evaded the necessity of deciding the legality of this usage; because the objection which has been urged to it, that it would engender laxity of practice and schism in opinion, I consider of little moment: since any irregularity or impropriety, which may characterise such compositions, would form a substantive ground either of prohibition by the Diocesan, or of criminal procedure in this Court. It is not, however, on the base of public policy or convenience that I must found my judgment, but on considerations strictly legal; and in this view I am bound to say that this Article is admissible.

"The argument has branched into two directions: first, the effect of the prohibition under the Statutes of Uniformity—secondly, the restrictive operation of Ecclesiastical Supremacy. With respect to the statutory restraint, it would, as I observed on a former occasion, apply as much to the versions of the Psalms, commonly called the authorised versions, as to the present selection; because no exception is made either in the Statute 12 Car. II. or 1 Eliz. in favour of any allowance of Ecclesiastical authority; and if they were to be construed strictly, they would not only render illegal the power which has been habitually exercised by the Sovereign, of permitting the use of various versions of Psalms, but _a fortiori_, the introduction under the same sanction of occasional prayers and thanksgiving. I consider the clause in the Statute 2 and 3 E. VI. which provided 'that it shall be lawful for all men, as well in churches, chapels, oratories, or other places, to use openly any Psalm or Prayer taken out of the Bible at any due time, not letting or omitting the service or any part thereof,' to be still in force, as being revived by the Statute 1 Eliz.: but this would give no protection to any version of the Psalms except the prose version established by the act, and much less to any Hymn. There is, indeed, one period of the service at which Anthems are expressly permitted; but the construction of this word must be limited to literal extracts from the Bible or Liturgy. This may be collected as well from the practice in the Cathedral Anthem books, as from the use of the word in the Preface to the Prayer book. There is but one exception which I am aware of, and that is in favour of an anthem, the words of which were composed by Henry VIII. which bore, therefore, the stamp of Supremacy at its birth. In the preface to the Liturgy it is stated, that Anthems, Responds, and Invitatories, which interrupted the reading of the Scriptures, be cut off: which referred to the practice in the Romish Church of chanting the Lessons in parts, with interpolations of _Ave Maria, Venite exultemus_, etc.

"It is however clear that these Statutes are not to be construed so rigidly, as to exclude from divine service all intervention of musical performances, nor would such performances subject the Clergy to penalties in the temporal Courts. There is a case in one of the old reports in the reign of Car. II. in which it was held, that the Clergyman was not subject to the penal operation of the Statute of Uniformity, by the introduction of a voluntary prayer before the sermon. Moreover, the uncontested permissions accorded from time to time by our Monarchs, for the reception, by congregations, of various versions of the Psalms, raise a strong presumption, that their performance was not restrained by any Statute.

"But these permissions are yet more important, with reference to the second branch of the argument, the restrictive operation of Ecclesiastical supremacy. If the grant of those permissions was not purely gratuitous, or an arbitrary assumption of controlling jurisdiction, we must infer from them that all versions of Psalms destitute of similar sanction are illegal. For the version of Sternhold and Hopkins, notwithstanding the preference assigned to it by the learned Bishop Horsley, I can discover no regular authority, though perhaps it may be presumed from immemorial unquestioned usage. The question of their insertion as part of the Liturgy, established by 2 and 3 E. VI. was then debated in Parliament, and carried in the negative. A version of the nine first Psalms, by Dodd, was privileged by James I, in 1603, and he himself composed a version of the whole, which was recommended, as well as allowed, by his successor. The version of Tate and Brady, was sanctioned by King William III. in Council, and recommended by the Bishop of London to the use of his Clergy. There is, lastly, another sanction in the reign of George I. granted by the Lords' Justices, representing him in Council, to the version of Sir R. Blackmore; and this is the more remakable, because not only did he, as Tate and Brady had done before, petition the Sovereign for this bare permission, but the major part of the Bench of Bishops concurred in a Certificate, 'approving and recommending it to the King's allowance.' Now these versions were not even recommended by the King, much less imposed on Congregations—they were only 'allowed and permitted to be used in all such churches, chapels, and congregations, as shall think fit to receive the same.' This is a decisive indication of the opinion of the Composers that such sanction was required, and of the Bishops, that even their approbation would not suffice, to authorise their introduction in their respective Dioceses. In 1559, Queen Elizabeth issued some injunctions, relative to the practice of the church, in which this provision occurs:—'It may be permitted, that in the beginning or end of common prayer, either at morning or evening, there may be sung an hymn, or such like song, to the praise of Almighty God'—but this was addressed solely to Collegiate Churches.

"It seems then, on the whole, that for whatever may be supplementary to the Liturgy established by Statute, and not repugnant thereto, authority must emanate from the head of the Church. Formerly that was in practice, as well as in right, the King and Convocation; but the functions and authority of the latter fell into neglect, after it ceased to hold the purse-strings of the Clergy—and some disputes between the High Church and Low Church parties in the reign of King William, gave the last blow to its active existence. During the last century, its voluntary jurisdiction in spiritual matters has been exercised by the King in Council, and nothing can be permitted to intervene in the service of the church without that, or legislative authority.

"It is however fit that it should be understood, that no advantage can be taken for the purposes of vexation, of this construction of the law. The Court may be called upon to exercise its controlling jurisdiction, and to admonish the party who may deviate from the limits which I have traced out; but it will never condemn in costs in such cases, except where very peculiar circumstances shall aggravate the technical irregularity into an offence—and I think it my duty to state, even in the present state of these proceedings, that no such circumstances exist here. I feel that the promoters of these articles were fairly entitled to a decision of the legal question to the best of my judgment, but if they proceed to call for sentence in this cause, and decline the mediation which I before suggested, I shall consider them as wanting not only in a sense of their own interest, but in a regard to Christian charity and practical religion."

The parties, agreeably to Mr. Vernon's suggestion, ultimately referred the dispute to the amicable adjustment of the Archbishop; who, in a spirit of conciliation, undertook to compile a new Selection of Psalms and Hymns for Mr. Cotterill's Church; and in consideration of the expence and loss which Mr. Cotterill's Work had occasioned to him, his Grace further took upon himself the charges of printing the new Selection.

This circumstance, while it is honourable to the character of the Archbishop of York, exhibiting him as the promoter of peace and union in the Church; affords an additional testimony, in favour of the modern practice of introducing into the Church, selections of Psalms and Hymns, accommodated to the popular taste and feeling.

James Montgomery (1771-1854)

James Montgomery, the son of a Moravian preacher, was born in Scotland, but spent most of his life in England. In

1792, he became an employee of a newspaper, the _Sheffield Register_. Montgomery took over the periodical in 1794, changing its name to the _Sheffield Iris_. He edited the paper for thirty-one years, relinquishing ownership in 1825. Montgomery wrote about 400 hymns, among which were "Angels from the realms of glory" and "Go to dark Gethsemane." He edited the eighth edition of Thomas Cotterill's _Selection of Psalms and Hymns_ (1819) and published _Songs of Zion_ (1822), _The Christian Psalmist_ (1825), and _Original Hymns_ (1853).

The "Introductory Note" to _The Christian Psalmist_ contained one of the earliest historical surveys of English hymnody. In the portion of the essay reprinted below, Montgomery also pointed out some of the characteristics of good hymn writing and expressed his dismay at the lack of craftsmanship exhibited in the hymns of some earlier and contemporary authors.

59   From "Introductory Essay" to _The Christian Psalmist_, 5th ed. (Glasgow: William Collins, 1828), pp. xiv-xvii.

A hymn ought to be as regular in its structure as any other poem; it should have a distinct subject, and that subject should be simple, not complicated, so that whatever skill or labour might be required in the author to develope his plan, there should be little or none required on the part of the reader to understand it. Consequently, a hymn must have a beginning, middle, and end. There should be a manifest gradation in the thoughts, and their mutual dependence should be so perceptible, that they could not be transposed without injuring the unity of the piece; every line carrying forward the connection and every verse adding a well-proportioned limb to a symmetrical body. The reader should know when the strain is complete, and be satisfied, as at the close of an air in music; while defects and superfluities should be felt by him as annoyances, in whatever part they might occur. The practice of many good men, in framing hymns, has been quite the contrary. They have begun apparently with the only idea in their mind at the time; another, with little relationship to the former, has been forced upon them by a refractory rhyme; a third became necessary to eke out a verse, a fourth to begin one; and so on, till, having compiled a sufficient number of stanzas of so many lines, and lines of so many syllables, the operation has been suspended; whereas it might, with equal consistency, have been continued to any imaginable length, and the tenth or ten thousandth link might have been struck out, or changed places with any other, without the slightest infraction of the chain; the whole being a series of independent verses, collocated as they came, and the burden a cento of phrases, figures, and ideas, the common property of every writer who had none of his own, and therefore found in the works of each, unimproved, if not unimpaired, from generation to generation.—Such rhapsodies may be sung from time to time, and keep alive devotion already kindled; but they leave no trace in the memory, make no impression on the heart, and fall through the mind as sounds glide through the ear,—pleasant, it may be, in their passage, but never returning to haunt the imagination in retirement, or, in the multitude of the thoughts, to refresh the soul. Of how contrary a character, how transcendently superior in value as well as in influence, are those hymns, which, once heard, are remembered without effort, remembered involuntarily, yet remembered with renewed and increasing delight at every revival! It may be safely affirmed, that the permanent favourites in every collection are those, which, in the requisites before-mentioned, or for some other peculiar excellence, are distinguished above the rest. This is so remarkably the case with the compositions of Watts, Wesley, and Newton, the most prolific writers of this class, that no farther illustration is needful than a recurrence to their pages, when it will be found, that the most neglected are generally inferior in literary merit to the most hackneyed ones, which are in every body's mouth, and every body's heart.

It may be added, that authors, who devote their talents to the glory of God, and the salvation of men, ought surely to take as much pains to polish and perfect their offerings of this kind, as secular and profane poets bestow upon their works. Of these, the subjects are too often of the baser sort, and the workmanship as frequently excels the material; while, on the other hand, the inestimable materials of hymns,—the truths of the everlasting Gospel, the very thoughts of God, the very sayings of Christ, the very inspirations of the Holy Ghost, are dishonoured by the meanness of the workmanship employed upon them; wood, hay, straw, and stubble, being built upon foundations which ought only to support gold, silver, and precious stones; work that will bear the fire, and be purified by it. The faults in ordinary hymns are vulgar phrases, low words, hard words, technical terms, inverted construction, broken syntax, barbarous abbreviations, that make our beautiful English horrid even to the eye, bad rhymes, or no rhymes where rhymes are expected, but above all, numbers without cadence. A line is no more metre because it contains a certain concatenation of syllables, than so many crotchets and quavers, pricked at random, would constitute a bar of music. The syllables in every division ought to "ripple like a rivulet," one producing another as its natural effect, while the rhythm of each line, falling into the general stream at its proper place, should cause the verse to flow in progressive melody, deepening and expanding like a river to the close; or, to change the figure, each stanza should be a poetical tune, played down to the last note. Such subservience of every part to the harmony of the whole, is required in all other legitimate poetry, and why it should not be observed in that which is worthiest of all possible pre-eminence, it would be difficult to say; why it is so rarely found in hymns, may be accounted for from the circumstance already stated, that few accomplished poets have enriched their mother tongue with strains of this description.

Thomas Helmore (1811-1890)

Thomas Helmore, an ordained priest in the Church of England, played a major role in the revival of plainsong in the Anglican communion. An important part of his work was arranging and adapting ancient chant melodies to accompany translations of medieval Latin hymns by John Mason Neale and others. One of Helmore's most significant publications was *The Hymnal Noted*, issued in two parts in 1852 and 1854. This included the first modern printings of DIVINUM MYSTERIUM, VENI EMMANUEL, and a number of other chant melodies found in recent hymnals. Helmore observed that the translation and adaptation of Latin hymnody had been part of the early English reformers' plan, but the task had been left incomplete due to its difficulty. He also claimed that, while the pieces in the book could be sung by various choral combinations, the most appropriate vehicle for the performance of his chant arrangements was the voice of the whole congregation.

60   Preface to _Accompanying Harmonies to the Hymnal
           Noted_ (London: Novello & Co., 1852), pp. [i]-iv.

The present volume completes the first portion of a work designed
to supply the acknowledged want of an English Hymnal. The
omission, at the Reformation, of one entire portion of the ancient
ritual treasured up in the Latin devotional books of Western
Christendom—the source from which our Book of Common Prayer
is derived—though necessary, could not be otherwise than injurious;
and although the course which for a time involved this palpable loss
to all who could understand the Latin Hymns, was the only
apparent alternative for the avoiding of greater evils, it must be
allowed that the translation into English of the really Catholic
Hymns, in such wise as to be capable of being sung to the old
Catholic tunes, was a work second only in importance to the
translation of the Psalter, the Offices, and the Liturgy, and their
adaptation to those holy strains in which, for many generations, the
incense of Prayer and Praise had (with no material change from the
forms of the early Church) ascended to the Throne of God.

The Reformers of the English Church, it is well known, desired
that these Hymns should be translated, as well as other portions of
the old Prayer Books. But it was not so easy a task to translate
verse as prose into the "tongue understanded of the people;" and
although the English version of the "Veni Creator Spiritus" in the
Ordering of Priests and Consecration of Bishops, as well as the
subsequent printing of Withers' Hymns (as it is asserted) by order
of Convocation, are plain manifestations of the wishes of the Rulers
of the Reformed English Church at two distinct periods of her
history, that she should have an authorised Hymnody, yet the too
general apathy, both of the clergy and of the laity, with regard to
ritual matters, combined with that secularity and torpor, which are
the natural results of the suppression of her discipline and
legitimate government, have hitherto prevented any such expansion
of her formularies by competent authority, as should include a
definite and satisfactory provision for this important part of
Christian worship.

The revival of Church principles, which has, by the grace of
God, so materially altered the present condition and the future
prospects of the English Communion, and of her affiliated
Churches, has at length turned the attention of many of her sons to

this long-neglected source of spiritual illumination and comfort. Individual exertions have been concentrated, and with the co-operation and under the sanction of the Ecclesiological Society, an attempt has been made by the Editors, not without painful consciousness both of the difficulty of the work, and their own responsibility, to supply the want so generally felt, by the preparation of the present Hymnal Noted, and its Accompanying Harmonies.

Some of the Hymns of the ancient Church, and principally of the Sarum Service-books, are here translated and set to their old melodies. Others are in preparation, and will form, when completed, a second part, giving greater variety and precision to the scheme of the work, which assigns each hymn to definite periods in the course of the Christian year.

The Hymnal is published in three forms:—the Words; the hymnal Noted; and Accompanying Harmonies.

I.—The English Words by themselves, in a cheap edition, for general use.

II.—The English words Noted, for the use of all who sing,—printed to correspond with the Directory, Psalter, and Canticles Noted, in the Manual of Plain Song, 18mo. edition.

III.—The present volume of Accompanying Harmonies, for the use of organists and others who play, and also for any who may find it expedient to add vocal harmonies to the Canto-fermo of the Hymnal.

For all the harmonies not individually attributed to others, the Editor of the music is himself responsible, as well as for the general form and style of arrangement.

To those kind friends, by whose compositions a greater variety is given to the work, as well as to all others by whose advice and encouragement it has been rendered less unworthy of admission into the solemn Service to which it is dedicated, the Editors desire to return their most hearty thanks—especially to the Rev. Samuel Stevenson Greatheed, M.A., late Fellow of Trinity College, Cambridge; to Charles Child Spencer, Esq.; to the Rev. W. I. Irons, B.D., for the words of "Coelestis urbs" and "Dies Irae;" to all others who have assisted us with translations or criticisms; and to Mr. Masters for his kind permission to reprint Mr. Spencer's harmony of the latter of the two above-named hymns.

The style of harmonization adopted is that founded upon the

Church scales, and brought to its highest perfection in the fifteenth and sixteenth centuries. While this is deemed in general more strictly suited to, and illustrative of, the genius of the melodies, the Editor would wish it to be considered, by skilful musicians, rather as suggestive of the received mode of accompanying the Canto-fermo, than as restricting them to the same harmony throughout all the verses of any hymn. An examination of the melodies themselves will be the best guide to that harmony of which, by the eternal and unchangeable laws of nature, all melody is but one part. The same melody may, however, be consistent with several progressions of harmony, and the most obvious (or, in other words, common-place) of these is not, it may be suggested, the most suitable for devotional purposes. Hence arises the peculiar advantage of the Church style; it does not oppose nature, but by artificial restrictions, relations, and combinations, raises and refines it, as in all other things, searching out hidden mysteries, and revealing that which is least discoverable to a superficial observation.

The Accompaniment of the first verse of each Hymn is here printed in the usual notation of Gregorian organ music (first used by V. Novello and S. Wesley), of which it will suffice to observe, that the lines drawn through the stems of minims do not indicate any increased speed of execution, and that the accent of the music is to be learnt from that of the words. The signature, in case of transposition, is guided by the following rule:—

IN TRANSPOSING MUSIC WRITTEN IN THE ANCIENT CHURCH MODES, FIND ON WHAT NOTE OF THE ALTERED SCALE THE DO (OR UT, OR C) OF THE ORIGINAL SCALE WILL FALL AND THE SIGNATURE OF THE TRANSPOSED KEY WILL BE THAT OF THE MODERN MAJOR SCALE OF THAT NOTE.

The Hymnal Noted stands (in a musical view) upon similar ground to that of the other restorations of the Gregorian music, or Canto-fermo, in the books before-mentioned. These books, printed in the Church notation, and restoring melodies, the antiquity of which reaches back, in many cases, *certainly* as far as any written records are left us, *probably* to the age of King David, and the first building of the Temple, claim to be, in a sense which no other music can be, the music of the Church. It has been, from time to time, set in order by learned and holy divines and musicians, and appointed by the authority, and consecrated by the use of the Catholic Church for many centuries at least, and some of it probably from the Apostolic times. Other music may be written for use in the Church, and tolerated, or approved of, or even preferred by individuals; but individual tastes are not the official and lawful exponents of the Church's will, and not one canon, rubric, or direction of the Church acting in her corporate capacity, has given formal authority to any other than the Canto-fermo or Gregorian music of the Western Church. And though the Editor would be one of the last to give up the license permitted of using in some portions of the Divine Service a more ornate and figurate style of composition, he claims for this simple music a restoration to its proper functions in the Church, feeling convinced that this is the surest means both of enlivening the true devotions of God's servants, and preparing us all for making a due choice, and use, of that more elaborate music for the choir, which too many would use throughout our Offices to the exclusion of this, which is emphatically, music for the people.

The Preface to the Accompanying Harmonies of the Psalter Noted may be referred to as giving such a general view of the doctrine of the Church Modes, and explanations of the Tones used for the Psalms, as may serve to introduce the subject to the students of Church Plain Song; and the brief notice prefixed to both editions of the Psalter and Canticles Noted, is a sufficient guide, if properly understood, to the right use of the Gregorian note used in those works and in this. But as many persons have found that notice too brief, a more full explanation is appended to this Preface, together with some few hints as to the manner in which the melodies of the Hymnal should be read.

In conclusion it may be observed that the present work is specially intended to furnish the means of various modes of musical performance, as, *e.g.* it may be sung in four parts, in the usual mode of choir harmony, with the melody in the Treble; or, in the same manner, with a Tenor reduplication of the melody in the octave below (as is always done in modern congregational use, though not as a recognized and legitimate mode for which the music is professedly arranged); or by men's voices only, with the melody in the Tenor; or, by a chorus of men's voices in unison, with organ accompaniment; or, by a chorus of Treble voices in unison, with organ, as before; or, by Trebles and men's voices in octaves, and accompanied with the organ; or, again, in either of the last three cases, a choral accompaniment, by a properly balanced choir, might be substituted for the organ. The Canto-fermo given in the Hymnal Noted is, however, alone suited, at present, for the people in general, as being best adapted to the immediate wants of most churches, and to the tastes of many devout Christians, to whom, for aid in singing themselves, a perfect balance of vocal parts is often nearly useless, and consequently a source rather of distraction and annoyance, than of edification and delight.

Nor is this feeling to be deprecated as being confined to the less musical members of the Church, for many testimonies can be adduced of such a mode of harmonic treatment being preferred by persons of undoubted musical taste, while instances are not wanting of musicians and composers of the greatest eminence, having been deeply affected by the simple grandeur of congregational unison.

What is principally needed in the execution of this style of music is vigor, concentrated power, and massiveness of effect, only to be obtained from large numbers of singers; and it may be safely asserted, that had not our people been so long deprived of music suited for such purposes, there would never have been cause for the complaints now unhappily all but universal—that in the Church of England there is no congregational singing. The modern cathedral music, intended exclusively for choirs, does not aim at producing—and the ordinary metrical psalmody has notoriously failed in sustaining—any such grand congregational effects; while the adoption in some places of an unecclesiastical, and secularized style, suited to the worst popular taste, and vulgar feeling, cannot too strongly be reprobated, as tending to bring down to the level of mere ordinary musical enjoyment, that portion of our worship on earth, which ought most to unite us to that of heaven.

John Mason Neale (1818-1866)

John Mason Neale was ordained a deacon in the Anglican church in 1841 and a priest in 1842; he spent most of his ministry serving as warden of Sackville College, East Grinstead, a home for elderly men. A subscriber to the principles of the Oxford Movement, Neale's primary service to the cause and to hymnody lay in his translations of early Greek and Latin hymns. His translations of "O come, O come, Emmanuel," "Of the Father's love begotten," "All glory, laud, and honor," "The day of resurrection," and other ancient hymns have achieved a secure place in modern hymnals. Two of his most important publications were _Medieval Hymns and Sequences_ (1851, 1853) and _Hymns of the Eastern Church_ (1862). The preface to the latter reflects on the neglect of Greek hymnody by the English church and the difficulties encountered by the translator. Neale also makes a pointed observation about hymnal compilers who used his translations without first asking permission.

61   Preface to _Hymns of The Eastern Church_ (London: J. T. Hayes, 1862), pp. [xi]-xvi.

The following Translations have occupied a portion of my leisure time for the last twelve years: and some of them have already appeared in more than one ecclesiastical periodical. So has also great part of the Introduction.

It is a most remarkable fact, and one which shows how very little interest has been hitherto felt in the Eastern Church, that these are literally, I believe, the only English versions of any part of the treasures of Oriental Hymnology. There is scarcely a first or second-rate hymn of the Roman Breviary which has not been translated: of many we have six or eight versions. The eighteen quarto volumes of Greek Church-poetry can only at present be known to the English reader by my little book.

Yet surely, if in the future Hymnal of the English Church we are to build an eclectic superstructure on the foundation of the Sarum Book, the East ought to yield its full share of compositions. And hence, I cannot but marvel that the compilers of eclectic Hymnals, such as the (modern) Sarum, the _Hymns, Ancient and Modern_, and others, have never turned to this source. Here was a noble field open to them; and to me it is incomprehensible that they should have so utterly neglected it.

There are difficulties in the task to which it is as well to advert. Though the superior terseness and brevity of the Latin Hymns renders a translation which shall represent those qualities a work of great labour, yet still the versifier has the help of the same metre; his version may be line for line; and there is a great analogy between the Collects and the Hymns, most helpful to the translator. Above all, we have examples enough of former translation by which we may take pattern.

But in attempting a Greek Canon, from the fact of its being in prose,—(metrical Hymns, as the   reader   will   learn,   are unknown,)—one is all at sea. What measure shall we employ? why this more than that? Might we attempt the rhythmical prose of the original, and design it to be chanted? Again, the great length of the Canons renders them unsuitable for our churches, as *wholes*. Is it better simply to form centos of the more beautiful passages? or can separate Odes, each necessarily imperfect, be employed as separate Hymns? And above all, we have no pattern or example of any kind to direct our labour.

These questions, and many others, have as yet received no reply; but will in time, no doubt, work out their answer. My own belief is, that the best way to employ Greek Hymnology for the uses of the English Church, would be by centos.

The reader will find, in the following pages, examples of different methods of treatment. The following are short *Idiomela*, &c. which might serve as separate Hymns:

5. *The day is past and over.* (Evening.)
20. *O the mystery, passing wonder.* (Maundy Thursday.)
28. *Christian! dost thou see them.* (A Sunday in Lent.)
35. *By fruit the ancient Foe's device.* (Easter Tide.)
65. *Those eternal bowers.* (All Saints.)
84. *The choirs of ransomed Israel.* (Transfiguration.)
124. *Are thy toils and woes increasing.* (Passion or Holy Week.)

Centos might perhaps be made from

The Canon for Easter,		p. 42.
"	Low Sunday,	p. 53.
"	Christmas,	p. 69.
"	Lent,	p. 24.
"	"	p. 107.

It has been with great thankfulness that I have seen such copious use made of my Mediaeval Hymns, and my Rhythm of S. Bernard, in so many modern Hymnals. Permission has usually been most courteously asked: though in some few cases, whole Hymns have been taken without the slightest request for leave, or subsequent acknowledgment. I would therefore request any compiler of a Hymnal who may wish to quote from the following pages, to be so kind as first to express that wish to the publisher, or to myself.

I trust the reader will not forget the immense difficulty of an attempt so perfectly new as the present, where I have had no predecessors, and therefore could have no master. If I have opened the way for others to do better what I have done imperfectly, I shall have every reason to be thankful. I have kept most of the

translations by me for at least the nine years recommended by
Horace; and now offer them as a contribution to the hymnology of
our own Church. And while fully sensible of their imperfections, I
may yet (by way of excuse rather than of boast) say, almost in
Bishop Hall's words—

     "I first adventure: follow me who list,

     "And be the second Eastern Melodist."

SACKVILLE COLLEGE,

   Feast of the Epiphany, 1862

14
The Twentieth Century

Ralph Vaughan Williams (1872-1958)

RALPH Vaughan Williams was the most prominent English composer of the first half of the twentieth century. His works included symphonies, operas, concertos, music for ballets, incidental music, songs, and church music. Many of these pieces were national in character. Among these were works based on English scenes (*London Symphony*), literature (*Pilgrim's Progress*), traditional tunes (*Five Variants of "Dives and Lazarus"*), and music by earlier English composers (*Fantasia on a Theme by Thomas Tallis*). In addition to composing anthems and service music for the English church, Vaughan Williams served as musical editor for the *English Hymnal* (1906). This book had a tremendous impact on subsequent hymnals in both England and America, and its wide-ranging editorial policies became standard on both sides of the Atlantic. The *English Hymnal* also introduced a number of new tunes into common use, including Vaughan Williams's SINE NOMINE—attributed to "Anonymous" in the first edition—and his arrangement of the English traditional melody KINGSFOLD.

In the section of the preface dealing with the music of the hymnal, Vaughan Williams noted that his goal was to provide a collection of tunes directed at the congregation rather than the choir and to include music of the highest possible quality, be it simple or complex. He also explained why the pitches of many tunes had been lowered and that the congregtion should always sing the melody in unison—two features that were highly influential on later hymnals. Finally, he demonstrated the eclectic nature of the book by listing the basic sources from which the melodies were drawn.

62   From Preface to _The English Hymnal with Tunes_
(Oxford: The University Press, 1906), pp. x-xvii.

THE MUSIC

The music of this hymnal is divided into two main sections; the
plainsong melodies and the comparatively modern music. The
modern music only is dealt with here. The plainsong is discussed
separately.

The Choice of Material.

The music is intended to be essentially congregational in
character, and this end has been kept in view both in the choice of
tunes and in the manner of setting them out. Fine melody rather
than the exploitation of a trained choir has been the criterion of
selection: the pitch of each tune has been kept as low as is
consistent with the character of the melody.

Where there is congregational singing it is important that
familiar melodies should be employed, or at least those which have
stood the test of time: therefore the "specially composed
tune"—that bane of many a hymnal—has been avoided as far as
possible.   There are already many hundreds of fine tunes in
existence, so many indeed that it is impossible to include more than
a small part of them in any one collection.

The task of providing congregations with familiar tunes is
difficult; for, unfortunately, many of the tunes of the present day
which have become familiar and, probably merely from association,
popular with congregations are quite unsuitable to their purpose.
More often than not they are positively harmful to those who sing
and hear them. The committee were therefore placed in the hard
position of having to decide whether they should risk momentary
unpopularity by discarding certain tunes, or whether they should
sacrifice the greater ultimate good for the lesser and more
immediate advantage. The problem, however, solved itself in a
happy and unforeseen manner because the insertion of several of
the tunes in question was not allowed by the owners of the
copyright. Thus the committee, while regretting that they are not
able for a few years to include such beautiful tunes as Dykes'
"Dominus regit me" or Stainer's "In Memoriam", yet feel that
nothing but gain can result from the exclusion of certain other
tunes, which are worthy neither of the congregations who sing them,

the occasions on which they are sung, nor the composers who wrote them.

The committee believe that many clergymen and organists are now realizing their responsibility in this matter, and will welcome a tune-book in which enervating tunes are reduced to a minimum. The usual argument in favour of bad music is that the fine tunes are doubtless "musically correct", but that the people want "something simple". Now the expression "musically correct" has no meaning; the only "correct" music is that which is beautiful and noble. As for simplicity, what could be simpler than "St. Anne" or "The Old Hundredth", and what could be finer?

It is indeed a moral rather than a musical issue. No doubt it requires a certain effort to tune oneself to the moral atmosphere implied by a fine melody; and it is far easier to dwell in the miasma of the languishing and sentimental hymn tunes which so often disfigure our services. Such poverty of heart may not be uncommon, but at least it should not be encouraged by those who direct the services of the Church; it ought no longer to be true anywhere that the most exalted moments of a church-goer's week are associated with music that would not be tolerated in any place of secular entertainment.

There are, however, many who recognize this bad state of things, but are timid about removing old favourites. Those who have this fear should remember that most of our "old favourites" are of very recent growth, dating at the earliest from the year 1861—a very short life for a hymn tune; also that it does not take more than a couple of years to make a tune which congregations like into an "old favourite", and furthermore that it is not by any means necessarily bad music which is popular. The average congregation likes fine melody when it can get it, but it is apt to be undiscriminating, and will often take to bad melody when good is not forthcoming. Is it not worth while making a vigorous effort to-day for the sake of establishing a good tradition? Especially should this be the case with children's hymns. Children at all events have no old association with any particular tune, and incalculable good or harm may be done by the music which they sing in their most impressionable years.

An attempt has been made to set a minimum standard in the music selected for this work. This does not mean that austerity has been unduly sought, or that difficult and colourless music has been preferred to that which is vigorous and bright. A tune has no more right to be dull than to be demoralizing. Indeed, anxiety to ensure the co-operation of the congregation may have caused the boundary to be occasionally overstepped, so that a few tunes have been retained which ought to have been rejected, but on this borderland individual tastes must necessarily differ, and the committee have done their best to select the most suitable tune for each hymn. To make the possibilities of selection wider, numerous cross-references have been given, which should be freely used, and a short appendix is added of alternative tunes to certain hymns for the use of those who do not agree with the choice of the musical editor.

The Manner of Performance.

(*a*) *Pitch.*—The pitch of all the tunes has been fixed as low as possible for the sake of mixed congregations. Except in the case of tunes with an extended compass the highest note is not above D or E♭. Some choirmasters may object to this on the ground that it places the hymns in the worst part of the boy-chorister's voice, and that it takes the basses and altos rather low. The obvious answer is that hymns are essentially for the congregation; the choir have their opportunity elsewhere, but in the hymn they must give way to the congregation, and it is a great mistake to suppose that the result will be inartistic. A large body of voices singing together makes a distinctly artistic effect, though that of each individual voice might be the opposite. And it may be added that a desire to parade a trained choir often accompanies a debased musical taste.

Where a tune occurs twice in the book it is usually given in two different keys, and in one or two cases a higher version of certain well-known tunes is given in the appendix. If this is not sufficient it is always possible to transpose the tunes to a higher key. Where a tune is only given once it is obvious why it should be printed in a lower key. Such a key is particularly suitable for village churches where the organist is rarely able to transpose. On the other hand, in churches where it is desired to give the first consideration to a trained choir, the organist will certainly be competent to transpose at sight into the key desired.

(*b*) *Unison singing.*—Every hymn is so arranged that it can be sung in unison accompanied by the organ. Certain verses are marked as being specially suitable for unison singing, and it is suggested that the first verse of most hymns should be sung in unison as well as all the doxologies. In any case the congregation must _always_ sing the melody, and the _melody only_.

In these circumstances it has been thought advisable occasionally to introduce harmonizations (especially those of J. S. Bach) rather more elaborate than usual. These will no doubt add greatly to the beauty and the popularity of the tunes. If some choirs find them difficult the tunes can be sung in unison accompanied by the organ; the organist will find no difficulty in playing them, if they are taken at the proper speed. It is a great mistake to suppose that untrained musicians are insensible to fine harmony. They may not be able to analyse the effect, but there can be no doubt that a well-harmonized tune makes a more powerful appeal than one in which the harmonies are bad or unsuitable. Choirs would be much better occupied in learning these beautiful settings of Bach (which are not hard if practised a little) than in rehearsing vulgar anthems by indifferent composers.

(_c_) _Choir and people._—There are churches in which the experiment has been successfully tried of making choir and people sing some hymns antiphonally. By this means the people are given a distinct status in the services, and are encouraged to take an intelligent interest in the music they sing, while the eternal war between choir and congregation, each considering the other an unnecessary appendage to the services of the church, is done away with.

The congregation might be encouraged to sing and appreciate the finer melodies if a system of monthly congregational practices were held, at which the less known tunes could be made familiar in some such way as the following:—The first two verses might be sung by the choir alone, or some body of singers with good voices who already knew the melody: at the third verse the congregation would be invited to join in, and would finally sing a verse unaided by the trained singers. A _hymn recital_, at which some of the less familiar hymns might be sung by the choir, would also be a pleasant variety from the Sunday evening organ recital.

(_d_) _Speed._—The present custom in English churches is to sing hymns much too fast. It is distressing to hear "Nun Danket" or "St. Anne" raced through at about twice the proper speed. Metronome marks are added to each hymn, which, the editor believes, indicate the proper speed in a fairly large building with a congregation of average size. The speed indications should not be judged at the pianoforte.

Another painful experience is to hear an organist trying to play through a C.M. or L.M. tune in absolutely strict time, regardless of the slight pauses which the congregation, with unconscious artistic insight, are inclined to make at the end of every line. Pauses have been marked wherever they should be made, and a sign, has also been extensively used to designate a very short break, less than the ordinary pause (⌒). Sometimes ⌒ and ' are used together, signifying a pause as well as a complete break in the sound.

Some of the hymns are marked to be sung "in free rhythm". This direction is especially applicable to unmeasured tunes, but all hymn tunes should be sung more or less freely; at all events a stiff clock-work rendering should be avoided. If this is borne in mind, and the hymns are not sung too fast, the bad effect will be largely avoided of those false accents which inevitably occur when several verses of a hymn are sung to the same tune.

(*e*) *Expression.*—Expression marks have been altogether omitted, as it is considered that subtleties of expression are entirely unsuitable for congregational singing. The organist can use his own judgement as to the general dynamics of each verse, and convey his idea to the congregation by his registering. All sudden "pianos" or small "crescendos" and "diminuendos" should be avoided as destroying the broad and massive effect which congregational singing should convey.

(*f*) *Notation.*—Both minims and crotchets have been employed, the former for the slower and more solemn hymns and the latter for those of a brighter nature. The point of division has been fixed at M. 85 for hymns in duple time, and 100 in triple time in the more ordinary hymns, but special rules have been framed to govern special cases.

Sources of the Melodies

No particular country, period, or school has been exclusively drawn upon to supply material, but an attempt has been made to include the best specimens of every style. In settling the form which each melody shall take, no rules have been made, but each case has been decided on its merits. The object has been to print the finest version of every tune, not necessarily the earliest. Thus the later forms of "Wachet Auf", "Nun Danket", and "London New", to give a few examples, have been preferred to the originals. But the old method of mutilating tunes to suit new metres has been as far as possible avoided—only in one or two cases have a composer's rhythms been very slightly adapted, and then for some very special purpose. In cases where such a slight adaptation from a composer's rhythm is made the general outline is never destroyed, so that the original can at any time be restored without disturbing a congregation. But adaptations already made have been occasionally retained when the result is a fine and popular tune: thus "Dix", "Narenza", and "Ravenshaw" have not been discarded, though the fact of their adaptation is duly acknowledged. On the other hand the committee are glad to be able to restore the true metres of such tunes as "Innsbruck", "Weimar", or "Les commandemens", which have been disfigured into dullness in so many hymnals.

The original rhythms of many of the old psalter tunes have also been restored, especially the long initial on the first syllable, which gives such a broad and dignified effect to these tunes. Attempts to adapt them to the procrustean bed of the nineteenth century hymn tune have merely taken away their character and made them appear dull. For the same reason no attempt has been made to square the irregular times of some tunes. These irregularities are always easy to sing by ear—and this is the way in which a hymn melody should be learnt—so that choirmasters should not let the fear of what may appear to be irregular deter them from using many splendid and essentially congregational melodies.

The following classification shows the chief sources from which the tunes come:—

A.   German.—(1) Lutheran chorale tunes 16th and 17th centuries. (2) Tunes from the 16th and 17th century Catholic song books (chiefly Leisentritt's, 1567, and the Andernach _Gesangbuch_, 1608). (3) Tunes of the 18th century, chiefly by Bach and Freylinghausen. (4) Modern German tunes. (5) German traditional melodies.

B.   French and Swiss.—(1) Tunes from the Genevan Psalters of the 16th century. (2) Ecclesiastical melodies from the _paroissiens_ of various French uses (chiefly those of Rouen and Angers). (3) French and Swiss traditional melodies.

C.   Italian, Spanish, Flemish, Dutch.—Ecclesiastical, traditional, and other melodies from these countries are also included.

D.   American.—Among American tunes may be mentioned Lowell Mason's tunes, certain tunes from "Sacred Songs and Solos", and a few "Western melodies" in use in America as hymn tunes.

E.   British Isles.—I. *Ireland*. (1) Irish traditional melodies. (2) Tunes by Irish composers.

II.   *Scotland*. (1) Melodies from the Scottish Psalters of the 16th and 17th centuries. (2) Melodies from the Scottish tune-books of the 18th and 19th centuries. (3) Scottish traditional melodies.

III.   *Wales*. (1) Archdeacon Prys' Psalter, which contains the famous tune "St. Mary". (2) Welsh traditional melodies. (3) Tunes by 18th and 19th century Welsh composers, which partake decidedly of the nature of their traditional melodies.

IV.   *England*.   (1) Tunes from Day's, Damon's, Este's, Ravenscroft's, and Playford's Psalters of the 16th and 17th centuries (the original versions of these, with the melody in the tenor, are occasionally included as alternatives to the modern version). (2) Tunes by Tallis, Gibbons, Lawes, &c., from their own collections. (3) Tunes from 18th century books—especially those by J. Clark and Dr. Croft. (4) English carol, and other traditional melodies. (5) Tunes by 19th and 20th century composers.

Part IV

American Hymnody

15
The Eighteenth Century

Thomas Symmes (1678-1725)

THOMAS Symmes was the son of the Puritan minister at Bradford, Massachusetts. After graduating from Harvard (1698), he served as pastor at Boxford (1702-1708) and at his father's church in Bradford (1708-1725).

Symmes's *The Reasonableness of Regular Singing*, published in 1720, was the opening salvo in a campaign by a number of New England ministers to reform the congregational singing of the Puritan churches. Their primary target was the so-called "Usual Way of Singing," in which each member of the congregation apparently felt at liberty to sing his or her own variations on the tune. Symmes's colleague, Thomas Walter, described the Usual Way as sounding "like *Five Hundred* different Tunes roared out at the same time" (*The Grounds and Rules of Musick Explained*, 1721, p. 5). The manner preferred by the reformers was "Regular Singing," in which rhythm and pitch were governed by musical notation.

The stand taken by Symmes, Walter, and others led to the publication of music instruction manuals and tune books, the institution of singing schools, and ultimately the development of choirs and introduction of hymnody into Puritan churches. In addition to *The Reasonableness of Regular Singing*, Symmes published two other writings promoting Regular Singing, *Prejudice in Matters of Religion* (1722) and *Utile Dulci, Or, a Joco-Serious Dialogue, Concerning Regular Singing* (1723).

63   From *The Reasonableness of, Regular Singing, or Singing by Note* (Boston: B. Green for Samuel Gerrish, 1720), pp. 3-9.

The following Considerations, have occasioned many People to think, that the Publishing something of the Nature of what is here effected, would be very Serviceable, *viz.*

1.   The Total Neglect *of Singing Psalms, by many Serious Christians, for want of* Skill *in Singing Psalm Tunes.* There are many who never employ their Tongues in Singing God's Praises, *because they have not Skill.* It is with great difficulty that this part of Worship is performed, and with great indecency in some Congregations, for want of Skill: It is to be feared Singing must be wholly Omitted in some Places for want of Skill, if this Art is not revived. I was once present in a Congregation where Singing was for a whole Sabbath omitted, for want of a Man able to lead the Assembly in Singing.

2.   The imperfect and irregular manner *of Singing* Psalm Tunes *in most Places.* Some of the *Tunes* are varied much (and much more in some Congregations than others) from the Pattern or *Notes* in our own *Psalm Books,* and from the *Rules* of *Musick.*

3.   The *Difficulties & Oppositions which some Congregations have met withal, in their attempting & accomplishing a Reformation in their Singing.* These arose in a great Measure from the *Misapprehensions & Mistakes* of some honest and well-minded People among them. Thus it has happened in some, tho' not in all Congregations, where Singing has been Reformed. It is hoped, that as the Contentions of *Paul* and *Barnabus*, were over-ruled to the more effectual spreading of the Gospel; so the Oppositions which some have made against *Regular Singing,* will prove a means for the more speedy and successful Reviving of the Duty of Singing Psalms and that in the most Decent, Regular Way.

4.   The *Success which has followed suitable Endeavours to remove those Cavils, which some* (while they laboured under their Prejudices to Singing by Rule) *have tho't were unanswerable Reasons in their Favour.* Experience has sufficiently shewn, (in scores of Instances) That the most vehement Opposers of *Singing by Note,* never fail of being convinced of their Mistakes, as soon as they gain a *Competent Knowledge* in the *Rules of Singing,* with Ability to Sing a small number of *Tunes* with some exactness. I have never known, (as I remember) or heard, of one Instance to the contrary.   The Reasonableness of *Singing by Note,* and its excelling the *Usual Way,* cannot be fully understood by any till they have attain'd some Skill in the *Rules of Singing;* yet there is so much Reason for Singing according to Note, more than for the other Way, as may satisfy any Rational, unprejudiced Person, that it is much rather to be chosen.

I shall now proceed in the plainest, most easy and popular Way I can, (for 'tis for the sake of common People I write) to shew, That Singing by or according to *Note*, is to be preferred to the *Usual Way of Singing*, which may be evidenced by several *Arguments*.

I. The first *Argument* may be taken from the Antiquity of *Regular Singing. Singing by Note* is the most *Ancient Way* of Singing, and claims the Preference to the other on that Account. Truth is older than Error, and is venerable for it's Antiquity; but as for Error, the ancienter it is, the worse it is. There are many bad *Old Ways*; Antiquity is no infallible Mark of Truth, *Mat.* 5.21. Yet the Argument may be of Service here, because those who plead against *Singing by Note*, urge with much zeal and warmth, that this is a *New Way*, and the *Usual Way* is *the good Old Way*, as they call it. Here I shall endeavour to prove their Mistake; and I suppose, that if they could be convinced, that *Singing by Note* was known to, and approved of, by the first *Settlers* of *New-England*, it would satisfy most of them as to this Point; and if this be not done, it may be, some will be so unreasonable as to think the Point not made out, tho' it could be plainly proved to bear an *Equal Date* to that of *Instrumental Musick*. It is more than probable, it was known and approved of by the *first Inhabitants* of *New-England*, For,

1. It was studied, known and approv'd of in our *College*, for many Years after its first Founding. This is evident from the Musical *Theses*, which were formerly Printed, and from some Writings containing some *Tunes* with Directions for *Singing by Note*, as they are now Sung; and these are yet in Being, tho' of more than *Sixty Years* standing; besides no Man that Studied *Musick*, as it is treated of by *Alsted, Playford* and others, could be ignorant of it.

2. If *Singing by Note* was not designed, Why were the Notes plac'd in our *New-England* Psalm-Books, and some General Directions there given about them? If they were designed for a Pattern for us to Sing by, either it was a true and exact Pattern or not; If it was not, either *Skill* or *Honesty* or both were wanting in our *Predecessors*, and surely you have so great and just a Veneration for them, as not to suspect either of these things of them; but if the Pattern was exact and was Sang by, then *Singing by Note* is of Ancient Date with us in this Land.

3. There are many Persons of Credit now Living, Children and Grand-Children of the *first Settlers* of *New-England*, who can very well remember, that their Ancestors Sung by *Note*, and they learnt

so to Sing of them, and they have more than their bare Words to prove that they speak the Truth; for many of them can Sing *Tunes* exactly by *Note*, which they learnt of their *Fore-Fathers*, and they say that they sang all the *Tunes* after the same manner; and these People now sing those *Tunes* most agreable to *Note*, which have been least practiced in the Congregation. But suppose *Singing by Note* was not practiced, and that the *Usual Way* was in our Congregations from the *First Settling* of *New-England*; it does not therefore follow, that *Singing by Note*, is not of the antientest Date, nor that the *Usual Way of Singing* is the best. For I suppose you will grant that there was a *Possibility* of their Singing in a Way which was not of the most ancient Practice among the People of God; and I will prove that there is *more than a Probability* of it, if they Sang not by *Note*, but in your *Common Way*: I will prove it thus; That Way of Singing which all the Books that treat of *Vocal Musick*, and especially of *Psalm Tunes*, describes to be the Way which was owned and taught as the true *Mode of Singing*, must in all probability be of ancienter Date, than that *Mode* or Way, which was never so much as mentioned in any one Book that treats of Singing. Now, all *Treatises of Psalm Tunes*, which I have ever seen or heard of, speak only of *Singing by Note*, as the true and proper Way of Singing *Psalm Tunes*; and if there can be one Book produced, which treats of *Vocal Musick*, that gives *plain Rules* for, and commends your *Usual Way of Singing*, above that of Singing according to the *Notes* in our *New-England* Psalm Books, then it shall be granted that you have far more Reason on your Side than could ever be discovered by any but your selves.

Object. But some will say, If *Singing by Note* is the ancientest Way, How came it that it was not continued, when or by whom was it laid aside or altered?

Answ. The Declining from, and getting beside the *Rule* was *gradual* and *insensible. Singing-Schools* and *Singing-Books* being laid aside, there was no Way to learn; but only by hearing of *Tunes* Sung, or by taking the *Run of the Tune* (as it is phrased.) The Rules of Singing not being taught or learnt, every one sang as best pleased himself, and every *Leading-Singer* would take the Liberty of raising any *Note* of the *Tune*, or lowering of it, as best pleas'd his Ear, and add such *Turns* and *Flourishes* as were grateful to him; and this was done so *gradually*, as that but few if any took Notice of it. One *Clerk* or *Chorister* would alter the *Tunes* a little in his Day, the next a little in his, and so one after another, till in *Fifty* or *Sixty* Years it caus'd a *Considerable Alteration*. If the Alteration had been made designedly by any *Master* of *Musick*, it is probable that the Variation from our *Psalm Books* would have been alike in all our Congregations; whereas some vary much more than others, and 'tis hard to find *Two* that Sing *exactly alike*. The Alteration being so *gradual*, it is no wonder that People are ignorant when it was made, or that there is any at all: As *Weights* or *Measures* (which are seal'd) with using them, *Seven* or *Ten* Years, may alter considerably, and the Person using them not discern it, till he compares them with the *Standard*, and then he is presently convinc'd of it. We are well inform'd, that in other Countries, where *Singing-Schools* are kept up, Singing is continued in the Purity of it: Where they are not, it is degenerated, as it is among us. Your *Usual Way* of Singing is handed down by *Tradition* only, and whatsoever is only so conveyed down to us, it is a thousand to one if it be not miserably corrupted in *Three* or *Fourscore* Years Time.

Jonathan Edwards (1703-1758)

Jonathan Edwards was born in East Windsor, Connecticut, and received his B.A. and M.A. from Yale College (now Yale University). In 1729, he became pastor of the Congregational church in Northampton, Massachusetts, where his preaching led to a spiritual awakening in his congregation and the surrounding territory. His most famous sermon, *Sinners in the Hands of an Angry God*, was delivered in 1741. A dispute with his congregation led to his dismissal in 1750, and in 1751 he became pastor of the Stockbridge church. He was elected to the presidency of the College of New Jersey (Princeton University) in 1757, but died a few weeks after taking office.

One of Edwards's letters, reproduced below, reveals the growing popularity of the hymns of Isaac Watts in the American colonies during the eighteenth century. Upon his return from a trip, Edwards discovered that his people had totally discarded metrical psalmody in favor of Watts's hymns. The pastor persuaded them to take a more middle-of-the-road approach by using both sources. Yet, the innovation of singing hymns was still new enough that eventually a few members raised objections to the practice,

though it may be surmised that this minority did not carry
the day.

64   Letter to Benjamin Colman (1744).   *Source*:
          Proceedings of the Massachusetts Historical Society, 2nd
          series (Boston: Published by the Society, 1896), vol.
          X, p. 429.

NORTHAMPTON, May 22, 1744.

REV'D & HONOURED SIR,—It has been our manner in this
congregation, for more than two years past, in the summer time,
when we sing three times upon the Sabbath, to sing an Hymn, or
part of a Hymn of Dr. Watts's, the last time, *viz*: at the conclusion
of the afternoon exercise. I introduced it principally because I saw
in the people a very general inclination to it: indeed I was not
properly he that introduced it: they began it in my absence on a
journey; and seem'd to be greatly pleased with it; and sang nothing
else, & neglected the Psalms wholly. When I came home I disliked
not their making some use of the Hymns: but did not like their
setting aside the Psalms; and therefore used them principally, and
continued the singing of the Hymns only in the manner that I have
spoken of, and thus we continued to use them: which at first I
suppose, was to universal satisfaction: and [so] it continued to be
till very lately, excepting one [m]an, one Mr Root; he after a little
while manifest[ing] a disgust, not by coming to me to say anything
[to] me, but by turning his back on that part of [our] publick
worship from time to time, and [going] out of the meeting House.
There was no appearance of dislike in any other person that I know
of, 'till lately I have heard some other persons have appear'd not
well pleased: which I suppose principally arises from what Mr Root
says you said to him concerning our singing those Hymns, more
than a twelve-month ago, and a message that he says you desired
him to deliver to me (tho' he never deliver'd it, or informed me of
it 'till yesterday) He says that he went to you on purpose to talk
with you on the affair, and that you charged him with this message
to me, once and again, "Tell Mr Edwards from me, that I desire
that he would by no means sing Dr. Watts's Hymns." This message
which Mr Root has spoken much of to others tho' he did not
deliver it to me, has I believe made some difficulty: and because I
was ready to think there was some mistake, and it is pity that

trouble should arise among us from nothing, I thought it would be best to write to you, that I might know the certainty. Therefore I would pray you Honoured Sir, to inform me whether Mr. Root did not mistake you, by writing briefly to me concerning this matter. Herein, Honoured Sir, you will much oblige

Your already greatly obliged son and servant
JONATHAN EDWARD[S]

William Billings (1756-1800)

William Billings was born and spent his entire life in Boston, Massachusetts, where he worked as a tanner of hides and held a number of minor municipal posts. An ardent patriot, Billings was acquainted with Samuel Adams, Paul Revere, and other supporters of American independence.

In addition to his other pursuits, Billings was active as a singing school teacher and composer of psalm and hymn tunes, fuging tunes, and anthems. He published six tune books, all but one of which contained exclusively his own music. His initial collection, the *New-England Psalm-Singer* (1770), was the first tune book to include music only by an American-born composer. With the exception of his *Music in Miniature* (1779), all of Billings's tune books were designed primarily for the singing school, rather than the church. Nevertheless, a number of his psalm and hymn tunes found their way into the congregational repertory of American churches in the late eighteenth century.

In the preface to the *New-England Psalm-Singer*, Billings begged "the Critic to be tender" with his volume, citing the composer's youth and inexperience. He also pointed out that, whereas most tune books placed primary emphasis on tunes in "common Metre"—a reflection of the popularity of this meter for congregational song—he attempted "to have a Sufficiency in each Measure." Despite his protestations of youth and inexperience, Billings revealed his own self-confidence in a section of the tune book's theoretical introduction, which was devoted to advice "To all Musical Practitioners." Here he declared himself to be free from the "rules" of composition that had been formulated by earlier musicians. While it is clear that Billings was not advocating a total abandonment of the "rules," some have seen in these statements a musical Declaration of Independence comparable to the political one of 1776. Billings's own music was obviously based on the English models available to him, but was also typified by a rugged, individual character.

65   Preface to *The New-England Psalm-Singer* (Boston: Edes and Gill, [1770]), pp. 2, 19-20.

Altho' this Composition hath cost me much Time and Pains; yet I thought little of exposing it to Public view. But being repeatedly importuned by my Friends, I was at last prevailed upon to commit it to the Press. And such as it is I now offer it to the Public, from whom, should it meet with a favourable Reception, it would compensate for all the Trouble I have been at, and the Time I have spent in the Prosecution of it. Perhaps there may appear in the eyes of the Accurate much Incorrectness that I was not able to discern; therefore would beg the Critic to be tender, and realize those Errors which through Inexperience may happen to have escaped the Notice of a Youth, in the Course of so large a Volume.

I would here take Occasion to return my Thanks to those Gentlemen who have put so much Confidence in this Performance, as to promote and encourage it by Subscription, before they would have an Opportunity of examining it. And I would acknowledge myself in a particular Manner obligated to that Gentleman who has honored me and this Book with his learned Philosophical Essay on Sound; *yet at the same Time I can't but be sorry that I am not allowed to give the Public the Satisfaction of knowing his Name: For somewhat contrary to Nature, Modesty in this Gentleman, has so far gained the Ascendency over Ambition, that the World must remain deprived of the Knowledge of him, 'till his Name shall shine on the Page of some future Work.*

It would be needless in me to attempt to set forth the Usefulness and Importance of Psalm-singing, which is so universally known and acknowledged, and on which depends no inconsiderable Part of the Divine Worship of our Churches. But thus much would I say, That he who finds himself gifted with a tunable Voice, and yet neglects to cultivate it, not only hides in the Earth a Talent of the highest Value, but robs himself of the peculiar Pleasure, of which they only are conscious who exercise that Faculty.

Authors in general, upon Subjects of this Nature, abound mostly in

Tunes of common Metre; but in this respect, I have deviated from them, endeavouring to have a Sufficiency in each Measure. In the Composition I have been as plain and simple as possible; and yet have tried to the utmost of my Power to preserve the modern Air and Manner of Singing. And should it upon Proof be found equal to the Attempt, I hope it will be as well an Inducement to the unskill'd in the Art to prosecute the Study of it, as an Entertainment to the more experienced in it.

Boston, October 7, 1770.

. . .

To all Musical Practitioners

Perhaps it may be expected by some, that I should say something concerning Rules for Composition; to these I answer that *Nature is the best Dictator*, for all the hard dry studied Rules that ever was prescribed, will not enable any Person to form an Air any more than the bare Knowledge of the four and twenty Letters, and strict Grammatical Rules will qualify a Scholar for composing a Piece of Poetry, or properly adjusting a Tragedy, without a Genius. It must be Nature, Nature must lay the Foundation, Nature must inspire the Thought. But perhaps some may think I mean and intend to throw Art intirely out of the Question, I answer by no Means, for the more Art is display'd, the more Nature is decorated. And in some sorts of Composition, there is dry Study requir'd, and Art very requisite. For instance, in a *Fuge*, where the Parts come in after each other, with the same Notes; but even there, Art is subservient to Genius, for Fancy goes first, and strikes out the Work roughly, and Art comes after, and polishes it over. But to return to my Text; I have read several Author's Rules on Composition, and find the strictest of them make some Exceptions, as thus, they say that two Eighths or two Fifths may not be taken together rising or falling, unless one be Major and the other Minor; but rather than spoil the Air, they will allow that Breach to be made, and this allowance gives great Latitude to young Composers, for they may always make that Plea, and say, if I am not allow'd to transgress the Rules of Composition, I shall certainly spoil the Air, and Cross the Strain, that fancy dictated: And indeed this is without dispute, a very just Plea, for I am sure I have often and sensibly felt the disagreeable and slavish Effects of such a restraint as is here pointed out, and so I believe has every Composer of Poetry, as well as Musick, for I presume there are as strict Rules for Poetry, as for Musick. But as

I have often heard of a Poetical Licence, I don't see why with the same Propriety there may not be a Musical Licence, for Poetry and Music are in close Connection, and nearly allied, besides they are often assistants to each other: and like true friends often hide each others failings: For I have known a Piece of Poetry that had neither *"Rhime nor Reason"*[1] in it, pass for tolerable good Sense, because it happened to be set to an excellent Piece of Musick, and to get respect rather for its good fortune in falling into such respectable Company than for any Merit in itself; so likewise I have known and heard a very indifferent Tune often sung, and much caress'd only because it was set to a fine Piece of Poetry, without which recommendation, perhaps it would not be sung twice over by one Person, and would be deem'd to be dearly bo't only at the expence of Breath requisite to perform it—for my own Part, as I don't think myself confin'd to any Rules for Composition laid down by any that went before me, neither should I think (were I to pretend to lay down Rules) that any who came after me were any ways obligated to adhere to them, any further than they should think proper: So in fact, I think it is best for every *Composer* to be his own *Carver*. Therefore, upon this Consideration, for me to dictate, or pretend to prescribe Rules of this Nature for others, would not only be very unnecessary, but also a great Piece of Vanity.

---

[1]A simple Fellow bro't a Piece of Prose to Sir *Thomas Moore* for his Inspection; Sir *Thomas* told him to put it into Rhime, accordingly he did; upon which Sir *Thomas* said to him, now it is Rhime; but before it was neither *Rhime nor Reason*.

16
The Nineteenth Century

Timothy Dwight (1752-1817)

TIMOTHY Dwight, a grandson of Jonathan Edwards, graduated from Yale College (University), served as a chaplain in the Continental Army during the American Revolution, and became pastor of the Greenville, Connecticut, Congregational Church. In 1795 he assumed the presidency of his alma mater, where he served with distinction until his death.

In 1797 the General Association of Presbyterian churches in Connecticut invited Dwight to prepare a revision and enlargement of Watts's *Psalms of David Imitated in the Language of the New Testament* (1719). The first edition of "Dwight's Watts," as the work was nicknamed, was published in 1801 and was widely used in Congregational and Presbyterian churches in New England. In addition to altering and completing Watts's work, Dwight included thirty-three of his own texts in the collection. One of these, "I love thy kingdom, Lord," is still found in many hymnals.

Dwight's Watts was but one of several attempts to adapt and arrange the poetic works of the English author in the late eighteenth and early nineteenth centuries. These collections illustrate the continuing influence of Watts on English and American congregational song during that era.

66   Advertisement from *The Psalms of David, Imitated in the Language of the New Testament ... by I. Watts, ... A New Edition . . . by Timothy Dwight* (Hartford: Hudson and Goodwin, 1801), pp. [5]-[8].

After the American Revolution, it became early the general wish of the Churches and Congregations in this country, that such passages in

Doctor Watts's *version of the Psalms, as were local, and inapplicable
to our own circumstances, might be altered, and made to accord with
those circumstances. In several succeeding instances, such an
alteration has been made. The General Association of this state,
however, thought proper, at their Session in June* 1795, *to request the
subscriber to attempt the work anew. To this request they subjoined
another; viz. that he would versify the Psalms, omitted by Doctor*
Watts. *At the same time, a number of the Clergy and Laity, of the
first respectability, recommended, that an addition should be made to
the number of Psalms, versified by Doctor* Watts *in proper metres for
the purpose of preventing a too frequent repetition of them in our
worship. They also recommended, that a number of Hymns should be
annexed to the Psalm-book, sufficient to complete a system of public
Psalmody.*

In May, 1798, *a motion was made in the General Assembly of the
Presbyterian Church for accomplishing the same general purpose; but
the General Assembly, being informed, that the business had been
taken up by the General Association, concluded to postpone any
further measures, relative to it, until they should see the issue of the
measures, adopted in Connecticut. After this work was completed, a
joint Committee was appointed to examine, on behalf of both these
Ecclesiastical bodies, the state and character of the work, and finally
to approve, or disapprove of it, as they should judge proper. Their
decision the reader has already seen, on a preceding page.*

*With the requests and recommendations abovementioned I have
endeavored to comply. Some account of what I have done is due to
the public.*

In making such alterations in Doctor Watts's *version as respected
objects merely local, I have in some instances applied the Psalm, or the
passage, to the Church at large, or to Christian nations generally; and
in others, particularly, to our own country. The latter I have done,
because every nation, like every individual, feeling its own concerns
more than any other, will find various occasions of adapting its praise
peculiarly to them.*

*In altering such passages, as were defective, either in the language,
or the sentiment, I found two objects claiming my attention—the errors
of the press, and those of the writer.*

The reverence for Doctor Watts *is in this country so great, that I
shall not be surprised to find myself charged with want of modesty, for
suggesting, that he was the subject of such errors. Doctor* Watts *was
a man of great eminence for learning, wisdom, and piety; and in*

usefulness to mankind has had few equals. As a poet, in writing a flowing, happy stanza, familiar without vulgarism, and elevated without affectation or obscurity, he has perhaps, never been excelled. The design of evangelizing the Psalms (if I may be allowed the expression) was one of those happy thoughts, which rarely occur, and will give his version a decided superiority over every other, as a vehicle for the praise of Christians. Still he was not distinguished as a correct writer, and must undoubtedly be charged with some of the errors, found in his Psalm-book. A part of those only have I attempted to remove. I should have ventured farther, had I not been originally cautioned to make no alterations except those, which should appear to be either absolutely necessary, or plainly important. In these alterations I have aimed to vary as little as might be from my original.

As the Editions of Dr. Watts's psalms have been very numerous, both in Great Britain and America, many typographical errors have crept into the modern copies of that work. These I have carefully endeavored to correct.

In versifying the Psalms, omitted by Dr. Watts, I have followed the free example, which he has set. When the reader is informed, that Dr. Watts was discouraged from attempting these, I am persuaded, that he will not think the latitude, which I have taken, unwarrantable.

In adding to the number of Psalms, versified in several kinds of proper metres, I have generally selected those, which were of frequent use. As the design was to prevent the necessity of singing the existing Psalms, of this description, too often, such a selection became indispensable. I have not versified any in the metre of the old 50th because of the incumbrance of the Chorus; nor any in that of the 113th. because I thought the number already sufficient.

The Hymns I have selected from various writers, with a design of extending and completing a system of Psalmody. I do not flatter myself, that a divine song will be found here, adapted to every religious subject; yet I hope, there will be no important deficiency. Had I followed my own judgment only, the collection would have been somewhat larger; but I found several judicious divines of opinion, that it would be expedient to make it still less. To the Hymns selected, I am persuaded, there will be no objection.

It cannot, without weakness, be supposed, that what I have done will meet the universal approbation of those, for whose use this Psalm-book is intended. The introduction of a Psalm-book into the use of Churches has ever been attended with difficulties. I have not satisfied myself; it ought, therefore, not to be expected, that I should satisfy others, whose judgment must doubtless be more impartial, and less biassed in my favour, than my own. I can only say, that I have intended well.

No doctrine will, I believe, be found in the book, which is not accordant with the general Protestant Orthodoxy. In this part of the performance I presume, therefore, I shall not be extensively censured. With respect to the rest, I leave it in the hands of the public, with my sincere wish, and earnest prayer to God, that it may please him to make it a means of assisting the praise, and promoting the edification and comfort of my fellow Christians.

TIMOTHY DWIGHT.
New-Haven, August 13, 1800.

The Boston Handel and Haydn Society (1822)

The Boston Handel and Haydn Society was founded for the express purpose of "improving the style of performing sacred music, and introducing into more general use the works of Handel and Haydn and other eminent composers." The Society gave its first performance, a miscellaneous program consisting mainly of arias and choruses from the oratorios of Handel and Haydn, on Christmas Day, 1815. The organization quickly became a major force in Boston concert life and continues as an active performing society to the present day.

As is obvious from its name, the Society looked primarily to European composers as the model for good church music. The rough, vigorous music of eighteenth-century American psalmodists such as William Billings and the homespun folk hymns that were popular in rural areas were deemed to be inferior to the "scientific" music of the great classical composers.

In addition to performing the works of European masters, the Society attempted to raise the level of church music in America through the publication of sacred music. The first significant step in this direction was taken with the issuing of the *Boston Handel and Haydn Society Collection of Church Music* (1822). The book was compiled by Lowell Mason (1792-1872), a bank clerk in Savannah, Georgia. Since Mason was relatively unknown at the time, the work was given the imprimatur of George K. Jackson, one of Boston's leading musicians; at Mason's request, his own name did not appear on the title page. This marked the beginning of a long and fruitful association between Mason and the Society. Mason later served as president of the organization (1827-1832), and the tune book he had compiled became very popular, with numerous editions printed through 1839.

The preface to the 1822 edition of the *Boston Handel and Haydn Society Collection* explains the purpose of the collection and the respective roles of the Society, Lowell Mason, and George K. Jackson in its compilation.

67 Preface to *The Boston Handel and Haydn Society Collection of Church Music* (Boston: Richardson and Lord, 1822), pp. [iii]-v.

The Handel and Haydn Society, having been instituted for the purpose of improving the style of Church Music, have felt it their duty to keep two objects continually in view; the first to acquire and diffuse that style and taste in performance without which even the most exquisite compositions lose their effect and influence; the second, what was indeed a necessary pre-requisite, to furnish the public with a selection of such compositions, both of ancient and modern authors, as are considered most excellent, and at the same time most useful.

With regard to the first of these objects, they reflect with great pleasure upon the success which has attended their efforts. A visible improvement has taken place in the style of singing, and consequently in the taste of the community. Not only the practice but the science and theory of music, have been the objects of great attention; the increase of patronage has been commensurate with the increase of knowledge and fondness for the art: and the various collections of psalmody, and the number of editions to which some of them have passed, are sure and certain indications of increasing refinement in the public taste.

These favourable appearances have animated the exertions of the Society with regard to what they have mentioned as the second object of their attention; and they have for some time been engaged with much labour, and at considerable expence, in collecting materials for the present work.

It is obvious that no collection of Sacred Music, can be so extensively useful in this country, as one of psalmody. The only question which can arise therefore, is with respect to the particular advantages to be derived from that which is now presented to the public.

The Handel and Haydn Society, have certainly no disposition to detract from the merits of the respectable collections which are now in use; and they wish to avoid any appearance of depreciating the efforts of those whom they consider as fellow-labourers for the promotion of a common benefit. But, while they give that praise which is justly due to these laudable exertions, and acknowledge that much has been done, they are confident that all scientific and disinterested persons will agree with them that much still remains undone. Many respectable teachers of music in various parts of our country have frequently requested the Society to publish a new collection, and the advantages they enjoy for this purpose have seemed to them to render a compliance with this request an act of duty.

Their combination as a Society, and their local situation, have given them an extensive and easy access to the fountains of Music in Europe, and have enabled them to cultivate with advantage an intercourse with gentlemen of taste and science in our own country. As a Society also they are able to sustain an expence beyond the power of individual exertion; and by that division which is so necessary to the perfection of mental as well as bodily efforts, their labours have been rendered more effective.

While there has been in our country a great improvement in the taste for good melody, there has not been a correspondent attention to good harmony. To remedy this defect has been the special object of the Society in the present work.

Many of the oldest and best psalm tunes, as they were originally composed, were simple melodies; and as the practice of singing metre psalms in public worship was only allowed, not enjoined in England, and was confined to the parish churches, it was not much attended to by the principal masters, who were chiefly engaged in the composition of Cathedral Music. When therefore the other parts were added to these simple melodies, metre psalmody being considered of minor importance, the harmonies were mostly added by inferior composers. And even when the harmonies were original parts of the composition, a beautiful air might be composed without any of that science which was necessary to direct with propriety the inferior movements.

Of late years however a great change has taken place in the public sentiment with regard to the importance of psalmody, and this has of course called the attention of the most eminent masters in England to the subject. Several of them have been recently employed in harmonizing anew many of the old standard airs, and also in selecting and adapting movements from the works of Handel, Haydn, Mozart, Beethoven and other great masters, whose mighty talents have been displayed and acknowledged throughout Europe.

These works are among the materials to which the Handel and Haydn Society have had access, and they have exercised their best judgment in making such selections from them as would most enrich the present work. They consider themselves as peculiarly fortunate in having had, for the accomplishment of their purpose, the assistance of Mr. Lowell Mason, one of their members now resident in Savannah, whose taste and science have well fitted him for the employment, and whose zeal for the improvement of Church Music, has led him to undertake an important part of the labour in selecting, arranging and harmonizing the several compositions. But what has most contributed to the confidence with which they offer the present collection to the public, the whole work has been finally and most carefully revised by Doctor G. K. Jackson. The obligations which the Society owe to that gentleman for his gratuitous and unwearied labours, they have endeavoured in some measure to express, by prefixing his name to their work.

The Society are fully aware of the cautious delicacy with which variations should be admitted into tunes that by long use have become familiar, and by the power of association with holy purposes have been in some measure sanctified. They have been careful, therefore to retain in general, the airs of the several tunes unaltered; but as the longest usage cannot reconcile science and correct taste with false harmony, it has been found indispensably necessary to introduce changes into the accompanying parts. The leading part, however, being unaltered the change will not be such as to shock even the most accustomed ear; while the increased richness of the harmony cannot fail to increase the delight of every lover of Sacred Music.

It is obvious that these improvements will create an additional interest in psalmody, both in schools and societies, and in congregations for public worship. If the inferior parts are tame and spiritless, there will be a reluctance in the scholars or members of societies, to take them. The consequence must be that very unsuitable voices will sing upon the principal part, and thus materially injure the effect of the whole. The same remark is equally applicable to congregations for public worship. With regard to private worship, the improvements in harmony which have now been introduced will operate as an incitement to family devotion. Where there are three or more voices to be found in the same family, capable of sustaining the different parts, a much more powerful effect will be produced by a noble and expressive harmony, than if all should be confined to the Air alone.

The Society are far from thinking, that with all their care and advantages, they have produced a perfect work. Imperfection is the characteristic of every human effort; and works of this nature especially will approach the ideal standard, only by a slow and gradual approximation. They invite therefore the critical examination of all lovers of music, and scientific musicians, that even the most trivial errors may be rectified, and another edition, should another be called for, be rendered still more worthy of the public patronage.

William Caldwell (19th century)

The precise identity of William Caldwell, the compiler of the four-shape shape-note ("fasola") tune book *Union Harmony* (1837), is uncertain, but he seems to have been a resident of Jefferson County, Tennessee, during the first half of the nineteenth century. County records indicate the presence of two William Caldwells—a father and son—during this period. Which of the two actually compiled the tune book is not known, but it is likely that the older William Caldwell paid for the printing of the collection.

The *Union Harmony* is representative of the oblong tune books used in southern United States singing schools in the nineteenth century. These tune books almost invariably contained a discussion of the "Rudiments of Music" and a selection of psalm and hymn tunes, fuging tunes, and anthems. A special feature of these books was the presence of tunes derived from oral tradition set to hymn texts, i.e., "folk hymns." While most fasola tune books by southerners included folk hymns, Caldwell was one of the few compilers to openly acknowledge the presence of this "unwritten music in general use" in southern evangelical churches.

68   Preface to *Union Harmony* (Maryville, TN: F. A. Parham, 1837), pp. [3]-4.

The subscriber in presenting his musical compend to the public, feels it to be his duty to offer some reasons for undertaking a work so arduous, and so responsible. He has not undertaken it for the purpose of amusing the critic with metaphysical disquisitions on the science of music, nor has he undertaken it alone for the purpose of adding one more, to the long catalougue of music books now in circulation in our country—but he has undertaken it with a view to discharge a duty that appeared to rest upon him, a duty, to the performance of which, he has been urged by many personal solicitations, and indeed, by a general pressing demand from the different branches of the church of Christ in the Southern, and Western country.   Many indeed are the music books now in circulation—but the demand is for a book of music suited to the taste of the different branches of the church. This has ever been kept in view in the composition of this work.—Many of the airs which the author has reduced to system and harmonized, have been selected from the unwritten music in general use in the Methodist Church, others from the Baptist and many more from the Presbyterian taste; and, in the selections he has made from other authors, he has been careful that the most substantial and lasting music should be found on the pages of the Union Harmony—He flatters himself that this book will be more acceptable and useful than any book of the kind heretofore published—for the following reasons:

1st. The first principles or rudiments of music are presented to the view of the learner, abridged, and simplified in such a manner that they may be comprehended by an ordinary capacity, even without a teacher.

2. By an unwearied attention to music as a teacher for fifteen years, he has had an opportunity of being well acquainted with the kind of music which will be acceptable and lasting; he therefore hopes and believes that every page will be found interesting. This book will be offered to the public in three parts.   The first containing all the plain church music now in general use.   The second, the more lengthy and elegant pieces adapted to the use of

schools and singing societies. The third, a few anthems, the most elegant and sublime, from various authors, to which is added an appendix containing a few tunes with choruses adapted to revivals of religion.

The giver of every good and perfect gift has been pleased to bless us with singing faculties, and to music we are indebted for one of the most refined and exalted pleasures which the bounty of heaven ever permitted to gladden the hearts of the children of men.

Then, most certainly, it is reasonable that we improve those faculties of our nature as we have opportunity that we may be prepared to exercise them in accents of acceptable praise to our Creator. "O sing unto the Lord a new song—sing unto the Lord of all the earth. It is a good thing to give thanks unto the Lord and sing praises unto thy name O thou most high." Music like all other sciences must be critically learned, or it can never be performed correctly, and if it is the duty of one, it surely is the duty of all to sing, and yet how many do we see daily enter the house of God and sit gazing at some idle fashion without ever opening their mouth to sing, while the devout worshipers are lifting their voices in tones of melody, speaking forth the lively emotions of their devoted souls in the praises of the Redeemer. It is admitted however that there are some who are not gifted with musical faculties; such are exempt from the obligation that rests upon all to sing, it is the remark of Dr. J. Edward, that it is the command of God that all should sing, and as it is a thing that cannot be decently performed without learning, those therefore who have musical faculties and neglect to improve them are living in sin, for it is an ordinance of Gods' worship in which *all are commanded to join*.

So far as could be ascertained, the authors name, is set over each piece of music in this work, many of the tunes however, over which the name of the subscriber is set are not entirely original, but he has harmonized them, and therefore claims them. As this book is designed principly for a school book, and as it is admitted by all in the present day, that children and youth are most susceptible of improvement, it is hoped that its simplicity and adaptation to the capacity of children, will not subject it to the chilling influence of criticism from an enlightened public; for surely that which is calculated to instruct the simple should not be offensive to the wise.

A few typographical errors have escaped correction, but it is hoped that a reference to the station, the *mi*, which is the leading note, will enable every individual who is capable of singing by note, to determine where each note should stand in the stave.

The large number of hymns inserted in that part of this book which contains church music, it is confidently believed, will render it more useful to the church of Christ, than any book of the kind now in circulation; and consequently more worthy of the patronage of an enlightened community. It is therefore dedicated to the Christian Church with an humble hope, that the feeble efforts of one of the least of its members, may tend in some degree to build up and beautify that spiritual temple, whose "walls are salvation, and whose gates are praise."

William Francis Allen (1830-1889)

William Francis Allen, a native of Massachusetts, graduated from Harvard University in 1851. Following a three-year stint as a private tutor in New York he traveled in Europe, returning to his home state in 1856. Allen moved to St. Helena, South Carolina, in 1863 as an agent of the Freedmen's Aid Commission to assist in the education of recently freed slaves. After holding various positions in different parts of the country he became professor of ancient languages and history at the University of Wisconsin, where he remained until his death.

In addition to writing numerous books, articles, and reviews in his areas of specialty, Allen served as a co-compiler with Charles P. Ware and Lucy M. Garrison of _Slave Songs of the United States_ (1867), one of the earliest collections of African-American spirituals to be published in the United States. Among the familiar spirituals included in this volume were "Michael row the boat ashore," "Nobody knows the trouble I've had," and "Rock o' my soul." The preface, which was written by Allen, describes some of the difficulties involved in transcribing the melodies from oral performance. He also points out the extraordinary effect created when these songs are sung by the people among whom they originated.

69   From Preface to _Slave Songs of the United States_ (New York: A. Simpson & Co., 1867), pp. [i]-vi.

The musical capacity of the negro race has been recognized for so many years that it is hard to explain why no systematic effort has hitherto been made to collect and preserve their melodies. More than thirty years ago those plantation songs made their appearance which were so extraordinarily popular for a while; and if "Coal-black Rose," "Zip Coon" and "Ole Virginny nebber tire" have been succeeded by spurious imitations, manufactured to suit the somewhat sentimental taste of our community, the fact that these were called "negro melodies" was itself a tribute to the musical genius of the race.[1] The public had well-nigh forgotten these genuine slave songs, and with them the creative power from which they sprung, when a fresh interest was excited through the educational mission to the Port Royal islands, in 1861. The agents of this mission were not long in discovering the rich vein of music that existed in these half-barbarous people, and when visitors from the North were on the islands, there was nothing that seemed better worth their while than to see a "shout" or hear the "people" sing their "sperichils." A few of these last, of special merit,[2] soon became established favorites among the whites, and hardly a Sunday passed at the church on St. Helena without "Gabriel's Trumpet," "I hear from Heaven to-day," or "Jehovah Hallelujah." The last time I myself heard these was at the Fourth of July celebration, at the church, in 1864. All of them were sung, and then the glorious shout, "I can't stay behind, my Lord," was struck up, and sung by the entire multitude with a zest and spirit, a swaying of the bodies and nodding of the heads and lighting of the countenances and rhythmical movement of the hands, which I think no one present will ever forget.

Attention was, I believe, first publicly directed to these songs in a letter from Miss McKim, of Philadelphia, to _Dwight's Journal of Music_, Nov. 8, 1862, from which some extracts will presently be given. At about the same time, Miss McKim arranged and published two of them, "Roll, Jordan" (No. 1) and "Poor Rosy" (No. 8)—probably on all accounts the two best specimens that could be selected. Mr. H. G. Spaulding not long after gave some well-

---

[1] It is not generally known that the beautiful air "Long time ago," or "Near the lake where drooped the willow," was borrowed from the negroes, by whom it was sung to words beginning, "Way down in Raccoon Hollow."

[2] The first seven spirituals in this collection, which were regularly sung at the church.

chosen specimens of the music in an article entitled "Under the Palmetto," in the _Continental Monthly_ for August, 1863, among them, "O Lord, remember me" (No. 15), and "The Lonesome Valley" (No. 7). Many other persons interested themselves in the collection of words and tunes, and it seems time at last that the partial collections in the possession of the editors, and known by them to be in the possession of others, should not be forgotten and lost, but that these relics of a state of society which has passed away should be preserved while it is still possible.[3]

The greater part of the music here presented has been taken down by the editors from the lips of the colored people themselves; when we have obtained it from other sources, we have given credit in the table of contents. The largest and most accurate single collection in existence is probably that made by Mr. Charles P. Ware, chiefly at Coffin's Point, St. Helena Island. We have thought it best to give this collection in its entirety, as the basis of the present work; it includes all the hymns as far as No. 43. Those which follow, as far as No. 55, were collected by myself on the Capt. John Fripp and neighboring plantations, on the same island. In all cases we have added words from other sources and other localities, when they could be obtained, as well as variations of the tunes wherever they were of sufficient importance to warrant it. Of the other hymns and songs we have given the locality whenever it could be ascertained.

The difficulty experienced in attaining absolute correctness is greater than might be supposed by those who have never tried the experiment, and we are far from claiming that we have made no mistakes. I have never felt quite sure of my notation without a fresh comparison with the singing, and have then often found that I had made some errors. I feel confident, however, that there are no mistakes of importance. What may appear to some to be an incorrect rendering, is very likely to be a variation; for these variations are endless, and very entertaining and instructive.

Neither should any one be repelled by any difficulty in adapting the words to the tunes. The negroes keep exquisite time in singing,

---

[3]Only this last spring a valuable collection of songs made at Richmond, Va., was lost in the _Wagner_. No copy had been made from the original manuscript, so that the labor of their collection was lost. We had hoped to have the use of them in preparing the present work.

and do not suffer themselves to be daunted by any obstacle in the words. The most obstinate Scripture phrases or snatches from hymns they will force to do duty with any tune they please, and will dash heroically through a trochaic tune at the head of a column of iambs with wonderful skill. We have in all cases arranged one set of words carefully to each melody; for the rest, one must make them fit the best he can, as the negroes themselves do.

The best that we can do, however, with paper and types, or even with voices, will convey but a faint shadow of the original. The voices of the colored people have a peculiar quality that nothing can imitate; and the intonations and delicate variations of even one singer cannot be reproduced on paper. And I despair of conveying any notion of the effect of a number singing together, especially in a complicated shout, like "I can't stay behind, my Lord" (No. 8), or "Turn, sinner, turn O!" (No. 48). There is no singing in *parts*,[4] as we understand it, and yet no two appear to be singing the same thing—the leading singer starts the words of each verse, often improvising, and the others, who "base" him, as it is called, strike in with the refrain, or even join in the solo, when the words are familiar. When the "base" begins, the leader often stops, leaving the rest of his words to be guessed at, or it may be they are taken up by one of the other singers. And the "basers" themselves seem to follow their own whims, beginning when they please and leaving off when they please, striking an octave above or below (in case they have pitched the tune too low or too high), or hitting some other note that chords, so as to produce the effect of a marvellous complication and variety, and yet with the most perfect time, and rarely with any discord. And what makes it all the harder to unravel a thread of melody out of this strange network is that, like birds, they seem not infrequently to strike sounds that cannot be precisely represented by the gamut, and abound in "slides from one note another, and turns and cadences not in articulated notes." "It is difficult," writes Miss McKim, "to express the entire character of

---

[4]"The high voices, all in unison, and the admirable time and true accent with which their responses are made, always make me wish that some great musical composer could hear these semi-savage performances. With a very little skilful adaptation and instrumentation, I think one or two barbaric chants and choruses might be evoked from them that would make the fortune of an opera."--*Mrs. Kemble's "Life on a Georgian Plantation," p.* 218.

these negro ballads by mere musical notes and signs. The odd turns made in the throat, and the curious rhythmic effect produced by single voices chiming in at different irregular intervals, seem almost as impossible to place on the score as the singing of birds or the tones of an AEolian Harp." There are also apparent irregularities in the time, which it is no less difficult to express accurately, and of which Nos. 10, 130, 131, and (eminently) 128, are examples.

Still, the chief part of the negro music is _civilized_ in its character —partly composed under the influence of association with the whites, partly actually imitated from their music. In the main it appears to be original in the best sense of the word, and the more we examine the subject, the more genuine it appears to us to be. In a very few songs, as Nos. 19, 23, and 25, strains of familiar tunes are readily traced; and it may easily be that others contain strains of less familiar music, which the slaves heard their masters sing or play.[5]

Robert Lowry and W. Howard Doane (19th century)

Robert Lowry (1826-1899) and William Howard Doane (1832-1915) were two of the most popular composers and compilers of Sunday school and gospel songs during the late nineteenth century. Lowry served as the pastor of Baptist churches in New York, Pennsylvania, and New Jersey, and as a professor at Bucknell University. Doane, a Baptist layman, was a businessman by profession. Both men pursued their musical interests as an avocation, frequently collaborating in the compiling of songbooks. One of their successful ventures was _Pure Gold for the Sunday School_ (1871). Unlike many Sunday school collections of the time, this one was designed for use by both children and adults. Nevertheless, the contents were similar to other such compilations in their provision of simple lyrics, tuneful melodies, and uncomplicated harmonies in the popular parlor-song style of the day. Among the songs first printed in this book that are

---

[5]We have rejected as spurious "Give me Jesus, "Climb Jacob's Ladder," (both sung at Port Royal), and "I'll take the wings of the morning," which we find in Methodist hymn-books. A few others, the character of which seemed somewhat suspicious, we have not felt at liberty to reject without direct evidence.

still found in some hymnals are "Take the Name of Jesus With You," "Savior, Thy Dying Love," and "To the Work! To the Work!" In the salutation to *Pure Gold for the Sunday School*, the compilers reflected on the importance of the material sung in the Sunday school, pointing out that in the present work "care has been had that no song without merit should find place here."

70   Salutation from *Pure Gold for the Sunday School* (New York: Biglow & Main, 1871), pp. [2]-[3].

Millions of Music Books have gone from this Publishing House, to aid Sunday School laborers in their Christian work. In every part of our land, the songs in these books are sung by youthful voices, and caught up by children of a larger growth in the great Congregation. The music of the Sunday School is now acknowledged to be an important factor in that grand educational force which is levering up the rising generation to a plane of personal morality and Christian enlightenment. It is admitted that the Sunday School is more potent in providing for the future well-being of Society, than any other instrumentality that affects to mould the coming constituents of the Commonwealth; while no one questions that the saving truths of the Scripture are nowhere brought to bear with greater converting power on the minds of our children, than in the Sunday School. How important, therefore, that the material of a Sunday School Song Book should be made up of the "Pure Gold" of God's Word, with the truths of that Word concreting themselves in Christian experience and life!

In the present work, the Editors have aimed at a compilation of Songs that would carry with them not only transient gratification, but permanent profit. In no case have the mere interests of trade been considered, but in every case the spiritual good of the singer has determined the selection. Hymns of doubtful historical statement and of questionable doctrinal character, have been studiously excluded. The one controlling consideration has been—how best to promote the spiritual efficiency of the Sunday Schools. Every other interest has been subordinate to that; and if this one end is not secured in "Pure Gold," it will not be from lack of conscientious labor and pure intention.

Nearly everything in the book is new, and has been prepared expressly for it. It is taken for granted that Sunday Schools do not wish to purchase over again the songs which they have used in other books. Care has been had that no song without merit should find place here. Every song has passed through the ordeal of a close criticism; and there is not one piece packed into "Pure Gold" for the mere purpose of filling up a page.

The hymns in this work are not all projected on the plane of childhood. That quiet revolution by which our Sunday Schools for children are passing up to the higher level of Bible Schools for all ages, has not been overlooked. Keeping that strictly in view, we have inserted hymns of Heaven which veteran saints can sing, hymns of Activity for the strong and buoyant, hymns of new Experience for the Christian child; as well as hymns of Invitation to the unconverted, and hymns of Confession for the penitent. All through these leaflets of "Pure Gold" will be found soul-stirring hymns of Praise to God and to Christ, which the whole School can sing. For the convenience of those who may not have time to examine the entire work, we mention a few which illustrate its general character:

"My Sabbath Home," page 7; "Who'll be the next?" 8; "Keep Step," 10; "Blessed River," 12; "Beloved of the Lord," 28; "'Twill all be over soon," 40; "Mansions of Light," 42; "Thy name alone can save," 46; "Beautiful Land of Song," 64; "We're going home," 71. "In the valley," 73; "Tell it with joy," 92; "Strike for Victory," 96; "Joyful Message," 98; "Wake the song," 101; "The Bright Forever," 108; "Jesus, I am coming," 113; "Here again we meet you," 128; "The Rifted Rock," 134.

In no book hitherto issued by this House has there been so large a number of excellent song-writers represented, and, consequently, such a variety of material, both as to topics and treatment. No expense has been spared to secure the contributions of pens already familiar to our Sunday Schools, as well as others whose fresh and pure lines will claim for them an equal place among the established favorites. In this respect "Pure Gold" will be found to contain an unusually large selection of rich, sound, and evangelical hymns.

The extraordinary popularity of "Bright Jewels," of which more than _three hundred thousand_ copies have been sold in less than two years, demonstrates that the Sunday Schools look confidently to this House for the best book of Sunday School Song. We have endeavored, in this work, not only to merit that confidence, but give assurance that it will not be forfeited. With the hope that our labors may, in some degree, help the Sunday School teacher in his blessed calling, and be instrumental in leading many souls to the dear Redeemer, we commend to our Sunday Schools everywhere this collection of "Pure Gold."

Ira D. Sankey (1840-1908)

Ira D. Sankey was the most widely known American evangelistic musician of the late nineteenth century. In company with Chicago evangelist D. L. Moody, he led the music in revival meetings throughout the United States and Great Britain, singing solos, leading congregational singing, and playing the organ. Sankey wrote the music for about 100 gospel hymns, the most famous of which was "The Ninety and Nine." His collection of _Sacred Songs and Solos_ was first published in England in 1873 and went through numerous editions. Sankey was also involved in the production of the _Gospel Hymns_ series of songbooks (1875-1891), which achieved the same sort of popularity in the United States that _Sacred Songs and Solos_ enjoyed in the British Isles. The following extracts from Sankey's autobiography describe his initial difficulties in securing an English publisher for his _Sacred Songs and Solos_ and how his most popular gospel song was written. The story of "The Ninety and Nine" illustrates the fact that many gospel songs of the time originated as solos that later found their way into the congregational repertory. The "Dr. Bonar" mentioned in this account was Horatius Bonar, the author of such hymns as "No, not despairingly" and "I heard the voice of Jesus say."

71   From _My Life and the Story of the Gospel Hymns_ (New York and London; Harper & Brothers Publishers, 1907), pp. 36-37, 42-43, 47-48, 268-271.

In June, 1873, we sailed for England, Mr. Moody taking his wife and children with him, and my wife accompanying me, having left our two children with their grandparents.

The only books that I took with me were my Bagster Bible and my "musical scrap-book," which contained a number of hymns which I had collected in the past years, and many of which, in the providence of God, were to be used in arousing much religious interest among the people in the Old Country.

. . .

Our sacred songs continued to grow in popularity, and I was continually beset with requests for the loan of my "musical scrapbook," in which alone could be found the songs that were then being sung as solos at our meetings. For a while I permitted many of my friends to have them, but soon found that it would be impossible to continue doing so, as persons having my book failed to return it in time for the meetings, thus preventing me from using the desired hymns at the services. To overcome this difficulty I had the words of a number of hymns printed on small cards. I hoped that these cards would supply the demand for the song, but as soon as the congregation observed that the cards were given out free to applicants, a rush was made for the platform, and the supply was exhausted the first day. I could not afford to continue this plan, and it was evident that something else had to be done. Having received a number of complaints from persons who had purchased copies of the "Hallowed Songs," which we were using in the meetings, that that book contained but a very few of the solos the people so much desired, I made an effort to have the publishers of that book print a few of the most popular pieces and bind them in the back of future editions of that book. This offer the publishers respectfully declined, saying that Philip Phillips, the compiler of the book, was in California, and that they did not care to make any alterations without his permission. I wrote them again, saying that I was an intimate friend of Mr. Phillips, and that I was sure he would be very glad to have this addition made to his book, but again the offer was declined, and here the matter rested for a while.

. . .

While here [Sunderland] Mr. R. C. Morgan, of London, editor of "The Christian," having heard of the work that was going on in the north, visited us for the purpose of writing up an account of the meetings for his paper, and while seated one day at the dinner table, I remarked to him that I was afraid what I had heard about the English people being slow and conservative was all too true. I spoke with considerable animation on the subject, and he inquired what I meant. I then told him of my attempt to give away my sacred songs, which were in such demand by the people, and that I could get no one to take them. He at once remarked that as he had been printing musical leaflets for a number of years, he would be glad to take some of mine with him to London and publish them in a small paper-covered pamphlet. So I cut from my scrap-book twenty-three pieces, rolled them up, and wrote on them the words, "Sacred Songs and Solos, sung by Ira D. Sankey at the meetings of Mr. Moody of Chicago."

Mr. Morgan returned to London the next day, and in about two weeks we received 500 copies of the pamphlet, which was first used at an all-day meeting, held near the close of our mission in Sunderland. The little book was sold at sixpence per copy, and before the day was over every book had been purchased. We immediately telegraphed for a still larger supply, which was also soon exhausted, and a few days later copies were seen not only in the windows of bookstores, but grocers', dry-goods establishments, etc. Thus began the publication and sale of a book which, together with the edition of words only, has now grown into a volume of twelve hundred pieces.

. . .

It was in the year 1874 that the poem, "The Ninety and Nine," was discovered, set to music, and sent out upon its world-wide mission. Its discovery seemed as if by chance, but I cannot regard it otherwise than providential. Mr. Moody had just been conducting a series of meetings in Glasgow, and I had been assisting him in his work as director of the singing. We were at the railway station at Glasgow and about to take the train for Edinburgh, whither we were going upon an urgent invitation of ministers to hold three days of meetings there before going into the Highlands. We had held a three months' series in Edinburgh just previous to our four months' campaign in Glasgow. As we were about to board the train I bought a weekly newspaper, for a penny. Being much fatigued by our incessant labors at Glasgow, and intending to begin work immediately upon our arrival at Edinburgh, we did not travel second- or third-class, as was our custom, but sought the seclusion and rest which a first-class railway carriage in Great Britain affords. In the hope of finding news from America I began perusing my lately purchased newspaper. This hope, however, was doomed to disappointment, as the only thing in its columns to remind an American of home and native land was a sermon by Henry Ward Beecher.

I threw the paper down, but shortly before arriving in Edinburgh I picked it up again with a view to reading the advertisements. While thus engaged my eyes fell upon a little piece of poetry in a corner of the paper. I carefully read it over, and at once made up my mind that this would make a great hymn for evangelistic work—if it had a tune. So impressed was I that I called Mr. Moody's attention to it, and he asked me to read it to him. This I proceeded to do with all the vim and energy at my command. After I had finished I looked at my friend Moody to see what the effect had been, only to discover that he had not heard a word, so absorbed was he in a letter which he had received from Chicago. My chagrin can be better imagined than described. Notwithstanding this experience, I cut out the poem and placed it in my musical scrap-book—which, by the way, has been the seedplot from which sprang many of the Gospel songs that are now known throughout the world.

At the noon meeting on the second day, held at the Free Assembly Hall, the subject presented by Mr. Moody and other speakers was "The Good Shepherd." When Mr. Moody had finished speaking he called upon Dr. Bonar to say a few words. He spoke only a few minutes, but with great power, thrilling the immense audience by his fervid eloquence. At the conclusion of Dr. Bonar's words Mr. Moody turned to me with the question, "Have you a solo appropriate for this subject, with which to close the service?" I had nothing suitable in mind, and was greatly troubled to know what to do. The Twenty-third Psalm occurred to me, but this had been sung several times in the meeting. I knew that every Scotchman in the audience would join me if I sang that, so I could not possibly render this favorite psalm as a solo. At this moment I seemed to hear a voice saying: "Sing the hymn you found on the train!" But I thought this impossible, as no music had ever been written for that hymn. Again the impression came strongly upon me that I must sing the beautiful and appropriate words I had found the day before, and placing the little newspaper slip on the organ in front of me, I lifted my heart in prayer, asking God to help me so to sing that the people might hear and understand. Laying my hands upon the organ I struck the key of A flat, and began to sing.

Note by note the tune was given, which has not been changed from that day to this. As the singing ceased a great sigh seemed to go up from the meeting, and I knew that the song had reached the hearts of my Scotch audience. Mr. Moody was greatly moved. Leaving the pulpit, he came down to where I was seated. Leaning over the organ, he looked at the little newspaper slip from which the song had been sung, and with tears in his eyes said: "Sankey, where did you get that hymn? I never heard the like of it in my life." I was also moved to tears and arose and replied: "Mr. Moody, that's the hymn I read to you yesterday on the train, which you did not hear." Then Mr. Moody raised his hand and pronounced the benediction, and the meeting closed. Thus "The Ninety and Nine" was born.

Part V

Vatican Council II

17
Vatican Council II (1963)

IN 1959, the recently elected Pope John XXIII declared his intention to convene an ecumenical council of the church. Vatican Council II opened in 1962 with more than 2,000 representatives from the Roman Catholic church and a number of observers from the Orthodox and various Protestant communions. The Council adjourned in December 1965, having promulgated sixteen formal statements.

Significantly, the first statement to be released was *Sacrosanctum Concilium* (Constitution on the Sacred Liturgy, 1963), which dealt with various features of worship in the Roman Catholic church. A number of these related to the participation of the congregation in singing. As is shown in the following extracts, Latin was still considered the preferred language for worship (Articles 36, 54) and Gregorian chant the preferred music (Article 116). But the document also allowed for services in the vernacular, encouraged singing by the congregation (Articles 30, 54, 113, 114, 118), and called upon composers to provide suitable materials for the people to sing (Article 121). These directives had a tremendous impact on the Roman Catholic church, and within a few short years Latin virtually disappeared from most parishes and Gregorian chant was replaced by various forms of congregational song.

72   From *Sacrosanctum Concilium* (1963). *Source*: International Commission on English in the Liturgy, *Documents on the Liturgy 1963-1979* (Collegeville, MN: The Liturgical Press, [1982]), pp. 10, 11-12, 15, 24, 25.

28.   In liturgical celebrations each one, minister or layperson, who has an office to perform, should do all of, but only, those parts which pertain to that office by the nature of the rite and the principles of liturgy.

. . .

30.   To promote active participation, the people should be encouraged to take part by means of acclamations, responses, psalmody, antiphons, and songs, as well as by actions, gestures, and bearing. And at the proper times all should observe a reverent silence.

. . .

36.§ 1.   Particular law remaining in force, the use of the Latin language is to be preserved in the Latin rites.

§ 2.   But since the use of the mother tongue, whether in the Mass, the administration of the sacraments, or other parts of the liturgy, frequently may be of great advantage to the people, the limits of its use may be extended. This will apply in the first place to the readings and instructions and to some prayers and chants, according to the regulations on this matter to be laid down for each case in subsequent chapters.

§ 3.   Respecting such norms and also, where applicable, consulting the bishops of nearby territories of the same language, the competent, territorial ecclesiastical authority mentioned in art. 22 § 2 is empowered to decide whether and to what extent the vernacular is to be used.   The enactments of the competent authority are to be approved, that is, confirmed by the Holy See.

§ 4.   Translations from the Latin text into the mother tongue intended for use in the liturgy must be approved by the competent, territorial ecclesiastical authority already mentioned.

. . .

54.   With art. 36 of this Constitution as the norm, in Masses celebrated with the people a suitable place may be allotted to their mother tongue. This is to apply in the first place to the readings and "the universal prayer," but also, as local conditions may warrant, to those parts belonging to the people.

Nevertheless steps should be taken enabling the faithful to say or to sing together in Latin those parts of the Ordinary of the Mass belonging to them.

Wherever a more extended use of the mother tongue within the Mass appears desireable, the regulation laid down in art. 40 of this constitution is to be observed.

. . .

113.   A liturgical service takes on a nobler aspect when the rites are celebrated with singing, the sacred ministers take their parts in them, and the faithful actively participate.

Further Reading

THE purpose of the following bibliography is to direct the attention of students and other readers to additional sources on the people and topics covered in this book. The list is necessarily selective and concentrates mainly on writings in English that are likely to be available in most college, university, and seminary libraries.

General Surveys

Bailey, Albert Edward. *The Gospel in Hymns*. New York: Macmillan Publishing Company, n.d. (reprint of 1950 ed.).

Eskew, Harry and Hugh T. McElrath. *Sing with Understanding: An Introduction to Christian Hymnology*. Nashville: Broadman Press, 1980.

Julian, John. *A Dictionary of Hymnology*. 2 vols. Grand Rapids: Kregel Publications, 1985 (reprint of 2nd rev. ed., 1907).

Reynolds, William J. and Milburn Price. *A Survey of Christian Hymnody*. 3rd ed. Carol Stream: Hope Publishing Company, 1987.

The Early Church and Middle Ages

The Early Church

Benson, Louis F. "The Relation of the Hymn to Holy Scripture," in *The Hymnody of the Christian Church*, pp. 57-75. Richmond: John Knox Press, 1956 (reprint of 1927 ed.).

McKinnon, James. "Christian Antiquity," in James McKinnon, ed., *Antiquity and the Middle Ages: From Ancient Greece to the 15th Century*, pp. 68-87. Englewood Cliffs: Prentice Hall, 1990.

___, ed. *Music in Early Christian Literature*. Cambridge: Cambridge University Press, 1987.

Sherwin-White, A. N. *The Letters of Pliny: A Historical and Social Commentary*. Oxford: Clarendon Press, 1985.

Wellesz, Egon. *A History of Byzantine Music and Hymnography*. 2nd ed., rev. and enl. Oxford: Clarendon Press, 1962.

217

The Middle Ages
Bullough, John F. "Notker Balbulus and the Origin of the Sequence." _The Hymn_ 16 (January 1965), 13-16, 24.
Crocker, Richard L. _The Early Medieval Sequence._ Berkeley/Los Angeles/London: University of California Press, 1977.
Doyle, Eric. _St. Francis and the Song of Brotherhood._ New York: Seabury Press, 1981.
Messenger, Ruth Ellis. _Latin Hymns of the Middle Ages._ No. 14 of Papers of the Hymn Society, 1948.
___. _The Medieval Latin Hymn._ Washington: Capital Press, 1953.

The Reformation
The Lutheran Chorale
Buszin, Walter E. "Luther on Music." _Musical Quarterly_ 32 (January 1946), 80-97.
Leupold, Ulrich S., ed. _Liturgy and Hymns._ Vol. 53 of _Luther's Works._ Philadelphia: Fortress Press, 1965.
Liemohn, Edwin. _The Chorale Through Four Hundred Years of Musical Development as a Congregational Hymn._ Philadelphia: Muhlenberg Press, 1953.
Nettl, Paul. _Luther and Music._ Trans. by Frida Best and Ralph Wood. Philadelphia: Muhlenberg Press, 1948.
Reed, Luther D. _Luther and Congregational Song._ No. 12 of Papers of The Hymn Society, 1947.
Riedel, Johannes. _The Lutheran Chorale: Its Basic Traditions._ Minneapolis: Augsburg Publishing House, 1967.
Swiss Reformed
Garside, Charles, Jr. _Zwingli and the Arts._ New Haven and London: Yale University Press, 1966.
Genevan Psalmody
Garside, Charles, Jr. "Calvin's Preface to the Psalter: A Re-Appraisal." _Musical Quarterly_ 37 (October 1951), 566-577.
___. _The Origins of Calvin's Theology of Music: 1536-1543._ Philadelphia: American Philosophical Society, 1979 (reprint from _Transactions of the American Philosophical Society_ 69 [1979]).
Pidoux, Pierre. _Le psautier Huguenot du XVIe siecle._ 2 vols. Basel: Edition Barenreiter, 1962.
Pratt, Waldo S. _The Significance of the Old French Psalter Begun by_

Clement Marot in 1532. No. 4 of Papers of The Hymn Society, 1933.

Terry, Richard R., ed. *Calvin's First Psalter [1539].* London: Ernest Benn Limited, 1932.

English and Scottish Psalmody

Frost, Maurice. *English & Scottish Psalm & Hymn Tunes c. 1543-1677.* London: SPCK; London/New York/Toronto: Oxford University Press, 1953.

Leaver, Robin A. *"Goostly psalmes and spirituall songes": English and Dutch Metrical Psalms from Coverdale to Utenhove, 1535-1566.* Oxford: Clarendon Press, 1991.

Patrick, Millar. *Four Centuries of Scottish Psalmody.* London: Oxford University Press, 1949.

Terry, Richard R. "A Forgotten Psalter," in *A Forgotten Psalter and Other Essays,* pp. 1-26. London: Oxford University Press, 1929.

American Psalmody

Chase, Gilbert. "The Musical Puritans," in *America's Music From the Pilgrims to the Present,* pp. 3-18. Rev. 3rd ed. Urbana and Chicago: University of Illinois Press, 1987.

Foote, Henry Wilder. *An Account of the Bay Psalm Book.* No. 7 of Papers of the Hymn Society, 1940.

Haraszti, Zoltán. *The Enigma of the Bay Psalm Book.* Chicago: University of Chicago Press, 1956.

Lowens, Irving. "The Bay Psalm Book in 17th-Century New England," in *Music and Musicians in Early America,* pp. 25-38. New York: W.W. Norton & Company, Inc., 1964.

Music, David W. "Cotton Mather and Congregational Singing in Puritan New England." *Studies in Puritan American Spirituality* 2 (1991), 1-30.

___. "The Diary of Samuel Sewall and Congregational Singing in Early New England." *The Hymn* 41 (January 1990), 7-15.

Owen, Barbara. "The Bay Psalm Book and Its Era." *The Hymn* 41 (October 1990), 12-19.

Stevenson, Robert. "New England Puritanism, 1620-1720," in *Protestant Church Music in America,* pp. 12-20. New York: W.W. Norton & Company, Inc., 1966.

English Hymnody

Benson, Louis F. *The English Hymn: Its Development and Use in*

Worship. Richmond: John Knox Press, 1962 (reprint of 1915 ed.).

The Sixteenth Century

Grubb, Gerald Tiles. "Myles Coverdale: Poet and Song Writer." *Review and Expositor: A Baptist Theological Quarterly* 40 (July 1943), 338-353.

Leaver, Robin A. "The Date of Coverdale's *Goostly psalmes.*" *The Hymnology Annual: An International Forum on the Hymn and Worship* 2 (1992): 210-215 (reprint from *IAH-Bulletin* 9 [1981]).

_____. *"Goostly psalmes and spirituall songes": English and Dutch Metrical Psalms from Coverdale to Utenhove, 1535-1566.*

_____. "A Newly-Discovered Fragment of Coverdale's Goostly psalmes." *The Hymnology Annual: An International Forum on the Hymn and Worship* 2 (1992): 218-226.

The Seventeenth Century

Curwen, John Spencer. "The Psalmody of the Baptists," in *Studies in Worship Music (First Series)*, pp. 93-107. 2nd ed. London: J. Curwen & Sons, 1888.

Goadby, J. J. "About Singing," in *Bye-Paths in Baptist History*, pp. 317-349. Watertown: Baptist Heritage Publications, 1987 (reprint of 1871 ed.).

Martin, Hugh. "Benjamin Keach (1640-1704): Pioneer of Congregational Hymn Singing, Part II." *The Church Musician* (July 1967), 8-11.

The Eighteenth Century

Davis, Arthur Paul. *Isaac Watts: His Life and Works*. London: Independent Press, 1948.

Demaray, Donald E. "Newton's Olney Hymns," in *The Innovations of John Newton (1725-1807)*, pp. 225-259. Vol. 36 of Texts and Studies in Religion. Lewiston/Queenston: Edwin Mellen Press, 1988.

Escott, Harry. *Isaac Watts: Hymnographer*. London: Independent Press Ltd., 1962.

The Golden Age of Hymns. Special issue of *Christian History*, 10 (1991).

Johansen, John Henry. *The Olney Hymns*. No. 20 of Papers of the Hymn Society, 1956.

Marshall, Madeleine Forell and Janet Todd. *English Congregational Hymns in the Eighteenth Century*. Lexington: University Press of Kentucky, 1982.

Rattenbury, J. Earnest. "Part VI: The Wesleyan Hymnody," in

Wesley's Legacy to the World: Six Studies in the Permanent Values of the Evangelical Revival, pp. 255-308. Nashville: Cokesbury Press, 1928.

Wright, Thomas. _Isaac Watts and Contemporary Hymn-Writers_. Vol. 3 of Lives of the British Hymn-Writers. London: C. J. Farncombe & Sons, Ltd., 1914.

The Nineteenth Century

Brunton, Grace. "Reginald Heber, Bishop of Calcutta." _The Hymn_ 11 (April 1960), 37-44.

Higginson, J. Vincent. "John Mason Neale and 19th Century Hymnody: His Work and Influence." _The Hymn_ 16 (October 1965), 101-117.

___. "Origins of _The Hymnal Noted_." _The Hymn_ 2 (April 1951), 5-8, 26.

Johansen, John H. "The Christian Psalmist." _The Hymn_ 22 (April 1971), 51-53.

Knight, Helen G. _Life of James Montgomery_. Boston: Gould and Lincoln, 1857.

Lough, A.G. _The Influence of John Mason Neale_. London: S.P.C.K., 1962.

___. _John Mason Neale—Priest Extraordinary_. Devon: A. G. Lough, 1976.

Messenger, Ruth Ellis. "John Mason Neale, Translator." _The Hymn_ 2 (October 1951), 5-10, 24.

Stevenson, Robert M. "John Mason Neale and Tractarian Hymnody," in _Patterns of Protestant Church Music_, pp. 139-150. Durham: Duke University Press, 1953.

Towle, Eleanor A. _John Mason Neale, D.D.: A Memoir_. New York/Bombay: Longmans, Green, and Co., 1906.

The Twentieth Century

Dickinson, A.E.F. "Hymnody," in _Vaughan Williams_, pp. 123-142. London: Faber and Faber, 1963.

Gore, Richard T. _Ralph Vaughan Williams and the Hymn_. No. 34 of Papers of the Hymn Society, 1981.

American Hymnody

Benson, Louis F. _The English Hymn: Its Development and Use In Worship_.

Foote, Henry Wilder. _Three Centuries of American Hymnody_. N.p.: Archon Books, 1968 (reprint of 1940 ed.).

The Eighteenth Century

Atkins, Charles L. "William Billings: His Psalm and Hymn Tunes," in _Addresses at the International Hymnological Conference, September 10-11, 1961, New York City_. No. 24 of Papers of the Hymn Society, 1962.

Chase, Gilbert. "Conflict and Reform," in _America's Music: From the Pilgrims to the Present_, pp. 19-37.

Hood, George. _A History of Music in New England with Biographical Sketches of Reformers and Psalmists_. New York and London: Johnson Reprint Corporation, 1970 (reprint of 1846 ed.).

Kroeger, Karl. "William Billings and the Hymn-Tune." _The Hymn_ 37 (July 1986), 19-26.

McKay, David P. and Richard Crawford. _William Billings of Boston_. Princeton: Princeton University Press, 1975.

Stevenson, Robert. "'Regular Singing,' 1720-1775," in _Protestant Church Music in America_, pp. 21-31; "Singing-School Masters in the New Republic," in ibid., pp. 59-73.

Temperley, Nicholas. "The Old Way of Singing: Its Origins and Development." _Journal of the American Musicological Society_ 34 (Fall 1981), 511-544.

The Nineteenth Century

Chase, Gilbert. "The Fasola Folk," in _America's Music From the Pilgrims to the Present_, pp. 170-191; "The Negro Spirituals," in ibid., pp. 213-231.

Jackson, George Pullen. _White Spirituals in the Southern Uplands_. New York: Dover Publications, Inc., 1965 (reprint of 1933 ed.).

Music, David W. "William Caldwell's _Union Harmony_ (1837): The First East Tennessee Tunebook." _The Hymn_ 38 (July 1987), 16-22.

Pemberton, Carol A. _Lowell Mason: His Life and Work_. Ann Arbor: UMI Research Press, 1985.

Sankey, Ira D. _My Life and the Story of the Gospel Hymns_. Philadelphia: The Sunday School Times Co., 1907.

Southern, Eileen. _The Music of Black Americans: A History_. 2nd ed. New York/London: W. W. Norton & Company, 1983.

Stevenson, Robert. "Negro Spirituals: Origin and Present-Day Significance," in _Patterns of Protestant Church Music_, pp. 92-105; "Ira D. Sankey and the Growth of 'Gospel Hymnody,'" in ibid., pp. 151-162.

Wilhoit, Mel R. "'Sing Me a Sankey': Ira D. Sankey and Congregational Song." *The Hymn* 42 (January 1991), 13-19.

Zellner, John F., III. "Robert Lowry: Early American Hymn Writer." *The Hymn* 26 (October 1975), 117-124 (Part 1); 27 (January 1976), 15-21 (Part 2).

Index

WACHET AUF 174
"Wake the song" 205
Walter, Thomas 179
Walther, Johann 37, 39
Ware, Charles P. 199, 201
Watts, Isaac 90, 109, 115-138,
  145, 147, 183-184, 189-191
"Way down in Raccoon Hollow"
  200
"We're going home" 205
WEIMAR 175
Welds, Mr. 93
Wesley, Charles 138, 141, 159
Wesley, John 138-145
Wesley, Samuel 163
Westminster Assembly 77-78
Westminster Confession 78
White, Mr. 95, 96
Whittingham, William 72-75
"Who'll be the next?" 205
Whole Book of Psalms, The
  (Sternhold & Hopkins) 71,
  73, 76, 79
*Whole Booke of Psalmes
  Faithfully Translated, The*
  (Bay Psalm Book) 82-90
William III 156
Williams, Capt. 95
Williams, Nathaniel 96
WINDSOR 95
Winthrop, Madam 95, 96
witch trials, Salem 94
Wither, George 107-109
*World Encompassed by Sir
  Francis Drake, The* (Fletcher)
  81-82

YORK 95, 96

"Zip Coon" 200
Zwingli, Huldreich 51-53, 54, 57

About the Author

DAVID W. Music is Professor of Church Music at Southwestern Baptist Theological Seminary, Fort Worth, Texas. He was previously Associate Professor of Music and Chairman of the Music Department and Fine Arts Division at California Baptist College, Riverside, California. He served for six years (1991-1996) as Editor of *The Hymn*, the quarterly journal of The Hymn Society in the United States and Canada, and coauthored *Singing Baptists: Studies in Baptist Hymnody in America* (1994).